IT COULD HAPPEN TO YOU

VOILA CRUZITA TREVIÑO

Gotham Books

30 N Gould St.
Ste. 20820, Sheridan, WY 82801
https://gothambooksinc.com/

Phone: 1 (307) 464-7800

Published by Gotham Books (September 3, 2022)

ISBN: 978-1-956349-50-4(sc)
ISBN: 978-1-956349-51-1 (e)

Because of the dynamic nature of the Internet, any web addresses or links contained in this book may have changed since publication and may no longer be valid.

The views expressed in this work are solely those of the author and do not necessarily reflect the views of the publisher, and the publisher hereby disclaims any responsibility for them.

It Could Happen

*T*he Entrapment of my Divorce; My life had changed overnight. In the most unspeakable way, you can ever imagine. It started when I mentioned to my husband that my co-worker/friend had a Spitfire Sports Car. She wanted to sell. I asked my husband if he wanted to test drive the spitfire sports car.

My husband decided to fill up the Spitfire. While pumping gas, this woman working at the gas station walked up to my husband and leaned against the sport car. She whispered to my husband ear. If you give me a ride to my house, I'll have sex with you. She said it as if she had done it before. Several months later. Around six o'clock before picking up my kids. I noticed another vehicle on my driveway; the bedroom light was on. I decided to ring the doorbell but no answer.

I went to the side of the house and, look inside the bedroom window. Oh my God! My husband and some women were naked alongside my bed; they were sweating hard like two pigs on a Pig-style position. I didn't have time to absorb what I had witnessed. The other woman (Annie) immediately ran to the bathroom, called 911. My husband just stood there staring at me, speechless. I dreadfully turned to my right. I heard a voice beside me, and I jumped with fear. There stood police. Annie had immediately called 911, declaring she feared for her life.

The Police; walked up to me and yelled, what's going on? I stood there confused; I didn't know what to say; finally. I said I was trying to get into my house. The police instantly stopped me. He then said the man inside the house said he doesn't know you. I yelled out, "what"? Are you kidding me"? I said, look at my driver's license. The police said Ma'am do you have a place to stay. I answered Yes, my sister lives around the corner. The police escorted me to my sister house. The police explained to my sister what happened. She said that's her house. My children and I were forced stayed at her house till I went to court. My husband and I were now facing our first domestic violence, except for. I would now be facing the most horrifying judgment of my life. I was now facing a life sentence in prison over a love affair. It's an Unbelievable true story; It Could Happen to You as it did to me with my life of truth. It's a complicated story to digest. I would start my story by introducing myself. Before I met my husband.

The Center of the Heart

I needed more than just justice; Annie, a woman who didn't know me, wanted to end my life over a love affair. My husband was now a stranger to me. What could have been a sample divorce? My husband and Annie stood in our divorce court together. After the divorce it turned out to be a tragedy, with a life sentence. When the divorce was finalized, I was charged with numerous Domestic Violence's, IRS arrest continued with the DNA as the wheels turned. The District Court Judge, who would relight the fire of hell. The Court System went to the extreme. I was first charged for numerous domestic violence and then arrested by the Federal Marshalls for Improper filing of Income Tax. The fear of being behind bars for the first time I was treated like a criminal. With no way out. The sound, I had never heard. I had been stripped off my clothes, I became another person. Who was I? I was no longer the woman they called Viola. The Federal Public Defender had his dilemmas, came to see me, said the Federal Judge. They wanted to know where her younger daughter's whereabouts. Who was ruled as non-existences? The fear of losing my daughter to a monster. Annie helped my ex-husband entrap me into a DNA hearing that made them millionaires. My husband didn't lift a finger to help his wife of twenty-three years. Jake was now another man. Annie wasn't satisfied being a millionaire; she then pulled another illegal stunt. I was now facing **forty-one years** in prison. Who was this woman? Why was she taking my family from me? She wanted to end my life; I had no life

----

to take? The challenges. That made me another person. I wanted to end the lives of all of those who made me suffer. Karma has followed in its own magical way. How could the court system take my life.

EVEN THOUGH My, immediate family wasn't a part of my childhood. There had been no gathering of Aunts, Uncles, Grandparents. We were invisible to our cousins whether separated seven houses down the same street or in another state. I was born in Santa Fe, New Mexico, Santiago H. Treviño and Miquela Lucero Treviño; my mother had nine children, five daughters, four sons. My father's education was up to the second grade. My father worked for my Abuelito (grandfather) in his field at a young age, his father's brought other workers from Reynosa, Mexico. Every morning when my father was old enough, he went to pick up the workers at five in the morning and drove them to my grandfather's field. They would do farming for my Abuelito crops. When my father was 16 years old, he joined the Army. After Boot Camp training, he got stationed in Germany for over a year, where he drove the Officers around in the Army Jeeps on base. He also worked as a mechanic on his Jeep and other vehicles on base. My father was later transferred to New Mexico, where he met my mother. He told us that he had gone off base AWOL to meet my mother and, the Army found out. My father then had his stripes torn off from a sergeant to a private for going AWOL. My father was head over heels in love with my mother. When my father completed his service with the Army, he got married, and they moved to Mission, Texas. My mother had never been, anywhere, out of the state of New Mexico. My mother was born in a small town called La Canada, New Mexico. Its located 25 miles North of Santa Fe, where Spanish and Pueblo Anasazi Indians resided. My Abuelito was born in Camino De Santiago in Spain; but, we never knew where our Abuelita (grandmother) was born. My Abuelito met my Abuelita in Mission, Texas. When my Abuelito married, he bought a considerable amount of land and three homes down the road from the fields, but the houses were apart from the main house, where the family lived. The second house was for the housemaid Litcha, a widow with two daughters and a son. The third house was where the worker stayed until the end of the weekend they went home to their families. They worked for my Abuelito, picking the crops on his land. My Abuelito had a lot of orange trees, grapefruit, and lemons, watermelons, and vegetables. I loved to eat oranges off the trees on my grandfather's field. Have you noticed the tangerines? The name has changed their no longer called tangerines. I remember when we went to visit my grandparents. I was about nine years old. One of my Aunts showed us a picture of my brother and me; we were both young. My brother was about nine months old. We both had curly hair. The picture showed both of us sitting inside a giant watermelon, eating like little pigs; our faces were full of watermelon from head to toe. The workers got paid $2.00 a day or by the bushels including room, and board. My Abuelito said you have to be careful who gets paid per hour sometimes; you hire a person and, their lazy, come to eat Litcha homemade food then, sleep in the fields till the end of the day. Payday was every Friday at 3 pm. After everyone got paid, my Abuelito talked to some of his workers about a crazy idea. My Abuelito asked his men if they were interested in making a little extra money. My Abuelito said to the men if they were interested in helping him dig for the box he had buried but, the truth was my Abuelito had heard there was a (Tesoro) Treasure. My Abuelito said under one of those big trees. A couple of men started digging after work for two days but found nothing. Then night, one of the men decided to stay and search a bit longer. Suddenly, the man noticed the man who chose to dig a bit longer had vanished. My Abuelito figured he found the Tesoro and ran off with it. My grandfather knew it contained money and documents of properties. My Abuelito would leave out of town once a month after all the workers had gotten paid. He wouldn't come back for a week.My Abuelita said my Abuelito was a womanizer; My Abuelito had a lot of money. He was a very slim handsome man. He dressed like a cowboy. If you were to run into him, you couldn't tell he only spoke Spanish. My Abuelito father came from a high official position. My father said his grandfather father was a General and had a high power in Mexico. My Abuelito grew up in a wealthy family and was the only child. When I went to visit my Abuelito. I was on a business trip, my aunt Nana's found out and picked me up at the hotel. I had a training meeting for the Albuquerque Job Corps Center. I taught them my color-coded transportation monthly report. I learned my Abuelito had Special Abilities. We talked about a lot of different things in life. We were sitting in my Abuelito kitchen. That night he sat by the window, and listened to the radio and watch the neighbor walking down the road. He spoke about how we were all mixed in bloodlines but the same in life. He mentioned that the Black people were not the only slaves. The Whites, Hispanic, Asians and, other races were too. Except the blacks lived in their master's land free with all their needs. They had everything, room, and board, food. They even had their church where they sang and danced at night. When their master died, the slaves received their clothes. They wore it on Sunday for church. Most of the blacks who considered themselves slaves wanted to be free. They wanted the one piece of paper showing freed. After being told by various political figures, many freed people believed they had a right to own the land they had worked as slaves and were eager to control their property. Some freedmen took advantage of the order and took the initiative to acquire land plots. Several of black land ownership increased markedly. The blacks who received their freedom used their master's last name and moved away. It wasn't what they were expecting. They ended up paying room and board. Paying taxes working as maids and ground- keepers. Same old crap he said life is like a wheel it turns and, turn and, life will never change unless you change. The Blacks, because of their color got Fame. What do you see now? When you turn on the TV, all you see is blacks, black. Because black Matters. What about the rest of the Cultures? We have a color TV, not black and white. The rest of us got washed out. Turn on your TV. All you see is more blacks than any other race on TV, Movies. Stop with Black Matter. We all matter; life is beautiful when we see color or all races in a movies like NCIS, has blacks, whites hispanics. Portuguese, derived from the Latin word Negro, meaning dark complexion or race, are called Negro for the color of their skin. African Americans a Negro spiritual, Every history, of impartial mind, knows that the negro rule the world. Do you think it would make a difference to you or me? Will the Negro problem be settled by voice. No God made us of color Now they benefit from higher appreciation; they are no longer members of the Negro race but can be classified among a higher type as made out are no longer. When they are up and liberated, they tell that Africa Negro has made these people understand their destiny linked. Now color throughout the world, hundreds of millions of darker people are looking toward one common union and future through the effort. The white world has always tried to rob and discredit people of color. They had the inheritance of their parents who had money. They managed to make them rich they knew how to manage as they were educated. Speak up, America. What makes you better than I because you have blue eyes or your skinner than I fat people are beautiful. We will always be different in life. You are no better than I or I of you. Say it. Money comes and goes but, you will always be you. The people born here made you famous are suffering when they get rich they take the money we made them rich to other countries. Do you even know who lives next door? Most white people protest for blacks. They should stand up for their children and families who need them. Don't make others better than our own; those of us who don't have a voice are the ones in need are right Infront of you. Money makes people crazy some take drugs, and others commit suicide, and some try black magic to get what's not meant for them. My grandfather said evil is bad and not worth doing. Why hurt a person you say you love or just because you want power there is no power in life. God is the power Karma will get you. We have made the world feel for their stories of being the only slaves and suffering. You want to know history. The truth is that all races have in the past and some today. We all suffer the same. My daughter's friend was tied up on the back of a car bumper and dragged to death, then left on the road to die. The family posted signs to help find who killed their son. Not a one. The police wouldn't help her. They assumed a Hispanic was dead on the street. The first thing that went through the police minds was a drug deal gone wrong. That's what he deserves. The truth is, if you're not in a gang, you are dead. When the Mexicans or Latinos/Hispanics. The people said the Mexican who came to America had taken their jobs. The jobs that you say were taken paid less than minimum wage for hard labor. Most women were hired as housemaids as they were trustworthy and kept their home and children clean. They didn't take anyone jobs except for the work you didn't want as an American. Not just were Mexicans slaves but, Mexican-Americans were not allowed in a movie theater unless they sat on the balcony. Mexicans were not allowed in swimming pools. They had to wait till the white people swam in the pool till the water was dirty; public schools were segregated from the white students. The Mexican were rejected from enrolling in their community school.

My sister Felix's high school band class went on competition, they decided to stop at a well-known restaurant when the waitress said, and the Hispanics band students were not allowed in a restaurant to eat in 1971. They would not serve Spanish or Mexicans. The white students said if our Mexican friends don't get served, we don't want to eat here either and got back on the bus. When arriving back home, their parents and friends heard what happened and they held up banners welcoming them home safe.

The school later received an apology letter from the owner of the restaurant and the governor to Santa Fe High Band.

My Abuelito said the Natives traded buffalo skins to keep the white men warm for firewater whiskey, and got drunk. They traveled and camped out in different places living free in the land where most of us had to pay rent and taxes. When they made peace, why did we give the Natives land all over the United States, and money for seeds to grow their crops? The Natives don't allow us in their land. They have their own government, police force, private schools, hospitals, and their laws. their reservation. The Natives own their land. No one can touch it Tax-Free. They have their freedom. Our government is still giving them money for water rights that the rest of us can't claim. The Natives and Blacks have made movies. The Natives are the riches cultures their making millions of dollars a day in their Casino on the reservation. Tax-free. Their still taking money from our government. Why aren't we treated the same way we have to pay the price. The Natives don't need help from our government. They can help their own. We are the people who spend all our money to make them rich.

My Abuelito lived to be 97 years old. He said no one lives for free as there is a price for everything in life. God has blessed the Natives who betrended Gods by the laws given. I wonder what my Abuelito meant by that as he died before I would know what he meant. The Natives are trying to be noticed but going about it the wrong way.

Did you hear when one of the Casinos had to get shut down, it was seen and proven by most of the employees and surveillance camera recorded that the devil himself played the gambling machines and spoke to a woman who had lost her money for her mortgage? It a true story Natives from all over the United States came to make Sacraments to demand that the evil spell would leave the Casino but did it work. They blocked the Casino was swarming with Bees. Most of the gamblers remember the day it shut down. It's hard to break a curse.

It draws you to gamble more than you can afford. All we can do is pray that whammy leaves you. Whammy No whammy. The list goes on to research what they own now and who paying for it? Even with all the Casinos, our government is helping the Natives with our tax dollars. Did the taxpayer agree to all these agreements? The government has given to the Natives.

We are one of the poorest states in the United States. Then we have people from other countries who bought businesses in the United States; their children attend our colleges. You will see most of them have high positions. As hard-working citizens, we can't open our businesses or buy our own homes because colleges take money from people from other countries. My son has been on the honor roll and has more knowledge than the doctor, yet he can't get certified because the certification is going to the immigrants with money. Some go to other countries to live a better life, and others come to the United States to seek freedom. The United States of America has helped other countries. Now America is distress who's helping us here in the land of the free. Most of us have worked most of our lives to have what we have and, now we can't live off of our retirement check. Instead of helping the elderly who worked for years to receive their retirement are having to work to make ends meet. Your life if heading that way you can stop it. Help your own not just does being retired hurt but, your health goes down south. The people who worked for their country should be cared for. Not the young healthy women that are having five, six, and even seven children and live off of government assistance. I know of a woman like that she has, her husband or boyfriend living with her, with her government assistance and his construction job. They drive a big truck and own a nice house and, here we are tax-paying citizens driving a car that will only us get around town. The seniors end up living in a bad neighborhood because that all they can afford. The government should only pay for two births, and, after that, they should figure out how to pay for a pregnancy and think before getting pregnant to pay for their own hospitalization and care for their child. If a man or women is getting any kind of government assistance and are able to work put them to work homeless get government assistance and get tax free money on the street it that fair to us who pay taxes. The disable and, elderly should be help as they need it and, worked for years to earn it. As we did thank God for our grandparent who helped us care for our children for those who had to work. If you come to our country, you should earn government assistance from our government and work at least five years before being eligible, as we all have here in the United States. Don't watch your friends or neighbors worry about having to work minimum wage and can't make ends meet. They end up with depression, and some commit suicide, has the highest rate of death. We should be enjoying our retirement traveling enjoying our grandchildren but, we can't afford it—Stand-up America for your country. The White life stories slaves; India has the highest number of slaves globally as an American. Whites are powerful, wealthy, greedy and, living off of their parent's inheritance. That's when different cultures changed; other races married rich men and, white women married Blacks. That's where the word gold digger originated. Even if we know it to be accurate, we won't admit it, just like most of the stories told, like love spells, don't ever try a love spell because you'll never know if he genuinely loves you. Why would you turn to evil when a man or woman doesn't want you? Besides, witchcraft isn't worth doing. God will punish you and, the love spell will ruin your life as you have taken their true happiness. How cruel is that it's plain selfish? Why can't you pray for your hopes and dreams? Miracles do happen. My Abuelito also spoke that basically, they forgot the rest of the cultures. The list goes on. We are one color in your heart. Authentic cultures work hard for what they have. Most of them learned how to survive with their trades to build, fix things to make a living for their families. They took jobs no one wanted and learned to do things of their cultures. They made the things that others would travel all over the world to buy their goods. My Abuelito is right about one thing he said we are all of one color as we all suffer the same rich, poor no matter of the color. My Abuelito spoke that the most important thing we could ask for is an understanding of life. Life is beautiful, like the rainbow in the sky. The sun and the moon that we see the stars at night. If it all went away, what would it be like if there were no color? The Natives, Blacks, Whites, and all the world's culture would be boring color is what Matters. We Matter. We are of one Color no matter what. Color is what makes life. I think to myself, what a wonderful world. I couldn't live not seeing the different colors in my life. We make it what it is. I have been there, done that mostly all the sad things in life. We of all COLORS MATTER don't forget who you are and what you stand for. Our blood is red; our skin is of different colors. We have hopes and dreams, as you do. I believe in God. You may believe in another god. What matters is love, trust, belief in hope, peace. I figure that when we die and go to heaven, we will not be of one race as God loves color. I overheard my father tell one of his stories.

Love Spell

It was about a young man in love with a girl with blue eyes and long blond hair, but she wouldn't give him the time of day. So, he decided to see the town Bruja (Witch). The Bruja asked him to bring her a lock of the young girl's hair. The next day he sat next to the beautiful young girl. Where she sat on the bench every morning waiting for the bus, he thought it would be the perfect time to get a lock of her hair. He was enormously nervous, scared and, shaking. He had a hard time trying to get the scissors out of the pocket of his pants. He finally grabbed the scissors, reached over, swiftly cut a piece of the girl's hair; he quickly took it to the Bruja. The Bruja then made the young man a Spell with the young girl's hair. The Bruja said to the young man; she will come to you. Then a few days later, the young man went back to see the Bruja and said to the Bruja, it's not working, but this cow is following me everywhere. The Bruja said it should have worked; you must have cut the cow's tail. Instead, they all laughed and wanted to hear more of my father's stories. My father told another story to the men.

Mr. Wilson

My father started to tell of a man who walked into the bar after having a few drinks with the men; he then stabbed his knife on the counter and yelled out I'll bet anyone here I can go to the Cemetery at midnight and stab here this knife on old-man Mr. Wilson's grave. They all laughed. You know that Mr. Wilson was the meanest man that ever lived. Just before midnight, he headed to the graveyard on that cold, windy night. The man stood right in front of old-man Mr. Wilson's grave; then kneeled, pulled out his knife, stabbed the top of old-man Mr. Wilson's Coffin. When he was ready to get up, his knife got caught on old Mr. Wilson's Coffin. The next day they found the man dead on top of old Mr. Wilson's grave. He died of a heart attack.

Memories' of My Siblings

ossip has controlled my family by the one person who started it all. The lies, why wouldn't they have confronted me. We no longer have the closeness we had before. I could have used a sister by my side, but now it's too late. Life had passed me by and, it doesn't matter anymore. We have the following funeral; my daughter and I used to be inseparable; now, she won't even allow me to know my granddaughter. On Christmas, I heard that my daughter had visited most of my family, but she never came to see me, but that was ok. I was sick in bed. I kept a lot inside of me. I don't think it's worth worrying about. My daughter has a lot to thank me for as I gave my daughter and son everything they had in life and was there for them; look around. You will one day find me, but it will be too late. I have no regrets as I was the best mother and father figure they could have ever had. God sees all trust me. Karma is a bitch.

My older sister stayed home with my mother, and I went with my brothers to work downtown. I never knew what she did all day. My mother wouldn't allow us in the kitchen. She took care of the household cleaning. My older sister didn't come out of her room except when we ate if that. When my sister grew up and graduated from high school, she joined the Army right after graduation. When my sister got out of the Army, she was a different person. I believed it changed her life. She asked if I would move to Albuquerque to attend college at UNM; we became roommates. She went to college, and I got a job. We first bought a car to visit our family in Santa Fe on the weed ends. Our first car was a Nova; it fits the name, Nova. Nova in Spanish means No go; that fits the name. The car lasted a year. My older sister and I bought a house. My father got sick and was transported to Albuquerque to be admitted to the veteran's hospital. My mother didn't drive. She moved in with us. The family house would be leased till my father was released from the hospital. A family friend found out my father was sick and asked to lease their house. My father's education was up to the second grade. My parents' friend wrote up the lease. She drew up the paper for my parents to sign a quick claim deed that later became a warrant deed. My parents lost their house. My father had to start all over after he was released from the hospital seven months later but, before then, my mother and my younger brother and sister came to move in with us. My older sister and I had a lot of fun shopping at the mall. We used to dress up nice for school and work. I got married the following day; Jake and I headed to Chicago for three months. My husband had to report for training. It was the most horrifying trip. The roads were icy; cars drove off the road, and people were severely injured. It was late at night when the vehicle lost control; I could have sworn I had seen my Jake head on the steering wheel, bleeding; I wondered how I would get back home. Suddenly he said, did you know the car spin to the other side of the road and, back I looked at him and thought to myself I had seen him dead leaning against the steering wheel. My older sister got married a couple of months after I did. I wasn't able to attend her wedding. I was in Chicago. When I went back home to get my things. I received from our wedding; I couldn't find any of my stuff, including my wedding dress; my sister and her husband moved to Edgewood, New Mexico. My second to the oldest, Sister Felix, who is dead now, would visit my older sister at her house in Edgewood when she could; she would take my mother with her.

My sister Felix called me at work. That she had gone to visit my older sister, but she wasn't home. She was working, but her husband was home with his daughters; Felix said she walked in to see my nieces, and they were locked up in their room. She was puzzled about the visit and decided to investigate on her own. She felt the need to protect my nieces from something but never said what. The girls remember their aunt Felix visiting them. Then life changed so fast. I got married, then she got married, and we moved on with life. Our kids grew up, and here we are, back to square one. I could have wanted advice on some of my life problems, but I had no sister or anyone. That's what sisters do for each other like my sister Felix tried to do for me. Life is short. My older sister and her husband have two daughters and a grandson.

Maria Felix: The second to the oldest, Felix, who we called for short her given name is Maria Felix but, no one ever knew her by that name. We called her Felix, and others knew her as Mary or Maria. She died at a very young age. As a young girl, my sister liked to stay at my grandma Lucero's house. My grandmother was always cooking and baking. Once my grandmother helped my sister baked a cake from scratch for her Girl Scout badge she wore proudly. I remember my mother and father bought two big dolls, one had dark hair, and the other had light brown hair. The one with blond hair belongs to Felix because she had light brown hair like her; Felix played with her doll and took it with her everywhere, even to Grandma Lucero's house. The dolls were almost as tall as my sisters. Felix would drag her doll from the doll's arm and, sometimes, from her hair. After Felix graduated from high school, she got pregnant with her firstborn George's high school boyfriend and got married. A year later, her daughter was born; then, she was forced to file for a divorce from her husband, had got an underage girl pregnant, and was forced to marry the young girl. Then five years later, she had another daughter from another man in her life but never married. Twenty years later, she met Jorge at work. Jorge Morales. We never knew if that was his real name as he used my nephew's name. Felix met Jorge at work; he worked as a custodian at the college. My sister worked at she was the Directors' Secretary. She had her own office Jorge would visit my sister at work. The men in the custodian department were complaining Jorge was not doing his job. Jorge was a short man with black hair and dark brown eyes. He originally came from a place called Guerrero, Mexico. Felix gave Jorge a ride to the church where Jorge was staying. A month later, Jorge moved into my sister's house. My sister said he was staying in the garage to fix odds and ends. She needed to done around the house after work and on the weekends until he found a place to stay. Less than two weeks later, my sister found out Jorge didn't know how to fix anything and just needed someone to support him. When Jorge moved into my sister's house, he brought a couple of cans of food, two change of clothes, and an old blanket with holes that needed washing. Then Jorge broke the news that he was fired from work. Since Jorge had nothing to do all day, he would follow my sister to work. Jorge went with her to work and waited around in her office. The director confronted Jorge that he could not stay at my sister's office and was asked to leave. My sister called me if I could loan her some money till payday. I said I'd be right there. When I walked into my sister's office, all her co-workers were out to lunch and, she was working. I walked up to her desk; I right away noticed she was wearing these oversized sunglasses. I started to joke around how the office couldn't have been that bright. She had to wear sunglasses. She then lowered her sunglasses and looked up at me. I couldn't believe it. She had a black eye. I asked what had happened; she said it was an accident.

We went to lunch, leaving the back way with me alone without Jorge noticing us leaving. Jorge was hitting and stalking her at work. Weeks later, I got another call from my sister. I went to her office and noticed Jorge in the parking lot in Felix's car, waiting for my sister to get off work. We thought Jorge had a job he was leaving with my sister to work every morning, but he stayed in her car with his coffee and breakfast burrito till she got out for lunch and then till she got off work. My sister called me about six o'clock that her car wouldn't start; I figured Jorge had the car radio running and the battery died out; she just needed a boost. I asked my mother to go with me late at night, and I was already at her house picking up the kids. My mother always needs to know everyone's business or, more like gossip, my mother asked Jorge what he was doing there. My sister immediately answered for him; she said he was looking for work. That weekend, Jorge and Felix were visiting my parents. When I got to my parent's house, I noticed Jorge was standing outside the bathroom door listening to my sister. And, I walked up to him and, said what are you doing? He just moved away from the door. I couldn't believe he couldn't allow her to go to the bathroom in peace. My oldest brother loaned Felix a cell phone. Jorge was standing by the bathroom door lessoning if she was on the phone. I said are you kidding me. What are you doing? Can't she take a shit in peace? My mother said when Jorge and Felix saw you coming, they both ran out the back door. I said Felix shouldn't be getting hit by that man and, most of all, following her to work, she can get fired. Felix's daughter had gotten married and, her younger daughter was living in the dorm.

My daughter and I were fixing up the house to put it up for sale. I didn't need any reminders of Jake living in the house. It would have been too big for the three of us anyway. I gave my ex- whatever he wanted; I just wanted out of the marriage. My sister suggested that we could stay in my niece's old bedroom. Her daughter got married and moved to Chicago with her husband

and, we could stay there and help her with the rent. It was just me, my daughter and grandson.

My daughter worked the night shift and, I worked the day shift. My sister didn't have a phone.

I asked Felix if we could have a phone connected in my niece's room. We paid my sister **three hundred dollars a month** for the one-bedroom. Jake came to my sister's house to visit after work; Jake was living with the other women at the time. Jake came when my sister's water heater broke; he helped fixed her water heater. Then he offered my sister to pay for our rent but, I said we didn't need his help.

One day my sister got home late from work. She had stopped at Kentucky Fried Chicken to pick up dinner for Jorge and herself. Jorge was mad at my sister Felix for coming home late from work. She couldn't call him. They didn't have a phone to let him know she would be home late. Jorge grabbed the container of chicken and threw it across the kitchen floor. Then he grabbed Felix from her hair, dragging her around the kitchen. We heard my sister screaming, and we ran out of the bedroom; I grabbed Jorge and threw him up against the wall. Jorge yelled out, don't hurt me, please don't hurt me. My sister yelled out; please leave him alone.

Lucky for me Jorge was a short petite man. Before releasing him, I told him that I would make sure they put him in jail if he ever hurt Felix again. My grandson started running around the house, saying, please don't hurt me. It was a joke for a while. That wouldn't be the last time my sister had problems with Jorge. There was a time my daughter, grandson, and I decided to go shopping. When we got home, we opened the front door and walked into the house carrying our bags. My sister's house had a powerful smell. We couldn't figure out what or where the smell was coming from. Then my sister called us to her bedroom. Jorge had shattered her perfume bottles all over her bedroom. She loved collecting different perfumes; her dresser was full of different perfumes; That was one of my sister's treats for herself collecting lovely perfumes. Jorge had broken all her perfume bottles. They were on the floor, her dresser and mirror, and her bed. The whole house had to be aired out.

My daughter and I helped clean up the mess. My sister married Jorge being he had moved into her house. My sister's co-worker tried to talk her out of getting married to Jorge but, she was desperate to have someone to be in her life who cared for her. Felix's co-workers were my friends at work. I used to work with them before I got another job. They called me and said they tried to talk my sister out of getting married to Jorge, refused to find a job, and followed her around. She couldn't have a friend or visit her family without his permission but, she wouldn't take their advice after my sister got married. I later found out my sister had been stranded in Guerrero, Mexico, with Jorge on her honeymoon. She ran out of money and didn't have money to get back home. I called my mother daily, and she never said a word to me that my sister Felix had been stranded for three days in Mexico. She called my motherhouse to send her some money to get back home, but my younger sister intervened. She alleged to Felix's son and my mother not to send her any money and teach her a lesson. I said didn't you realize what's going on.

I asked if anyone called the University; she needed to get home and work; she didn't have money to eat or a place to sleep; Jorge's family had taken the little money my sister had. I asked when did she last call. My mother said two or three days ago I said are you kidding? I couldn't believe it. When she calls, tell her I will figure out how to send her money on Western Union to get something to eat, and I will get her a prepaid bus fare to come home, but I won't pay for Jorge he can stay there where he belongs. My sister refused to leave Jorge behind. She used the money I sent her to get a ticket for Jorge. When my sister arrived home, my mother informed my sister and Jorge, you won't believe who sent you money to get home. The one person you less expected to send you money. Do you know who it was? It was Viola. I asked my sister how she managed to be in Mexico for three days without money. She said they were having some all day and night Fiesta and, they got free food and could sleep on the floor in town. I thought to myself; my sister must have had an Angle watching over her. I had gotten concert tickets from a place I volunteer at, and I invited my sister and, of course, she wouldn't go without Jorge. I also invited my older sister and her husband and her younger daughter to go too. My sister went to buy Jorge a beer before we were seated. Jorge must have been drinking before going to the concert; he started yelling out at the performers, calling them names. We were all embarrassed but, Jorge kept yelling and cussing and jumping as most drunks do. Jorge yelled over and, over you, F N Mexican, you can't sing. Suddenly, my sister had disappeared. When we finally found her, Jorge had gotten a beer bottle and hit her over my head because she wouldn't buy him another beer. She would have got him another beer but, she didn't have any money. When she came back, we noticed she was full of blood and, we all got up. My older sister and her husband took her to the emergency room to get stitches. Jorge walked back to my sister's house. Eight months later, my sister was admitted to the hospital. They found out she had diabetes and wasn't taking care of herself. I later heard she was in the hospital. She had her leg amputated at that time. My son and I went to see her at the hospital. She said to my son, is that you and he said yes, and you know how much I hate hospitals. The smell makes me sick and, they laughed. She tried to get up; she said, look, you just missed my daughter and her family. They came to see me; look at the picture of my grandchildren, she smiled. She said my daughter wants me to stay with her in Chicago. I said you should go, but my sister wouldn't leave Jorge behind. I wish that my sister could have had the strength to leave Jorge. When my sister transferred to a Rehab

Center, Sal and I sometimes visited Felix; I went alone. When she was in therapy, I couldn't believe how hard it was to balance on one leg. After visiting with my sister on my way back home, I cried and thought to myself; I couldn't believe how this could happen to my sister. She had suffered so much in her life and, now, this. She was in therapy for about three weeks and, then She went home with Jorge. After she got home not more than a few days later, my son received a call from my sister. My son went over to help his aunt and found Jorge had been mistreating her. Jorge made Felix iron his shirt so he could go out to the bar. He was using my sister's debit card as he didn't work. Jorge knocked her down and threw his shirt at her face, and she fell on the floor. Jorge yelled, do it again. Iron it, right? Can't you see the sleeves are wrinkled; he yelled. I can't go out looking like that. Jorge laughed at her as she struggled to get herself back up. My son could hear Jorge yelling at his aunt. My son rushed to help his aunt. He walked in and, seen Jorge yelling at his aunt. My son helped her up and, said can't you see she can't get up from the floor? Jorge said she is my wife and I can do whatever I want with her. That's not true; a marriage certificate isn't anything but a piece of paper with both of your signatures. My son said, get your stuff; you're going with me now. Jorge just stood there. My sister left with my son. I'm not sure where my son took my sister someplace safe. The next day Jorge went out looking for my sister and couldn't find her. He went to my parents' house and the University to ask her co-worker where she was and, they refused to give Jorge any information regarding my sister. That was the last time my sister saw him. Jorge once told me he lived with another woman before my sister and, she couldn't get rid of him either. The woman's brother couldn't get him to leave their sister's home. Jorge said to me; you see these scars there from a knife her brothers had stabbed him. To get rid of him, but they couldn't. I asked how did she finally leave you. Jorge said he got and when he got home, she was gone. The house was empty. I am sure Jorge has found his next victim. Since my sister, he doesn't know; my sister has passed. One of my best memories of my sister was when she played the saxophone in a high school band. When she played in the parade, I never missed watching her play; I was proud of her. I would stand there in front of the crowd, and I cried. I was so proud of her. The high school band was good they went on the competition. I remember when my sister had gone to Oklahoma with her high school band. They got down to eat at a restaurant. The waitress called the manager, and the owner came out. He said they did not serve Mexicans but would be more than glad to serve the rest of the team. The whole team stood up and said, we're a team and left the restaurant. When they got back home, the whole town heard what had happened. They were cheering for the band. The Governor and the High School class of 1969 received an apology letter from the restaurant and the Governor of Oklahoma. I remember walking into my sister's house and, my sister was in her bedroom all alone crying for her daughter, who moved away after she got married. She moved to Chicago with her husband. Our family never knew how to show their feeling; she hoped her daughter knew she cared. Her older daughter had gotten married to a nice guy she met in high school and, my sister had three grandchildren. After my sister died, her younger daughter moved to Las Vegas, Nevada, to pursue a job in teaching, then years later, after her mother had died. She got married. I wanted to go to her wedding with my sister Felix, I went to Vic's wedding to have family standing by her side, but she wasn't that happy to see me as one of her living family members. Her older sister and her family were there. They had come from Chicago. I could kick myself. My sister had mentioned her grandkids' names to me, but she was occupied with her sisters. My sister had shown me a picture of her daughter's family she had in the hospital. She said these are my daughter's kids and her husband. I hoped Felix's oldest daughter me their address or phone number. I didn't want to miss out on life without my family and friends; I wanted to keep in touch. I miss my nephew. May God give him peace and happiness in heaven. My sister had many bad relationships but took care of herself the best way knew how. She worked till she no longer could. No matter how old you are, you can make it on your own most women believe that you need to be married to have a family. That's not true. No one should mistreat you. Don't be in a relationship with anyone when you know deep in your heart you hate being with that person and, the outcome could be worse trust in your feeling. Who the hell did Jorge think he was? Life is too short. You're the only one who can make yourself happy look in the mirror and making yourself happy, not anyone else. Don't ever believe it when they say I'm sorry or I love you and, the other big one is he won't do it again. It never worked for my sister. Men used her weakness. She needed to be love even if it hurt. It can happen to men as well. Women abuse men too.

* * * Don't fear failure. Get up and learn from it * * *

We never had a mother who taught us what that we needed to know. My father gave my mother everything she needed and never laid a hand on her. Our mother never knew what her daughters and sons had to deal with in life. We learned from friends, and, in reality, I was with my sister at her worst times. My sister just wanted someone to love her. She was a hard worker and a great Secretary. If only others had seen how wonderful my sister Felix was inside, she had a big heart. Jealousy and, gossiping was her weakness. My old boss Eva always said the person who gossips about others could only imagine what they're saying about you, the gossip you hear is usually not true they just have hatred inside them. My father always said jealousy is the biggest sin in life.

* * * Look around on what you have, not what you don't have * * *

* * * Stress is nothing but psychological pollution * * *

My sister was working at the courthouse when a girl was sabotaging her work, and her boss threatened to fire her. she went home crying every night. I was working at T-VI as the Amnesty program secretary under the director. I asked him if he would consider hiring my sister, who had excellent credentials. He considered it and hired her. The girl that was tampered with her files and the documents she had typed for the director. The girl got my sister's job; she couldn't do the work she ended up quitting. Karma got her. She couldn't find a job after that incident. Three years later, Felix transferred to the University of New Mexico. At the time, I was working as a medical transcriber at home. My sister Felix had a big heart no matter what; I still loved her and always will. My sister asked my son if he would take her to see me. When she got out of the hospital, she visited me at MDC; she walked with a cane. I was so excited to see her and my son; I wanted to cry. I will never forget what my sister said to me, don't worry, pray to St. Jude, light him a candle for his blessings. That's the only thing that stuck to me from her visit. My son and sister had put money on my books to buy what I needed; I never received the money. While I was at MDC, my sister died and, I was unable to attend her memorial service. I did go to Felix graveside and felt sad I never went back. I remember Felix said to me one day; you know what? Our mother tried to get us to go against each other. You need to be careful what you say to her. My mother didn't have any sisters, so I didn't know what it was like to have a sister. Now believe that to be true; they didn't communicate. I would rather not talk much to anyone unless I have the facts. You know my Dad said the persons you think you can trust are the ones who started the gossip.

I remember my sister's making her salsa. My sister always made salsa. She never ate anything without her salsa. On the Easter holiday, She made chile Rellenos (stuffed green chile, cheese). And her Salmon paddies. We ate them faster than she could cook them. When Felix cooked, it came from the heart?

The oldest brother: My mother and father favored their firstborn son. They had three daughters and wanted a son. My oldest brother was special to my parents as they wanted a son. I remember when my parents had bought my brother two-pedal cars, a blue car, a red tractor with an umbrella, and he got a red bicycle when he was nine. I reminisce about my brothers asking our oldest brother to let them take a ride on his bike. He rode it till it got dark. My younger brothers had asked to let them take a ride on his bicycle. I said let him ride it till he gets tired, then he would let them ride his bike. And, he did the next day. My brother was so happy with his new red bike. One day my brothers got together and decided to build a ramp on the side of the house with boards and blocks to Pop Wheelies on my brother's red bike. They had the best time ever. I didn't like my brother's bike because it was a boy's bike. It was too high for me to ride. I borrowed my oldest brother's bike.

I was having a hard time riding the bike; I decided to give it up when trying to get off it; I fell and hurt myself. Three days went by; I went to see my grandmother Lucero down the street. I knew my grandmother would be home baking, cooking, or cleaning. I sat down in the living room on the bed and, said grandma; I'm going to die. I lost a lot of blood and, I feel weak. My grandmother sat down in her living room, and she laughed at me till she cried. I didn't think it was funny; only she knew what my problem was. My daughter had a similar problem. I came home one day and explained what had happened at school. I tried to clarify what to expect. My daughter then said, when did my brother start his and,

----

I explained that boys don't have that problem and, she? Yelled out What, why not, my daughter refused to talk to her brother for weeks and, he couldn't figure out what was wrong with his sister. When my oldest brother was seventeen years old, he joined the Marine Corp. He was stationed in Maine, where he graduated.

When he completed his service in the Marine Corps, he bought a trailer and parked it on the lot next to my parents. He then bought a house and got married to a good person. God must have blessed me, brother. My oldest brother's wife is the best thing in his life and, his stepdaughter and grandchildren his been blessed. I hope God is with my oldest brother and, his wife seems to be struggling with illness as I suffer from diabetes. I hope life will change for them as were not getting any younger and can't fight battles like we used to. My brother has always been the big brother. He doesn't hear gossip but finds out the facts.

Second, to the oldest Brother: Had also joined the Marine Corp. He was stationed in San Diego, California , I when I was living in Long Beach, California; my brother and his friends would visit me on the weekends. My parents surprised me one day they came to visit me. They came with my sister Felix and my younger sister Eva and her boyfriend. They stayed for two days. When I got home from work. I noticed my younger sister and her boyfriend were still in my apartment.

I called my mother and asked why they left my sister and her boyfriend behind and, my mother said my sister told them I had asked them to stay. How could I? I didn't know my sister's boyfriend? I was working and didn't know they were leaving. We lived in Navy Housing and paid seven hundred a month for a two-bedroom. We didn't have room. We were living in Navy housing and, they had rules. I asked my sister where they were going to staying. She said, they had moved the baby to your room and put their stuff in the baby's room. My sister was pregnant, and her boyfriend had a broken leg. Months went by my sister was getting bigger and, her boyfriend didn't have a job. Because of his broken leg.

I took my son every morning to the babysitters, and I went work Jake had duties on his ship for three weeks.

My sister was pregnant, and felt trapped and started to cry. I said to my sister that I could ask my boss if he could hire you. You could work in the back checking out wines. The only ones who would see her would be the waitress. He hired my sister on the spot. We went to work together and, her boyfriend stayed at my apartment all day waiting for the mailman. He even got the mail for the neighbor and hand-delivered it to them. Her boyfriend was receiving an unemployment check at my mail box. Her boyfriend took off his cast and, was out visiting the neighbors. My sister said she heard there was a job opening for maintenance on base? He worked for three in half weeks and hated to work.

They went out to eat every night after I got home from work. I picked up my son from the babysitter's house the minute I got off work; my sister's boyfriend would grab my car keys to go out. Without asking to use my car. One day, I picked up my son from the babysitter's house; I noticed my son had a fever and planned to take my son to the hospital after picking up some of the baby's stuff at home. I said to my sister's boyfriend that I needed to take my son to see the doctor. My sister's boyfriend became angry and said he needed to use my car. I said you have to wait till I get back. My sister's boyfriend got mad and threw one of my son's toys at me and hit me on the head because I wouldn't lend him my car. My son was ill, and I had to take him to the ER. I was bleeding from my head. When my brother and his friends walked into my apartment, my brother said to my sister's boyfriend, get your stuff and get out. My sister went with him. My brother took them somewhere for the night and got them on the bus to Albuquerque, New Mexico, the next day. I never said a word to my brother. I should have said Thank you to him but, we never knew how to show our gratitude. My brother met his wife in the Marine Corp and later got married and moved to Arizona. We used to talk till after he moved to Arizona. Then something happens and, he stops talking to me. I would think it had to do with gossip again. I can't remember most of my brother's children's names. They're all grown up, now and, maybe married and, have children of their own. We haven't talked for over thirty years. He never said what the reason was that he was mad at me.

The days and years are going by so fast and are not getting any younger. The last time I saw my brother was at my sister's Eva funeral, and we didn't say a word to each other. I didn't recognize his wife. She looked old, and she was younger than I. It's not like I didn't try. In early December 2019, my brother's youngest daughter died of cancer. She decided to give her body to science in the hope of finding a cure. That was my last wish. I asked my older brother for her phone number. I called to introduce myself but was denied to speak to her by her sister. I asked my older brother if she may want to see her family before she passed on instead of showing up to a funeral. That was the reason I wanted to talk to her. But my brother and his wife took my idea and went to see her, which was my idea. Oh well, God knows that all that matters.

My Fourth Sister: She was the fourth girl born after me; she never left my mother's side. She had seizures; my mother had to keep an eye on her. She had a boyfriend but never got married. She lived with him and their two daughters and grandchildren, whom she loved her. My daughter was close to her Aunt Eva and, my son was too. Her Saints and Angles are around her now. My Sister and I were close at one time. I would pick her up from work every day when she worked at Bob's Burger on Central. she was the manager, and, sometimes, she would babysit the twins for Bob and his wife. After work, my sister and I would go to the gas station when we needed gas up the hill on central, where my sister met the father of her daughters.

I remembered one time when the girls were about 7 or 8 years old. My sister took the kids out trick or treating and, her youngest daughter's costume was of a cat. The kids rode in the back of the Truck. My sister was driving and hit a speed bump; somehow, her daughter's tail got caught on the tailgate and, they couldn't get her untangled. They started yelling, stop by the time my sister heard them. My niece had ruined her costume. The kids couldn't stop laughing. Then there was the time we took my second to the oldest sister. Youngest daughter trick or treating and, most of the houses had their houses decorated for Halloween. There was a boy who laid on his lawn pretending he was dead with blood all over him. When the boy decided to jump up off the ground and scare the kids, my niece ran, crying and screaming. He ran after my niece to apologize for playing dead, but she just kept running, threw her bag of candy over my head, and kept running. They had a hard time catching up to her. We later found my niece at home crying. She ran two blocks without looking back.

My sister has always been a hard worker all her life. She died at work where she was working at the Casino when it first opened and, she died. Her family, neighbors, and co-workers loved her. She has been missed.

The Third Son: He also was in the Marine Corp and, stationed in San Diego, California but, got a dishonorable discharge. He would also come to my apartment in Long Beach, California, on the weekends. I remember he had to be in a Parade and got up late. I asked him if he needed a ride to the base and, he said no; I asked him how he got to my house? He said he hitchhiked by waving a dollar bill. After getting discharged from the Marine Corps, he moved back to New Mexico, where he moved in with friends. We didn't see him much. We heard he had been moving around here

----

and there with his friends. My brother came over to see my older brother, but he was at work, so they left. An hour later, my mother got a call that my brother was in a car accident with a family friend and his girlfriend. Was his friend killed in a car accident? I was at my mother's house when my mother got the call from the hospital that my brother had died. The person who called gave my mother the wrong information. It was his friend who had died, and his girlfriend survived the accident. My nephew, who lived with my parents, drove my mother and father to the hospital. His body was swollen; he was unrecognizable. He was in the hospital for three weeks, then transferred to a rehab center for therapy for another week was discharged from the hospital; he was paralyzed from the accident; he was in a wheelchair, wearing a halo on his head down to his feet, and needed a place to stay. I ended up being the only one who would take him in. He was unable to do anything for himself, including bathing himself. When he asked me to help him take a bath, I didn't know what to do. I ran the bathwater then I had to undress him. I got a towel to cover his private parts; then, I got the wheelchair close enough to the bathtub and pushed him carefully into the bathtub. My God, he was a grown man. I couldn't pick him up and, he couldn't help me. I could see in his eyes how embarrassed he was. I took care of my brother for over a year till he got his settlement. I cleaned after him. I knew it was hard for him at first. After living with us for a couple of months, he started to get a little bossy. One day the electricity went off throughout the neighborhood and, he started yelling, the electricity was off. What the hell, didn't you pay the damn electricity bill. I said there was no electricity in the whole neighborhood; I couldn't believe he yelled at me like that after caring for him without asking him for one cent. It wasn't as if he paid for anything; he didn't have any money till my sister helped him get his social security. He had gotten three months after living with me but, he never said a thing to me. He used most of his money to buy marijuana. That was the reason he had so many friends visiting him. I found out after he moved to his new house in Rio Rancho, New Mexico. I figured my brother used marijuana for his pain and suffering. I will never forget when I decided to go home after work and stop for a quick look around the kitchen to see what I could make for dinner. Then I would go pick up my kids from my mother's house. I walked into the house and kicked off my high heels by the entrance of the door. I went straight to my brother's room to see how he was doing. My brother right away asked if I could empty his stool pan. He had his friends come to visit. I could smell how bad it was and refused to look into the pan. I almost vomited with the smell. It was horrifying. I held my breath and started off to the master bathroom to empty his stool pan. At the time, I was proceeding towards the bathroom, crossing the kitchen hall. Then all of a sudden, I slipped on something and fell. Oh my God. I started to glide and, turn, I couldn't get up. I kept slipping and sliding. I was all full of my brother's muck, poop finally got up on my knees and leaned against the kitchen wall. I finally got up and walked around to the master bathroom. I turned to my left and, look in the mirror, holding what was left on the bucket, holding my breath. I could see a line on my face where I had been crying. I was sick to my stomach. I almost vomit. I started the shower, holding my breath. I got in the shower. I kept putting soap all over but, I couldn't get rid of the smell. I decided to take a bath till my hands and feet were wrinkled. Then I took another shower. I had to dry myself quickly and go to my parents' house to pick up the kids. I knew it was getting late. I had been in the bathtub and shower for over an hour. I cried to my parents' house. My mother asked what happened and, I had this lump on my throat that I couldn't speak. I started to tell my mother what had happened. I was upset, and she could tell I had been crying. When I finally said that, my brother had me dump his poop in the toilet and, I slipped, you know the rest. My mother couldn't stop laughing. She almost peed on her pants. I couldn't help seeing my mother laugh. I started to laugh too. Then there was the time we went to the car wash to wash my brother's wheelchair; he had soiled. When we started to spray the wheelchair at the car wash, it flew up in the air with the water hose pressure. We had to run and retrieve his wheelchair, hoping they didn't damage it. When we got it, we started to laugh? One of us ended upholding the wheelchair while the other washed it. We all got home soaking and wet.

My brother had been living with us for nine months. Then one day, he moved out without saying a word. He went to stay at my sister's house a block away. I asked my sister why he had moved out? She said he had moved to her house because he said we had taken his VCR. I couldn't believe it; he didn't even ask me where his VCR was. My younger sister told my brother that we had taken it as always the gossiping is my curse as I'm always the target. I said to my sister are you kidding me? We have three VCRs in the house. Why would we need to take my brother's VCR? A month later, my brother's friend visited my brother at my sister's house and told him the girl who did his grocery shopping stole his VCR. By then, my sister wanted my brother out of her house. She said he was a pig and asked that I exhibit the wall full of snot.

The next day I got home from work; I couldn't believe it; there he was, he had moved back to my house, without explaining why he had moved out and without asking to move back in. He ended up living with us there for another seven months. One night I heard my brother screaming; I went to check to see what was going on. He was on the floor, pleading with God to help him, he yelled out as he crawled across the room like a snake. God, if you help me get my settlement. I promised I would help my family. He had promised my niece that he would help her with her down payment on her car if he got his settlement. She was working and would have paid him back. He got the settlement and said he couldn't help her. He had other priorities. Instead, he loaned the money to his friends and gave money to the church hoping God would forgive him. But you can't buy God.

Karma is a bitch. When his friend heard my brother received his settlement, they were all over him. He got a little over **one million dollars** and didn't say a word to me; I noticed all of his stuff was gone. His friend said your brother bought a house in Rio Rancho, and moved out. He then bought two other houses in the same area where he lived and rented them out. His tenants didn't pay the rent for several months and destroyed most of the rooms. He then had a hard time finding new tenants. The houses were later foreclosed. Karma will follow. When my brother moved to his new home in Rio Rancho, New Mexico, he returned to get the rest of his belongings. He said here, and he handed me a check for one hundred dollars. He didn't want to pay me in cash; he had proven he paid for helping him out. I thought to myself is that all were worth it to him, Karam is a bitch.

I never mentioned charging him rent. Where did that come from? I thought to myself; rent is that all I was worth? After all, they did for him. I figured he couldn't have appreciated the fact that I took care of my brother when he couldn't even wipe his ass. My brother had just received over **one million dollars** as of this day; I have never asked my brother for a penny. My mother always said never to promise a Saint or God for a favor or pray if you're not true. He made a promise; he didn't keep his promises to God. That was a bad omen. Then there was a time. My brother had offered to help my son buy a car. My son gave my brother all the money he had worked to get a car. My brother told him he could help him get a good car. But, instead, my brother swindled my son and refused to help him get a car, and wouldn't give him back his money. I went to see my brother and asked my brother for my son's money. My brother told my son he didn't have it; I said are you kidding. The damn ass hole is a millionaire and, he can't give you your money back. I went and asked my brother for my son's money. He pulled the money out of his sock; I can't imagine why my son visits my brother; he doesn't deserve to have a nephew like my son. I thought to myself, what a thing to do to a fifteen-year-old. He worked hard for his money; my brother is ungrateful; it doesn't matter how much he preaches about God. God knew what he did and, so did I. Years later, you wouldn't believe what he did when I reached out to my brother that I needed a place to stay for a couple of days at the most. I had been placed on probation and an ankle monitor. My counselor contacted my brother and asked if I could stay with him till my apartment became available and; my brother put one of his girls on his cell to talk to my counselor; she said, why can't you put her in a Shelter.

I thought to myself, my brother lives alone in a five-bedroom house, including his upstairs one-bedroom apartment attached to his house. I gave my brother a home when no one else would and took care of him. I believe in Karma one day; he will be all alone, no one to ask for help as the rest of those who threw me to the wolves. God knows the truth of how much I suffered over a love affair. You won't believe it. I was blessed; God helped me. I got my apartment sooner than planned. When you visit my brother, he starts talking about God. Preaching I can't stand a two-face that's what he is. He needs forgiveness; I know God sees everything and what he did. **You can't buy God.** When my brother became a millionaire, he treated his family as an outsider and said terrible things about me. What did he even have to say about me? God knows his shit does stink. I went to visit his friend who died in a car accident. There was a broken brick with his friend's name on it at his gravesite; I bought a headstone for him. I was able to pay payments on it and, I delivered the brick to my brother, the millionaire, and, I said, now his friend has a headstone. He never said thank you or anything. I took a picture of the headstone and gave it to my brother. The reason I took a picture was so he could see that there was just a brick with a number and his friend's name that I replaced, not him with the million dollars he had. It said from his friend and family it was beautiful. My son got a call from my brother; would you believe it? My brother called and asked if my son could help him out with a hundred dollars for firewood. Even if he still owes my son money. It was a cold night. My son asked me what he should do; I said I would go half with him. I know how it feels to be without heat and no money. My son had paid for a cruise his son wanted for his birthday. My son wanted to spend time with his son on his twenty-first birthday. His son wanted to go to Mexico. I couldn't imagine why he couldn't speak Spanish. It turned out to be a disaster because his son changed his mind the days before the cruise. First, he said he lost his passport and driver's license; I wonder how it was possible that why he would have his passport with him. My son tried to cancel the cruise or reschedule but, he couldn't. Later his son and his mother called and said she would try to get his son his driver's license and passport. I don't know how she managed to get them, but they went on the cruise as scheduled; my grandson made the trip unpleasant and didn't want to do anything about it. Then the worse part was he was horrible with my son. I knew his mother bribed my grandson by getting him another tattoo; the day before the cruise. My grandson wanted the cruise in the first place. For some reason, he decided he didn't want to go. I was upset with my grandson for mistreating his father on the cruise. His father had saved for the cruise he wanted so bad, then he had the nerve to treat my son as an alien because he had changed his mind. Well, that trip was a big mistake.

Tattoo: Leviticus 19:28 You must not cut your body to show sadness for someone Who died or put a tattoo on you. I am the Lord.

My youngest sister: Was born when I was away in school. I helped my mother with my sister when I got out of school; we were close. When my sister graduated from High School, she moved into the trailer next door to my parent's house with her boyfriend, who was only thirteen years old and, my sister was eighteen. I remembered when her boyfriend's mother came over to my mother's house and demanded her son go home as a minor. My mother said she hadn't seen him. My sister was hiding him at her place. Now she has two sons and is still living with her boyfriend, the father of her two sons. The courts in New Mexico would consider them husband and wife as they have been together for over twenty years. Her older son moved with his girlfriend next door. At the property, my father left me. I have the original copy of the property that my father left me; it's all in the county records with my father's sound signature, my other sister Felix, and mine. Her younger son goes to school and also takes guitar lessons. I heard him play at my sister's facing. When we all met at the community center to say goodbye to my sister Eva, my younger sister walked up and handed me a necklace. They had put with my sister ashes for each one of sisters and brothers.

Youngest brother: My brother lived with my parents for about two years after graduation and, then he met a girl who got pregnant and, ends up raising the child thinking it was his son and, care for him as his own. He took him everywhere. My brother had mentioned at my parents' house that he had two weeks of vacation leave but, he had nowhere to go; I then suggested if he would want to go to Disney Land and take my kids, he said ok then somehow my sister heard of the trip and, decided to go with them. My brother drove to California with my kids and nephew, and his mother. I gave my kids spending money and gave my brother money for the trip. When the mother yelled out to him; he's not even your son. Even after he knew he wasn't his son, my bother kept seeing his son that wasn't his. To this day, he considers himself his son. Later my brother met another girl who had two children. I heard he had a child from my brother. I have not met his family. We're not sure if he ever got married. My mother said my brother could not have children due to a childhood accident on a motorcycle. If he thinks he has a child, it won't show as his DNA. Most people believe a mother knows and, my mother believes it? My brother and I have not spoken for years. The rumor went I took critical papers from my brother, home, or Truck when he was living with my parents, and I was the target again but, the person who took them will have their day. Karma is real.

Again my younger sister must have said I had taken them as they did when my oldest brother's house was robbed taking his movie videotape. There were high heel prints, so he believed it was me later; he found out who took them gossip like when my brother was told I had taken his VCR, it was stolen by one of his trusted girlfriends. I have a curse of gossiping and, non-trustworthy.

You know it's funny when you try to help someone in my family; it backfires my family won't ever be there for my kids or me. A stranger would come to our rescue before my own family. My youngest brother didn't attend my funeral when my mother died, but some of his Air Force friends came. After my mother died, we lost contact of each other. Even after my father was left alone, he didn't visit his father. It became impossible to visit my father as my sister built a fence; they had to call or honk to enter the property my father had given to me. When the second to the oldest sister died, my brother of her death but, he said he had plans to go on vacation to Florida and didn't show up. I couldn't believe it. It's not like Florida won't be there when the funeral is over. He didn't make it to his mother and sisters' funerals or even my nephew, whom he was close to. He was my mother's favorite and the youngest. My mother's first favorite was my oldest brother, her firstborn son. Then my other brother, the third-born son—the millionaire they haven't seen in any funerals except. When the greedy ass hole needed something, my oldest brother and his wife went to see him after my oldest brother got out of the hospital; his dogs had attacked him. They went shopping for him and bought him food and whatever else he needed. When he was a millionaire, he didn't care a rat's ass on how any of us were doing. When he needed a place to stay and help and I didn't have food, do you think anyone came to help me?

My family doesn't know how much I suffered. I couldn't go to them as they had all been told I was the wrong person when the natural bad person would soon be suffering from their dilemma like they say what goes around comes around. That's just how life is. I believe my youngest brother now lives not more than twenty minutes away. He worked at the Air Force Base for several years as an Air Craft Mechanic. It's been over twenty years and, they haven't seen or spoken to. All I know is my brother's girlfriend answers the phone and takes his message or answers for him and that they have been traveling. That would be the end of what I know about my brother.

The Favorite Child

Everyone has a favorite child. No matter what you tell your children, there will always be a favorite. My mother always had a special place for the boys in my family. I was the third girl born to my family, which was frustrating to my parents, being most mothers want to give their husband a son. When I was born, it must have torn my mother's heart to had given birth to another girl. In those days, your parents had nine to thirteen children. Well, my mother got pregnant again. This time she had a son, the joy it brought to my parents. I was still a baby, but she placed me aside;

after my brother was born. I grew up like one of the boys. Because the three of my brothers were treated special, my younger brothers and sisters never had to work or do anything my brother, and I worked when we were growing up. The second to the oldest sister was always by my parent's side. Even though my mother talked severely of her, it was mostly my sister. When my sister died, I thought to myself. My mother took my sister to keep her from suffering here on earth, being she was responsible for most of her suffering. My grandmother Lucero once told me that my mother was caring for a baby girl my age for some distant family member and, the baby girl got sick with pneumonia and died. The truth was my mother couldn't bear to tell my father his daughter had died when the mother came to retrieve her daughter Maryanne. My grandmother told her she had caught pneumonia and died and had replaced me with her daughter. In those days, there were no doctors to care for the sick at some homes. The father left my mother some money for Maryanne when she cared for her before she died to ensure she was put in a good school and cared for. My mother saved the trust fund for caring for me and putting me in a good school. After my grandmother, Lucero mentioned that I was given a trust fund for school and then sent to Harwood Private School. I didn't want to go, but my mother took it to the grave if the story was true. I did find the birth certificate after my mother and grandmother had passed on. I don't know but, I think my siblings sensed I was not part of their family. I was always treated differently, as if I didn't fit in with the rest of the family. I could pass as looking like one of my sisters. My soulmate looks like Johnny Carson, the TV Host. We all have some stranger who looks like you but, to me, whether or not I was so-called adopted, they will always be my parents because they raised me and my brothers and sister are my families. If I found my birth parents, the family who cared for me as my family brought me life. That's just the way it is. I can't imagine looking for parents after being raised by a stranger. There is a birth mother and the mother who gave your life.

My Parents

Never express their love to us; they never embraced each other or said, I love you. I had gone to visit my brother at that Veterans Hospital. When I got home, I started to think, Wow, my brother is sick, he could die, and I couldn't say how I felt. It would be one reason for writing my story is for my oldest brother and my children. May our Father God keep my brother with us for many years to come? And hopefully will receive a donor soon. My brother hoped the family would reunite but, it would take a big miracle to find each other after so many years lost and all the gossip told by the only person who could have started it all. My brother's wife got up and gave my son and me a hugged and, we hugged her back; I turned around, waved goodbye to my brother, and said I'd call tomorrow. Isn't that sad that I couldn't hug my brother? It's just the way our parents raised us. You won't find a family photograph of all of us together as a family. You may see school pictures of two or three of my brothers and sisters but none of me. I figured they couldn't afford it; besides, I didn't particularly appreciate taking my picture. I'm just not photogenic.

Moving to Santa Fe

My parents saved enough money to buy the town bar in Mission, Texas. My father's friends and the field workers went to the bar after work. My father purchased the bar and ran it for three years. Until one dreadful night, a good friend of my father walked into the bar looking for his wife. He found her with another man dancing and having fun. It was a busy night; the men and my father didn't notice his friend till suddenly, they heard a loud sound; it was a gunshot.

My father's friend shot and killed both the man and his wife, then turned the gun, killing himself. After that incident, my father closed the bar and moved to New Mexico. My father's saying is,

**They desire nothing,
so much as they ought not to have**

My Grandpa Felix Lucero and Grandma Florinda Gallegos Lucero were living in Santa Fe, New Mexico. Before my father and mother bought the house. We lived next to in the same house my Uncle's and his family lived down the street from our house in a double pink house; one side was where my grandparents lived and, on the other side, my Uncle lived with four of my cousins who didn't know or recognized us as their cousins. We didn't talk to us because we were too poor for them but, the truth was we never took the time to know us.

When we moved to Santa Fe, New Mexico, my father bought a house where we grew up. I remember the man who sold my father our house. He had a green Army coat with a lot of medals? Was he a General in the Army? After Mr. Sandoval sold my parents our house, they may have had some agreement because he lived in Cuartito in the back of our home for several months. One day after school, he was gone. He left his Army coat behind. That I had admired, I used that coat as my favorite blanket on cold winter nights till I went away to school.

I never knew whatever happened to it. It kept me warm on those cold winter nights. I will never forget my blanket and will always be grateful for leaving me his coat and my favorite blanket. My father had added on to the house it had three bedrooms 2 ½ baths. My parent slept in one room; the boys slept in the room closes to my parent's room, and the girls slept in the far end of the house. My parents believed the boys and girls should stay in a distinct area of the house. All the bedrooms were the same size. The living room was the biggest, and the kitchen was also significant. It was on the side of the house. When my father bought the house; it only had a one-bedroom, living room, and kitchen; it had an outhouse, but we didn't use the outhouse too long. My father had an indoor bathroom build in our house.

My father added a bathroom between the boy's and girls' bedrooms. Then little by little, he added on to the house till it was big enough for all of us nine kids. We were the first in our neighborhood to have an indoor bathroom. The rest had an outhouse. My Dad did all the indoor plumbing before the rest of our neighbors; we also had a Color TV, so my mother could watch her TV shows as my father said, but most of all, my mother liked talking on the telephone. We never went to see a doctor when we were growing up but, we didn't need to because my father had enough experience as he helped my Abuelita when he was a young boy. My father coached my mother on how to care for us. As my mother never had brothers or sisters, she grew up with her grandmother.

Healing of Herbs

My mother suffered from migraine headaches most of the time when we were young. She would put slices of potatoes with vinegar on her forehead; then, she got a bandana to keep the potatoes in place on her forehead. When a child had a stomach ache as an infant, my father called it empacho was another ailment that had to do with the blockage of undigested food in the stomach. Most children get with all the milk they drink as infants. My mother would use a bar of soap, cut it in the shape of a pen and, put it into the infant or a young child's butt. We laughed and swore never to complain of a stomach ache or a toothache. When a child or an adult has pink eye my father got a half spoon of sugar and put two tea spoons of warm water mixed it with the spoon he then he got a dropper squeezed the sugar water into the dropper and put it in the child's eye to cure pink eye. When a child is in there terrible two some start at terrible ones it the worse and hardest time to raise a child they run around get into every. A child can get traumatized if you yell at them. They will become fuzzy and can't sleep. You need to care for them and, not yell. There no medication of cure for it all it takes is to be patient. I remember my sister Felix complaining of a loose tooth; my father got some thread long enough to reach the doorknob and, tied it to my sister's tooth and, slammed the door shut and, out went my sister's tooth, hanging on the door. Her mouth was bleeding and, she was crying. We just stared with fear.

Most of these objects families used no longer believed in. One of the ailment symptoms was mal de Ojo, which usually affects infants primarily if sick with mal de Ojo. That would cause the child to cry and become fussy, have a fever, vomit, and have aches and pain; to keep a baby-safe, they placed dried deer's eye on the baby's crib for protection and pinned it on the crib. The dried deer eye is sold in most religious shops. An adult having mal de Ojo makes them distant, afraid of their surroundings, anxiety, insomnia, irritability, and depression.

My father said my nephew had Susto, becoming ill from a terrible accident or someone hurting you. My nephew refused my Dad's healing abilities; when he lived with my parents, he was insolated in his room till he died in his late forties. He refuses to see a doctor because he believes doctors wouldn't understand what was wrong with him. Doctors don't know what Susto is. The fear of their surroundings and commitments. Like getting married, staying in one place too long, his surroundings change, depressed, unable to share his feelings, and who would rather keep his distance, anxious, constantly tired, irritability nothing seems right. A doctor would recommend you see a psychiatrist who is also unaware of how to cure Susto. One must heal the mind and spirit through the power of natural herbs, prayers, and mostly faith. With the help of curanderismo, whom many relied on are hard to find. A psychologist cannot help you. When are you hurt by someone who should have respected you, your family, most of all, the people who believe he couldn't have hurt you? There is many fake Curanderismo. Some people use God's name in vain using God Blessing; Your faith and prayers help trust me.

My father also took care of Teddy, the family dog. He was an outside dog. He wouldn't stay in his dog's house at night. He wondered around the neighborhood; he would get into a fight with other neighborhood dogs. Teddy would come home wounded. My father would put some stuff that smelled horrible but, Teddy didn't mind; he only allowed my father to hold him when he was hurting. When Teddy had nasty wounds, my father would get the needle and thread and stitch him up. When we had time to play, we played with Teddy; he played jump rope with us. When Teddy tripped, Teddy would walk over and grab the end of the rope once in a while; we would say, it's ok, Teddy jumped and, Teddy refused and barked at us, holding the end of the rope. He was such a good sport. Teddy was with us all the time except when they had to go to school or town to work. He stayed home when we said, stay Teddy. Teddy had light brown hair and, he looked like a medium-size Collie and German Shepherd. Then one day, we were playing on the street with our sleds. When a car lost control and almost hit my younger brother Alex. Teddy ran and pushed my brother out of the way; the car hit Teddy he was, instantly killed our neighbor Mrs. Marquez cried for the loss of our dog. She cared for Teddy. My father put Teddy in the back of the Truck and, he buried Teddy up in the mountains where he could be free.

Going to School

I remembered my sisters going to school. I wanted to go to school too, but I was too young. It seemed forever for me to be able to go to school. I stayed at home with my mother and younger brother. Finally, the day had come.

My parents got me school supplies. My mother made lunch for my first day of school. I wanted to run all the way to school. It was the best day of my life. I was so happy to go to school.

Then one day my sister Felix couldn't find one of her shoes we started looking for her shoe. When we found her other shoe, we were late for school. When you were tardy to school, you got sent to the principal's office; the punishment was you had to stay after school or stay in for recess for being late most of the time. I was already in trouble when I realized I didn't have my tablet.

I returned from the principal office when the teacher asked me for my assignment. I answered my teacher.

I left my tablet at home on the top of the dresser.

I didn't know how to say the word dresser in English, so I said dresser in Spanish, not knowing. The teacher would punish me when the teacher heard me say dresser in Spanish. The teacher refused to hear us speak Spanish in the classroom. I was only five years old and didn't understand much except for the only language I knew. My parents, Grandparents and, most of the people I was around spoke Spanish. I sat quietly at a small desk, trying to absorb what the teacher was saying. But, it was hard to understand my teacher. She spoke very fast and very loudly. I tried to figure out what she was saying; I couldn't understand English. It was an unfamiliar language as Spanish was the only language I had ever heard. Two weeks had gone by; I had learned very little English. The teacher then yelled out, come to the front of the classroom. I didn't understand what she was saying to me. All the kids in the classroom turned around and looked at me. The teacher then pointed down toward the front of the class. I then got up and walked up slowly towards the front of the classroom. The kids observed quietly on their seats as we all carefully examined me. I was habitually the quietest one in the classroom and, very shy, I walked up very slowly and gently. My teacher yelled, put out your hands, another word I didn't understand, then she yelled again, put out your hands. She then grabbed my hands straight out. I kept them in the position she had placed them. Then she yelled, turn them upright. I almost cried; I couldn't understand what upward meant. The teacher then grabbed my hands again and turned them, facing the palm of my hands. My teacher became very angry. I wasn't sure what was going to happen next. I noticed my teacher pick up the ruler from her desk and ask that I stay still another word I didn't understand. I stood there in the position I had been placed on. When I saw the teacher approaching me with my ruler, she was furious with rage on my face. I wouldn't dare cry. I was shaking so hard I almost peed on my pants. I held my breath. I wouldn't dare cry in front of all my schoolmates. I looked at my little hands but, yet the teacher didn't miss once. When I got home from school, I laid on my bed crying as I put my hands between my legs for comfort till I fell asleep. I woke up when my mother called us for dinner. I couldn't eat my dinner: that night, my hands were throbbing with pain. I didn't want my mother to notice my hands. I didn't eat any of my dinners because I couldn't hold my spoon or fork. I carefully put my plate under the table and feed it to Teddy, the family dog. Then after the dog licked it clean, I picked up my plate from the floor and put it on the sink. The next day in school, I tried so hard to hold my pencil with my fingers to write but, I couldn't. I kept praying. Please, God help me make it through this day, and, God, I ask for a speedy recovery. Amen. I didn't feel like playing and didn't have an appetite. I continued giving my food to Teddy every night. It continued for several days. In those days, grandparents and, adults including teachers, were allowed to discipline other children except for my parents. They said they were responsible for their children and, to them, you have no business hitting one of their children. Therefore it's not your job. We didn't discipline your children don't come to our home and, run our household. I never said a word to my parents that the teacher made my hands bleed. I was afraid of what the teacher would do to me if I told.

My mother sent us to school with school lunches. It was either egg and potatoes. Sometimes she added bacon or sausage or just a plain bean burrito, and a jelly sandwich on a tortilla and, then my mother put it in a brown paper bag. Rather than in white bread and put our in a lunch box. One day this boy sat by me for lunch and asked what I had for lunch. I said it's a burrito and, he said his Mom always made the same sandwich every day ham and cheese sandwich, jelly or peanut butter sandwich with an apple or banana, and a bag of chips. He then asked if I wanted to trade? I have an apple and chips we traded and shared our lunch. I said, ok, homemade burritos are popular and nothing to be ashamed of.

I have this old memory; when I was seven years old, my mother bought a birthday cake in December close to Christmas on my birthday. We rarely celebrated birthdays, primarily mine being so close to Christmas.

My mother came home with a cake it had a sugar Santa Claus on top of the cake. My mother took Santa Claus off the top of the cake to put candles on the cake, and they sang Happy Birthday to me. My brother and sisters were so happy too. My grandma Lucero who was visiting that day took the sugar Santa Claus home with her. I wanted to say something, but you respected your elders in those days. I watched her put it in her apron pocket and take it home with her.

My grandmother Lucero was nice enough to get us some clothes. Some of the clothes were from my cousin's. We never questioned my grandmother, Lucero, where she got the clothes. We were just grateful.

Then the worst experiences happened to me; I couldn't believe what my cousin had done me. My grandmother brought some used clothes that my cousins didn't want anymore. She had gotten new clothes for school.

I opened the bag, and there was a beautiful white dress with lace, which I thought was the most beautiful dress. I was so excited to wear it to school the next day. When I got to school and sat down, I noticed the girls were laughing at me. I wondered why I was dressed up in my new dress. Then one of the boys who sat next to me in school whispered, do you know that you're wearing a slip? I was so embarrassed I turned around, got up and, ran all the way home crying. I was so humiliated I never wanted to go back to school again; being poor, I didn't know the difference between a fancy dress or a slip. I then wore another one of the dresses my grandmother brought in the bag. My cousin recognized me in school wearing one of her old dresses; she grabbed the dress, ripped it right off my back in front of all of her friends, she screamed out, "that's my dress, where did you get it." I caught loose from her and ran home and took off what was left of my dress.

I then grabbed all the clothes my grandmother had given me. I then improvised all the clothes I had from my cousins. I cut the sleeves, changed the neckline, and other parts of the dresses, then cut the dress with lace made a belt. My cousin never recognized her own dresses my grandmother had given me. My cousin's friends and the other girls liked my new dress or my new fashion.

When we were young, we weren't close to any of our parent's families. Most of my father's family lived far away. I knew I had a lot of cousins but, my mother had her way with my father. She didn't get along with my father's side of his family, so my father was sad most of his life. Although one of his sisters wrote letters to my father in Spanish, my mother didn't read Spanish, which helped. One day I went to visit my parents. When my father received news that his twin sister had died, I could hear my father crying in the bathroom. My mother said my father's twin sister had died.

My father was so sad. I just got my paycheck today, and I can get you an airline ticket to go to your twin sister's funeral. My father didn't say a word for a while; then, he came out of the bathroom. I could see he had been crying. He didn't know what to say; he was so happy. I knew my father wouldn't go without my mother. I then said, "Mom, I can get you and my Dad two airline tickets to go to my father's twin sister's funeral. Mom, either you go with my Dad, or I have to go with him. My mother agreed right away. I then called one of my Aunt, the one who wrote to my father. When I called my father's sister, my father was going to the funeral. She was so happy she said she would pick them up at the airport and stay at my house. I knew then I wanted to meet my father's sister.

Good Days and Bad Times

I was seven years old; my mother bought a birthday cake in December, close to Christmas on my birthday. We rarely celebrated birthdays, primarily mine being so close to Christmas. My mother came home with a cake it had a sugar Santa Claus on top of the cake. My mother put candles on the cake, and they sang Happy Birthday to me. My brother and sisters were so happy too. My grandma Lucero was visiting that day. My mother lit up the Santa Claus cake. After I blew out the candles, my grandmother took the sugar Santa Claus home with her. I wanted to say something but, in those days, you respected your elders. I watched her put it in her apron pocket and take it home with her. She was the only relative I know that came to visit. The school would be starting soon. My parents went to Woolworth to shop. They came home with school supplies for all the kids. My mother did all the shopping she bought the boy's clothes first. My father never paid any attention to what my mother bought. Instead of my parents taking all nine of us kids to the shoe store, my father would get a piece of paper and have us take off our shoes and put our feet on the paper, and he would trace our feet and take it to the shoe store. We got our shoes at Buster Browns shoe store. We wore what they bought us. We were just happy we had a new pair of shoes. We never had two or three pairs of shoes to decide which one to wear. The only problem we had was to find the other shoe or sew our shoes together with glue so we could run without falling or tripping. We had to make them last. My mother had her way with my father. She didn't get along with my father's side of his family, so my father was sad most of his life; although one of his sisters wrote letters to my father in Spanish, my mother didn't read Spanish. I went to visit my parents. My father had received news that his twin sister had died; I could hear my father in the bathroom crying. I didn't know my father's twin sister, but my father was sad. I told Dad I just got my paycheck. I can get you an airline ticket to go to your twin sister's funeral. My father didn't say a word for a while; then, he came out of the bathroom. I could see he had been crying. He didn't know what to say; he appreciated that he could attend his twin sister's funeral and see the rest of his family. I knew my father wouldn't go without my mother. I then said Mom, I can get you and my Dad two airline tickets to go to my father's twin sisters.' funeral; either you go with my Dad, or I have to go with him. My mother agreed right away. I then called one of my Aunt, the one who wrote to my father. When I called my father's sister, my father was going to the funeral; she was thrilled she said she would pick them up at the airport and they could stay at her house. I knew then I wanted to meet my father's sister.

Making Adobes

O ur mother taught my father how to make adobes. My mother asked my father to dig a big hole in the backyard and, our father took my three brothers and me up to the mountains to get the dirt he started digging. My Dad made a screen to help gets rid of all the big rocks, then he added water to the dirt and added straws. Then my father made these frames with nine squares in each tray. We filled them up with mud and let them sit overnight. In the early morning, my Dad took them out of the frames and, he stood up the adobes on their side. They were now blocks; we called them adobe's to add on to our house. We thought we were playing in the mud but were working making adobes blocks all that time. My Dad added on to the house and, he made a fireplace in the living room. Those Adobes kept us warm in the cold winters and Kool in the hot summers. My mother used the fireplace to roast Pinon (pine nuts). We could hear the crackling and the smell of the pinon nuts as we all gathered around the living room, watching the fire cook the pinon nuts. We couldn't wait for the pinon nuts to cook and cool down so we could eat them. We had gone up to the mountains to gather. It was so much fun. We ran from one pinon tree to another, gathering pinon nuts in our lard buckets to see who picked the most pinon nuts. There were many pinon nuts in the house with nine children, enough to last long. The Pinon tree grows pinon nuts every three years.

Shopping in Albuquerque

My parents went shopping in Albuquerque, New Mexico. It was an all-day trip. My mother enunciated my grandmother they were going to Albuquerque to visit her sister and go shopping. We got a visit from my grandfather. He would come to our house when my parents weren't home. My sisters would run and hide.

My mother had taken the boys with them; I don't remember them being around. My sisters must have seen my grandfather coming. I saw my sister hiding in a big barrel full of laundry. She was afraid of him. My grandfather was a tall man. I could see him walking down the street. My mother went to visit my grandmother, and I went with my mother. I saw him at my grandmother's house lying on the bed, smoking his pipe. He must have been over seven feet tall. That was tall for me.

His legs hung off the bed. He was a dirty older man. When my parents went to Albuquerque, he came over to the house; and tried to hurt my sisters sexually.

My grandfather caught me as I ran across the living room. When he caught me, he dragged me from my arm, then carried me to my parents' bedroom and threw me on the top of the bed. I kicked and, screamed calling him names as he held me down on the bed. Then he sat on top of me as he undid his pants. He took out the thing he used to pee with: he put his thing on my face; I yelled terrible words at him. I picked up my head and yelled out, help his going to hurt me. Let me go; then, I bit it hard when he put it close to my face. My grandfather jumped with anger. I managed to get away. When he got off me, I struck him and ran outside. My grandpa Lucero ran outside to get me; I ran around the house then went inside the house to the back door, ran into the kitchen, locked all the doors, and, I yelled out from the window, you dirty older man in Spanish. When my mother and Father get home, I'm going to tell them. When my parents got home; I told my mother what my grandfather had done; my mother became angry with me for saying that about her father; she grabbed me from my hair put my face close to the fire. I was so scared my mother put my head in the oven or fireplace. I could feel the heat on my face. I remember my mother holding on to me by my hair. For most of my life, I had nightmares. I could feel the hot heat on my face for years. I would get up in the middle of the night. I could hear my mother yelling at me while she put my face on the fire; she burned my eyelashes that never grew back. That was a reminder I carried with me all my life when I was twenty years old. I was so mad about something. My mother said about my son fighting with his sister and, I yelled out; did you even talk to my son about what happened. Then I said to my mother; after she argued with me. For some reason, I thought of my mother's father, and I yelled out. I hate you for allowing my grandfather to do what he did to me and not just me but my sister. He was a dirty old man. My father overheard me and became angry with my mother but, it was too late then my grandfather had been dead. After my grandfather died, I remember looking down the road. I could see my grandfather walking toward our house. I yelled I'm glad you're dead. I hate you. I realized I had to forgive him to stop the nightmares. My parents frequently went to Albuquerque, New Mexico, to do most of their shopping and visit my Aunt. We knew they would be away most of the day. We looked around the kitchen

to see what we could make to eat. Then my oldest brother decided
to bake a cake. We read the directions on the back of the box and
added the ingredients we needed. My brother came out with the
idea that we should add a little yeast to the cake mix. My mother
said the yeast made the bread rise and, we figured it would make
the cake bigger. We added three packs of yeast, set the temperature
at 350 degrees, put the cake in the oven. Then we sat in the living
room to watch TV till the cake was ready, not more than fifteen
minutes later, we heard a big bang it sounded like a bomb we
jumped up and ran to see what it was. The cake blew up. From
the oven, door hinges flew across the kitchen. All the parts were
all over the floor from the oven door hinges. We spent three hours
cleaning the mess, putting the hinges back on the stove. Well, that
took care of that there was no cake. It was all over the kitchen
floor. It wouldn't have tasted good anyway with all the yeast we had
put in the cake. When My mother opened the stove the next day,
the oven door fell off. The next day When my mother went to the
kitchen to bake something, the door fell off. We thought for sure
we were in trouble but, my mother figured we just needed another
Stove. We looked at each other, and though she didn't notice, we
had blown up the cake. When we have left home alone, there was
never a dull moment. My third brother decided to play Superman.
He put down some mattresses in the ground for A safe landing.
Then jumped from the house to the shed; his cape got caught on.
A nail on the top of the roof, he hung there choking. We heard
him pounding on the Wall; we all ran out to see what was going
on. My brother was on top of the roof Hanging. We ran up to
the roof to pull him down; he was more upset we had ruined. His
Superman cape, we had to tear his cape to cut my brother loose.
My brother Cried for his cape and didn't care if he almost died.
Then there was the time my brother had this brilliant idea that
we should go to my grandma Lucero's house to ask for a cigarette,
supposedly for my father, but it was for us to smoke. We said to

my grandmother it was for my father because he ran out. She was happy to give us a cigarette. My father would have never asked my grandmother for a cigarette. My brother wanted to feel what it would be like to smoke like a grown-up. We got the cigarette my brother lit it up. He took the first drag. He did ok, then. I took a drag; I started choking; the smoke came out of my nose, eyes, ears. I felt like I would die. After trying to smoke that cigarette, I never wanted to smoke again. The smoke was all over. I thought for sure we were going to get caught.

Working Downtown

My father made my brothers shoe shine boxes, just like the ones they sold at the store. The groundkeeper at the plaza saved my brother's shoeshine boxes in the bottom of the plaza platform, so my brothers didn't have to carry them around while they sold their Newspapers. We went to the New Mexican to get the News Papers at 2:30 pm every day of the week and sold paper till they were all sold. My brother's shoeshine boxes were safe until we came back the next day to the plaza in the morning. My brothers had to retrieve the shoeshine boxes early in the morning before the groundkeeper started work at seven in the morning except for Saturday and, Sundays on Fridays, my brothers, carried their shoeshine boxes home. The groundkeeper was off Saturday and Sunday that was our busiest day of the week. The Newspaper was ten cents during the week on Sundays. They were a quarter we got paid more on Sundays.

My younger brother was with me most of the time. He was about four in a half year old and hadn't started school yet. When my father made him a shoeshine box, my brother right away wrote on his shoeshine box fifteen cents on both sides of his shoeshine box. That was how much the shoeshine boys charged for a shoeshine. He wrote the number five backward. My younger brother watched one of the other shine boys shinning a man's shoe by lighting the shoe shine with a match. My brother decided to try the boy's trick but, it didn't work as well for him; it was a good thing he was fast because he almost caught the man's pants on fire by lighting up the shoe polish for a better shine. When we first got to the plaza, we helped the artists set up their stands; then, my brothers would start working. They would walk around the park looking for customers.

The boys would run to get the customer first, as did the other little shine boys, who were a little older than my brothers. My brothers, I stood together when they went to shined shoes and sold their News Papers. One of the artists asked me to model for him. I was about nine years old. I sat on the chair while the tourist noticed the Artist's work at the park. One of the artists had me pose for him; when he finished the portrait, he said he would let me have it, but the tourist asked me to buy it from him. I had posed for. That was the only way the Artist made any money for their work. I thought to myself, what would they want it for and? The Artist said they wanted it for their home or office, so I never got any of the portraits I had posed. Most tourists didn't have the time to have their painting done as they didn't have the time to sit in for an hour.

My father would take us to the New Mexican to pick up the Sunday Newspaper at three in the morning on Sunday morning at the New Mexican. Then we went home to get some sleep. At the end of the day, we would go home, reach into our pockets and give my mother our earnings for the day. our hands were full of dimes, and nickles quarters. most of the time we made three dollars a day. including the twenty-five Newspapers, we sold on the street or my brother would go to the business offices like the Court House the State Capitol, the Attorney, and, where ever the people worked. We went to work early in the morning someone would leave us some money on top of the wall there would be dimes, nickels, and pennies or a quarter which usually added up to a quarter's worth of change. whoever it was we would say Thank You where ever you are. One day we were going to the Plaza to start work we played and ran till we got downtown. I looked down on the ground and there was a twenty-dollar bill that was a lot of money to find on the field as we walk on the path to work. We all decided to buy ourselves a big meal at Lota Burger on our way to the Plaza, we ordered a Lota Burger with double meat double cheese and a tub of Dr. Pepper times four. the large drink was called a tub because it was like a tub. we had to hold it with two hands. The girl rang out our order and yelled out you won the red star. I look at her and wondered what was going on she said you get your meal paid congratulations. we sat outside and said a free meal now that we have money and laughed. We were so full we dragged ourselves to pick up the shoe shine boxes from the custodian. later that day we went to the Restaurant across from the Plaza. we sat at the round table we just barely reached the table our chins sat right on it. I remember I ordered spaghetti. my brothers ordered something else. but no more hamburgers. The manager saw us eating and said hello to us. then he told the waiter not to charge us as it was on the house. we look at each other and said wow no one wants the twenty dollars. We went back to selling our Newspapers. then we decided we had a plan, we went to Safeway grocery store and bought all kinds of stuff my mother could use in the kitchen. flour, baking soda, can foods, and other stuff. each one of us carried the bags home. My mother didn't say a word. when my father got home from work around Eleven Thirty at night. I heard my father yelling from the boy's room. Where did you get the money for the groceries then I heard my father say Voila get over here. my father was hitting my brothers with the belt and I was next he was so mad his face had turned red and he was biting his tongue to the right of his mouth. Oh my God, what did we do that my father would be so angry? All I heard was your mother. Then a month later my second to the oldest brother got jumped by some big boys they turned my brother upside down and grabbed all the change my brother had dropped he had from working. we had to take money home or we would get whipped. I gave my brother all the money I made with my tamales and burritos. my grandmother and I only knew I sold tamales and burritos mostly to the Natives. would you believe I had done a good deed and what do you think happened? My father said when I get home tonight your going to get punished. I went outside and hid in the back of the old sofa I fall asleep when I woke up I had a medallion of St. Judge on t the palm of my hand it was so beautiful.My father forgot about punishing me. Then again my mother said I said bad work to her.My father went outside to the front of the house and got a branch from the apricot tree and brought it into the room and said I don't want to hear you talking back to your mother after about the third whip I couldn't feel the rest my body went numb. In the end, I looked at the damage on my legs and looked in the mirror to see my back he marks were purple-red when I touched them lightly I could feel the throbbing throughout my body I couldn't move. I hated my mother and father and said back to my father one day I will leave this house I hate you God going to punish you for hitting one of his children he gave you. Why did you have so many kids you can't even remember my name? You call me in Spanish you stupid and point at me I would answer that not me you must be thinking of someone else your an idiot. but I would say it out loud or here comes the belt. I taught my children never to use the word stupid it's a bad word I'm sure that would have made my mother dearest happy. we were well respected by others we had respect for our elders and never took what wasn't ours never said bad words once a man said you have to come with me your mother is in danger I went with him and I noticed he was passing the Santa Fe opera I said this isn't the way home I felt an empty bottle on my feet I rolled it over and grabbed it hit him he stopped the car and I jumped out of the car and two old ladies were on the way to the opera and they stopped to help me. they asked if I wanted to go to the opera that was the first time in an opera everyone was dressed nice. in the end, they took me home. another miracle I was about nine years old. I grew up taking care of myself and have been all my life I have a few good friends and my son who I visit a lot and he calls me every day he's wonderful son and works hard. Some of my old and new memories, as a child we got up early in that morning to go out and sell the Newspapers at seven in the morning but before going to sell our newspapers. We went to church. My brothers and I would go to church every Sunday before heading downtown to sell their Newspapers; the best day to shine shoes was on a Saturday and, selling Newspapers was on a Sunday.

We would head up to the church to give thanksgiving to God for protecting us when we went to work, and, of course, I would thank God for blessing my homemade burrito and tamales I sold to make my share of the money.

We gave the church a quarter from each of us: that was a lot of money for us, but it was all worth it. A candy bar was twenty-five cents. We could have used it to buy that candy bar but, God comes first. We figured the church needed the money to pay the electric and gas bill to keep us warm and comfortable while the Priest gave service. All four of us were the first ones in church for mass every Sunday. In those days, females were not allowed to enter the catholic church unless they had a hat or small vail on the top of their heads. We always sat on the third row in front of the church. Where we could see and hear better and, every Sunday that small short chubby bald man who was the Usher would come up to us in the middle of the service and, ask us to give up our seats for the elders who came in late, he asked us to stand in the back of the church. We were small and couldn't hear the Priest from the back of the church. Then one Sunday, I finally stood up to the short bald man who was a volunteer at the catholic church. That one Sunday morning, I got up and said no, we were not giving up our seats. We were here first; we've been here since 6:30 in the morning. Why don't they get up early and get their own seats?

Everyone looked at us, and I ran outside crying, and my brothers followed me. None of the Catholics ever spoke their mind in the church or out of the church. They all just sat there and stared at us and said nothing. We sat outside of the church waiting to sell our Newspapers as the people would be leaving mass and, I sat on the side with my bucket of tamales and burritos. We then went downtown to sell the rest of our Newspapers. We sometimes finished around ten o'clock at night before curfew. The policeman would remind us. They would walk up to us and say: "Hey kids, it's almost time to wrap it up." We knew we had to pack it up and go home.

Except for one day, my mother decided to call the police department. She said the four of us were out late past curfew. Sure enough, the police caught my brother first.

I could see my brother yelling out of the police car. There she is. I asked my brother why he had told the police to take me too. He said he didn't want to go by himself. The policeman who took us to the detention center was new. When kids went to the detention center, the first thing they did was shave off their hair before being booked. Most people knew if you were bald, you had been in the detention center. Thank God there was police who walked into the booking office, recognized us, and called my father that we were at the detention center and were being held. My father right away drove to the detention center and picked us up. Thank God he got there just in time. We didn't get our hair shaved or, like some say, our head shaved. We were so afraid of being locked up.

When my father could, he would give us a ride home.

On his new truck, I wondered why they made a new vehicle every year. Why not every three years? That way, you can enjoy it and get it paid off? It would also help when you need parts to fix your truck.

My father had to get home to eat supper and go to bed to get ready for his next job most of the time. We walked home. Sometimes we worked late, and it was dark. We could barely see the path home. We had to pass by the Santa Fe National Cemetery at night most of the time; we ran fast past the path to get home. The Cemetery was on the right side. I didn't dare look in that direction l just ran all the way home.

Out of the blue, my mother decided to scare us. My mother was accompanied by my older sister when she brought a white sheet. My older sister didn't notice my mother had the sheet. When all of the sudden my mother hid behind a bush and put the sheet over her head and, ran towards us, when my mother ran towards us my sister saw my mother, and she thought it was a ghost my older sister screamed and ran all the way home we couldn't catch up to her, my mother tried to get the sheet off. Still, my sister was already gone. She ran all the way home and hid under the bed. It was her favorite place that's where she felt safe.

I remember one of my brothers had a sweet tooth and spent most of his money on candy. He hangs out by himself. Once, he went to the drug store and, seen a giant chocolate bar in a big box in front of the drug store. It said five cents a whole nickel; he bought the biggest chocolate bars in the box and ate it all. The chocolate ended up being a laxative. In those days, laxatives were in a silver package. You had to know how to read the package. The chocolate bar my brother had seen was in a big box. The chocolate bars that my brother bought were broken up and wrapped on clear wrap in big pieces were in the front of the counter. It didn't have a label. The box did say laxative, but my brother couldn't read. Our father had this new turquoise truck he had just bought. Who would have thought he would stop and ask us to ride home with him, but there was a problem my brother had diarrhea. He got rid of his underwear but, the smell was over well-being. We got on the back of the truck, hoping our father wouldn't notice or smell my brother.

When we got home, we right away went to the backyard. I got the water hose and sprayed my brother down. Then my older brother ran into the house, got my brother some clean clothes. After spraying my brother with the water hose, we all got wet from head to toe and had to sneak into the house dripping wet through the bedroom window. And, changed clothes. We ended up having a lot of fun: We laughed and played in the water for a while. Then we all went to have dinner. We never said a word. When we worked at the plaza, my brothers and I got a lot of tips from our customers; we could afford to buy whatever we wanted and still take my mother the money we had earned for the day. We didn't have any interest in toys. We didn't have time to play.

I went to my grandmother early in the morning to use her kitchen to make my tamales. I made it with pork and red chile.

I soaked the corn husk in hot water, then laid out the corn husk and added the mesa to the husk; I cooked the red chile with meat, my grandmother helped me wrap the corn husk, and tie it around the tamale with a string, made from the husk I tied it tight. The hardest part of making tamales was steaming the tamale. It took forever. I made my homemade bean burritos just like the ones my mother used to make us for lunch. I sold my tamales and burritos to the other shine boys and the Artist but, I mostly sold to the Natives. Who were my best customers because they could not leave their post where they laid out their Jewelry, Pottery and, Rugs that were all handmade? They worked with genuine turquoise, not like the plastic that is now used made in China. They improvised the natural turquoise that's sold now. They don't go to the mines for turquoise like the Natives used to. Now you see Made in China.

The Natives worked across the park at Governor Place.

I sometimes sit down with the women and talk about life. I was just a little girl, but I loved to listen to their stories. My grandmother and I would make a corn-colored necklace to sell. When I could. The tourist loved them as a souvenir from New Mexico.

The sad thing about working when you are young, you don't have friends, kids in school look down at us because we had to work. We had a lot of grown-ups who were our friends, and we had was each other. When we grew up, we became strangers. We worked and gave our mother what we had earned for the day selling Newspapers and shining shoes. My mother made herself a fanny pack where she put all the money we earned and my Dad's paycheck. She called it her purse. She made it out of the extra material she had from making our clothes.

My mother invented the fanny pack, every time I see a fanny pack, it reminds me of my mother but, hers wasn't so bulky. I guess you can say like mother like daughter.

I also came out with the idea of the Huggies Pull-ups around 1977-1978. I wrote to Huggies about my pull-up new invention. I got the address from the diaper bag.

I wrote to them about my idea of contriving the diapers to training underpants disposable that's where they got the idea of Huggies Pull-Up. After my son's kidnapping, I had forgotten about calling or writing back. I have a new vision for the latest truck to get built, but what dealer would I contact with my new idea?

When we worked downtown, my mother would go with my father to the plaza to see what we were doing. My mother would sit at the park till my father was ready to go home for lunch. It started raining hard. My father picked up my mother to take her home. When they were driving home, they saw a woman walking home in the rain. My parents stopped to ask her if she needed a ride. The story went.

The Maid from the La Fond Hotel

My mother and father were on their way back home from town. My father said it was raining really hard that day. My parents saw a woman walking home in the rain. My parents offered the lady a ride home. When the lady sat in my father's truck, she said to my parents she was on her way home from work. She had to get home in a hurry because she was worried about her daughter, who liked to party. When my parents dropped her off, the lady said, if you're ever in the area. I worked at the La Fonda Hotel as a maid just asked for me. One day my parents were in the area and decided to take the lady up on her offer and see how she was doing. They went to the La Fonda Hotel. They asked the girl at the front desk and asked for the woman by my name she gave them; the clerk said the woman you're looking for died a while back and was no longer with the Hotel. My father said no and described the woman. My parents had given her a ride home. The clerk again said, yes, that's her but, she died. Isn't that strange? My parents had given her a ride a few weeks earlier. My parents believe the lady still haunts leaving La Fonda Hotel and rushes home to her daughter. True story.

Loretto Cathedral Monastery

My father had two jobs during the day. He worked at the bus station picking up mail and taking it to the post office, and, sometimes, he delivered packages and drove passengers to their homes from the bus station. When her father had a Nun as a passenger, he picked her up at the bus station. She asked my father to take her to the Loretto Cathedral Monastery where the Nuns resided; he dropped her off in the front entrance, after sitting for several minutes for the Nun to return to pay her father. He finally decided to go inside and see what took the Nun so long to come out and pay him for driving her to the monastery. Her father walked inside the front entrance and asked one of the Nuns he had just dropped off one of the Nuns and, I never came out to pay him. The Nun said, wait here for a minute and, I called mother superior, who came out and asked what this Nun looked like and; my father said that's her on the picture on the Wall. She answered, that's impossible. The Nun you drove has been dead for several years. My father said that sister Teresa. Mother Superior answered how strange that was. The Nun's name was Teresa. My father said that how she had introduced herself. Mother Superior said someday she might come home. Then my father had another true story.

My father worked as a Merchant Police

My father worked the night shift as a Merchant Police for Mr. Sanchez, a short chubby man. It was his second job at night; his job was to check the stores to ensure they were secure; most stores closed by five o'clock. My father wore a uniform with a gun and drove a small white car with a blue light on top. He would check all the doors to ensure they were locked and put a business card on the doors to make sure they were locked. My father also worked as a mail carrier for the bus station during the day.

The Old Women in Black

My father told us about a woman he ran into while he was working as a Merchant Police. My father said an old lady walked up to my father and asked, where was the bus depot? In a very soft voice, my father could barely hear her. It was late at night, and my father said it was about three blocks down that road, but it was very dark. I'll take you as she followed my father. The woman was dressed all in black with shiny black shoes. She covered her face with a black scarf, but my father was able to glance at what she looked like but wasn't sure, although he did have a gut feeling about her. The woman in black was taciturn as she followed my father and just walked alongside my father till they arrived at the bus station. When they got to the bus station, my father directed her to the ticket agent and, he went on his way. My father went back to the building; he was supposed to be checking before meeting with the lady in black. The building where my father met the women in black had blown up. My father approached the fireman and asked what had happened and, he told my father the water heater blew up and started a big fire. After my father finished his rounds, my father went back to the bus station to ask if the woman in black got on the bus Ok. The ticket agent person said no, it'd been a slow night. My father said he knew there was something about the Woman in Black. She looked so much like his grandmother. My father started to think of the old lady in black. You know, my father said, if it wasn't for the woman in black keeping him away from the building, he could have died. My father believes his grandmother saved my father's life. True Story.

Years later, while my father was working for Mr. Sanchez. My father got frostbite on his feet. Mr. Sanchez had to work my father's shift till my father got better. My father lost three weeks of his income because he couldn't work. When my father felt better, he took the brothers and me to the mountain to pick trees for Christmas to sell. The ground was hard as a rock. My father broke one of the shovels digging, fighting the hard ground. He walked around looking for the best trees. I stood by my father's side. He always got the best Christmas trees and the most beautiful ones for our home. I remembered how cold it was. I felt like crying, but I wondered how my father felt doing all the hard work. My tears rolled back, knowing if I cried, my tears would have frozen on my cheeks with my teardrops. And laughed and, besides, I didn't want my father to think I wasn't strong enough to go with them. My three brothers sat in the truck watching my father and me until my father cut down the trees. Even if my brothers waited inside the truck, it was cold. When they came outside to help my father load the trees, it got cold fast. Their hand was almost frozen. We had two or three pairs of socks in each hand. We made sure we put them on the right. The holes would make our hands cold. My father used a pair of gloves that Mr. Sanchez had issued my father with his uniform. They were nice gloves but too big for us to wear. Then my brothers came out to help load the truck. My brothers were minor; they could barely lift the trees, with all three of my brothers pushing them up the truck. It was high for them to reach the top of the truck, but then they knew when they were finished, it meant it was time to head back home?

The trees my father dug up the trees with the ball. He would put to the side and, he would drive up to Los Alamos, New Mexico. My father would knock on people's homes and ask if they would be interested in having a tree planted in their yard. My father took all kinds of trees in the back of his truck: Pinon, Cedar, Blue Spruce, and a lot more. My father would bring them to the truck to select a tree and where they wanted it planted in their yard. In those days, you could ride in the back of the truck. all of us kids rode in the back. My mother went with us on those trips.

My parents never applied for food stamps or got help from anyone. When my father couldn't find a job, he would improvise by selling wood and digging out trees to transplant people's yards. One time they got a job cleaning bricks; my sister Felix was perfect and fast; I was so jealous as my sister piled up the bricks so perfectly stacked; I can still see it. I miss my sister. Now that's for richer for poor they cared for each other.

My father worked odd jobs that no one else wanted. He was a dishwasher and, bus driver, and a Merchant Police at night watchman. He wore a uniform. Sometimes we watched our father work if they happened to be downtown selling our Newspapers. Curfew was at 10 pm all kids had to be home by 10 pm, besides most of the stores closed at 5 pm. My father would let my brothers take turns shining his shoes for work. If they did a good job, he would give them ten cents. My father worked as a Merchant Police. He drove a small white car with a blue light on top. He would check all the doors downtown to ensure they were locked and secure; he would put a business card on the doors to let them know they had checked. Once when my father was working as a Merchant Police, he said an old lady walked up to my father and asked him where the bus depot was. My father said I'll take you to where it's because it's a way up the street and dark. She was a short older woman dressed all in black with a black scarf on my head covering my face and, she spoke in a low voice and, walked very slow she followed my father to the bus station. My father walked her inside the bus station and directed her to the front desk to the ticket agent. Then my father started back to the building where he would have been checking before being distracted by the lady in black who he took to the bus station. My father looked down the street. There were Firetrucks, and the Police were down the road. My father asked the policeman what had happened; he said a big explosion the water heater exploded. After my father took the old lady, he decided to finish checking the buildings. Later before his shift was over, he decided to go back to the bus station to ask if the old lady was black; he wondered if I had gotten on the bus as scheduled. The ticket agent said, no, it's been a slow night. My father said he knew there was something about the lady in black. My father had a gut feeling about the lady in black. He said he thought it was his grandmother. She had saved my father's life. Could she have been his grandmother?

My parents never applied for food stamps or got help from anyone. When my father couldn't find a job, he would improvise by selling wood and digging out trees to transplant people's yards. One time they got a job cleaning bricks; my sister Felix was perfect and fast; I was so jealous as my sister piled up the bricks so perfectly stacked; I can still see it. I miss my sister. Now that's for richer for poor they cared for each other.

My father worked odd jobs that no one else wanted. He was a dishwasher and, bus driver, and a Merchant Police at night watchman. He wore a uniform. Sometimes we watched our father work if they happened to be downtown selling our Newspapers. Curfew was at 10 pm all kids had to be home by 10 pm, besides most of the stores closed at 5 pm. My father would let my brothers take turns shining his shoes for work. If they did a good job, he would give them ten cents. My father worked as a Merchant Police. He drove a small white car with a blue light on top. He would check all the doors downtown to ensure they were locked and secure; he would put a business card on the doors to let them know they had checked. Once when my father was working as a Merchant Police, he said an old lady walked up to my father and asked him where the bus depot was. My father said I'll take you to where it's because it's a way up the street and dark. She was a short older woman dressed all in black with a black scarf on my head covering my face and, she spoke in a low voice and, walked very slow she followed my father to the bus station. My father walked her inside the bus station and directed her to the front desk to the ticket agent. Then my father started back to the building where he would have been checking before being distracted by the lady in black who he took to the bus station. My father looked down the street. There were Firetrucks, and the Police were down the road. My father asked the policeman what had happened; he said the water heater exploded. After my father took the old lady, he decided to finish checking the buildings. Later before his shift was over, he decided to go back to the bus station to ask if the old lady was black; he wondered if I had gotten on the bus as scheduled. The ticket agent said, no, it's been a slow night. My father said he knew there was something about the lady in black. My father had a gut feeling about the lady in black. He said he thought it was his grandmother. She had saved my father's life. Could she have been his grandmother?

Harwood High School

My parents decided to send me away to school to a Private School I hated the sound of leaving home. I didn't want to move I was afraid. It was an hour drive away from home. I went with my parents to see if I liked the school, I hated the thought of going away. I would have to live there but, I could go home on the weekends and holidays but, even that sounded like it would be a long time before I could go home. I lived with girls who lived further away from home than I did. They were my age and older. The girls I went to school with me came from all over the United States and from places I had never heard of. Our parents were asked to put allowance in our books. I had something called a trust fund; most girls came from wealthy families and were sent off to a private school like me. When I went away to school, my parents bought me my first doll. It came in a small suitcase with a doll cloth it was the best doll ever and, the only doll I ever had but, I was a little too old to play with dolls. For Christmas, my parents got me a cotton candy machine. I had fun with that in school with the girls; we made cotton candy almost every day after school. Some of the girls down the hall would come over and, the kitchen cook would provide me with some sugar for my cotton candy machine.

The allowance that we received was used to shop for personal things and clothes; primarily, the other girls bought makeup. You know how girls liked makeup we were teenagers. I wasn't too interested in makeup; I used a tiny bit, mostly eye shadow. The school had a professional makeup woman who came to show us how to use makeup. She also taught them how to walk and a lot of stuff young girls wanted to know to be a lady.

We had bowling night; I wasn't too interested in bowling but liked movie night.

I looked forward to going home on the weekend. One weekend the dorm mother decided to do her overkill on dorm check in our rooms. We were all in the dining room having breakfast. The dorm mother called my roommate and me to our room. She put on her white glove in her right hand and started to wipe all around our dorm, and, just before she left, she wiped the top of our bedroom door and found dust. She said to us we would not be getting our weekend passes. We turned around and ran downstairs and, straight to see Ms. Moor's in her office. She was our school principal. She was a tall skinny woman who kept her hair pinned up? She was single and went home in the evenings after finishing all her paperwork. She returned to work the next day before breakfast. We knocked on Ms. Moor's door and waited for her to call us to come in. When we walked into her office, we all started to talk at the same time. Ms. Moor yelled, stopped and, talk one at a time. One of the girls said Ms. Moor, the dorm mother tricked us. She wiped the dust off the top of the door with a white glove. Ms. Moor, my parents are on their way to pick me up from Santa Fe, and I have to go home. Ms. Moor said not to worry; we could go home for the weekend. We felt much better and were able to go home to hang out with our friends and family. There were times our parents were unable to come to pick us up on the weekend. We would go out shopping downtown or stay at the dorm. When I was with my friends in Santa Fe, we would have a lot of fun. We were best friends forever. When I went home to Santa Fe, the first thing I would do was unpack and call my friends. Then I would meet Rosemary down the road, where she would pick me up on her white Impala Convertible with red interior and white walls tires. Rosemary picked up the girls. We then stopped at her parents' house to say hello. Her mother would feed us. Her mother always said, eat up, girls, your too skinny but, then all mothers want to fatten up their kids. When we finished dinner, we all went to see the rest of our friends and, if we had a gig, we would put all our instruments in the back of the guy's truck. When we stayed in school, we would go downstairs in the basement and play records and dance and, my friends would sing along with our records. Those were the days of Miniskirt, hip huggers, bell-bottom pants; we were the best-dressed girls in town. We worked and shopped. No boys were allowed except for our friends at the school. It was the girls and the guys who were our best friends.

There was a saying we had as teenagers
Hugging is a shame; kissing is the same.
One night of fun, nine months of pain.
Then comes the baby's name.
Should we name him human nature?
When a boy sticks his information into
a girl's combination to increase the
population in the coming generation.

The boys next door would watch us from the window down in the basement, and, sometimes, we would sneak them in through the window. No one ever came downstairs; the principal allowed us to play our records downstairs in the basement. There were old pianos and a big stage it looked like an old theater. Where we played most of the time, that's where I met Johnny. He taught me how to play the drums. We started dating after graduation Johnny graduated one year before me. After he graduated, he joined the Air Force. It would have been three years that Johnny was in the Air Force. When his mother called me that Johnny had died, she said his airplane got shot down. Then another one of my old boyfriends died too. We dated before I met Johnny, we stayed best friends. He was a golden glove boxer when we were dating. We both moved on. He had been living with another girl when he died on December 23, 1971.

He was fixing his car and, the jack broke and, crushed his body, he died instantly.

When I was in school at Harwood, there was one place I loved going to. It was downstairs to the kitchen to help the cook early in the morning. She was a short black woman. At first, I helped by getting ingredients for her. Then one day. I asked her if I could learn to cook. My mother never allowed us in the kitchen. When we were small, we couldn't even get Kool-Aid. Not till dinner time. That was my mother's area and job. The cook and I got along so well we laughed and talked about how it was for her back home. She had two sons and her husband, all she knew was how to cook, so here she was the cook for over three hundred girls and staff. I learned a lot from her. She gave me orange tang to take to my room to make drinks with the girls and sugar to make cotton candy with the cotton candy machine.

The weekend before Christmas vacation, we were all said goodbye and hugged, crying; we would be going home for three months on Christmas vacation.

My parents drove over to pick me up around two o'clock. Most of the girls had already left for the airport, or their parents had already come for them. A week before, we were going back to school. My parents got a call one week before we had to report back to school. They said there was an electrical short and we would have to stay home another extra two weeks. I called my friends; we missed each other. We were looking forward to seeing each other at school. We couldn't wait to get back to school.

Cruising and Playing in our All-Girls Band

My friends and I cruised, driving up and down Cerrillos Road, and drove around the plaza and back. The boys and our friends would go to the drive-up to order hamburgers, fries, and soda. And park to see if we would see someone we knew. They would flag each other's down then we would meet at Highway Department Parking Lot, where most teenagers parked their cars and talked as we watched the other cars passing by. We sat on the top of the hood of the car.

There was a time I was driving my oldest brother's car. He had a white convertible and, we decided to stop for a soda. When the carhop came out to get our order, she instantly said this my fiancé car and, then my friends started to play with her and, said that's funny, she's his girlfriend. That's why we were in his car. The carhop jumped into the car to grab my friend's by her hair. We all grabbed her and pulled her out of the car. She didn't get fired, and no, she wasn't hurt. When I returned the car to my brother, I asked my brother if he knew a carhop at the A&W drive-up. He said no I said, well, she said you were getting married. He then asked who she was. I said I heard them call her Josie. My brother said, I don't know a Josie. She had a crush on my brother but, he didn't know it. I think he was dating another girl that summer when he joined the Marine Corps.

When I went home on the weekends. My best friends Rosemary, Joann and Terry, Liz, and the other girls hung around together.

I learned to play the drums at school in the school basement. There was all kinds of different instruments, including a drum set. The boys next door came over after dinner and, we played around. Johnny taught me how to play the drum; we also had a record player I had in my dorm we played our records, danced and, sang till dinner time. We had the basement, to ourselves. We could have the sound blast and, no one could hear us.

Rosemary decided to start a band. With some of our friends. My friend's brothers would escort us to most of our gigs, we went to the best parties. We had a lot of fun on the weekends. Sometimes we'd see some of the girls from Santa Fe High, where I would have attended high school. The other girls would crash wedding parties trying to find a husband. Most wedding crashers were bad girls and dressed up to find a man with money and a nice car. Rosemary played every instrument you imagined and had the most magnificent voice you ever heard in English and Spanish.

Our band was called **Leather and, Lace** it was an all-girl band. Rosemary had gigs set up. For us when I got home on the weekends. We played at birthday parties and, a couple of weddings, oh and, we once played at a barn house parties. We were doing a gig at the plaza. When a young man asked if we were interested in going to California and his company would pay all of our expenses, we would be interviewed for a magazine. Well, we did end up on a magazine all four of us girls. It changed our lives. One of the girls was hurt. So we decided to keep it out of our life and not mention it again. We had a lot of friends being in a band, and we met a lot of people. I met a man at one of our gigs at a birthday party he was having for his daughter.

He ended up being Senator Montoya. I had no idea who he was at the time.

He asked me if I was working; other than playing the drums, I said I had just graduated high school. The Senator said there was a program that hired kids my age. He then said he would set an appointment to meet with him in his office on Monday at eight o'clock in the morning. First thing Monday morning, I went to his office. That's when I found out he was the Senator. He had the most prominent chair and office I had ever seen. I got an interview that morning at the State Capitol for the Department of the Bureau of Revenue.

I was directed to a lady named Eva Garcia. Who was a native woman and the best supervisor in the whole world? She directed me to my desk. Then she introduced me to everyone in the office and then explained my duties, and what my job tiled would be. I stared as a file clerk. That was my first paying job with taxes, taken out of my paycheck and, accrued vacation.

The only time Eva called us in her office was to thank us for a great job. She never believed in gossip. She said if they say something about someone else you, you can only imagine what they're saying about you.

I later transferred to the PERA Bldg. for a higher position and, a pay raise in a different department for the Services of the Blind.

My older sister then moved to Albuquerque, New Mexico. About fifteen years later, my old boss, Eva, became ill. I took some days off and went to stay with my boss till she died. We talked about everything. How she would miss most of her family and friends who she was close to and, I will miss my; best friend and, my first real boss. We all respected our boss; you never know when your office clerk will be there for you, that's the outcome of a great boss.

Treat your employees good they may be your only friend after your old and your health has gone down south. The person you think will care for you has moved on to their own dilemma, and the person you least accept will be there for you. We hope our children will be there for us, but in most cases they won't be there but, trust me when it comes to take what you worked so hard for.

I worked hard to raise my children to keep up with the Jones as my soulmate articulate. It's almost like my brother getting in a car accident. Who would have thought I would have him living with me. The only difference is my boss appreciated me being there for her and, as did her son. Instead, my brother spoke badly of me after I was the only one who would care for him.

Moving Back to Albuquerque

My older sister completed the Army; she wanted to go to Albuquerque, New Mexico, to attend UNM. She asked if I would move with her to Albuquerque; being I had lived in Albuquerque, I had graduated high school; since I had gone to school in Albuquerque, I knew my way around most of the town.

I was working at the Santa Fe State Capitol. I started at the Bureau of Revenue then transferred to the PERA Building for Services for the Blind. I gave my two-week notice. We became roommates we went shopping she knew all the great stores to buy clothes. We dressed nicely, and we looked good. I had to dress up for work, and she went to school. We did everything together; then we first bought a car to visit our family in Santa Fe and get back and forth to my sister's college and, I had to get to work. I remembered once when my sister went to pick me up at work, I grabbed hold of the door handle and, slipped on a patch of black ice and, ended up under the car my sister wondered where I was and, all I could see was the bottom of the vehicle and, prayed that my sister wouldn't move the vehicle. My older sister got out of the car to see where I had gone and, I yelled out for help. She helped me get up from under the vehicle. Then we started to laugh.

My sister and I bought a three-bedroom house. Our family would come and visit us once in a while.

Father Got Sick

On March 10, 1980, My father became ill. He was diagnosed in his mid-fifties with diabetes; he was transported from Santa Fe and admitted to the Veterans Hospital in Albuquerque, New Mexico. He went on a diabetic coma. My mother doesn't drive and has four small children at home. My sister Felix stayed to care for her younger brothers and sisters and with her seven-month-old son. My sister drove my mother to Albuquerque to stay with my father at the Veterans hospital. My mother stayed with my older sister and me at our house. My father would be in the hospital for several months. After work, I took my mother to the hospital to visit my father. We had my nephew, George. My mother brought George with her. My sister Felix stayed in Santa Fe to care for the rest of the kids. Three months later, Felix got a call from the Navy she would be leaving in a week.

Then my mother, and my younger brothers, and a sister came to live with my sister Sarah and me. My Dad got out of the hospital; my parents went to the insurance company to pay for the house insurance. The agent then said to my parents they no longer owned their home. The insurance person said my parents should get an Attorney. So we went down to see an attorney who had an office across the street from the courthouse. My parents got tricked and signed a Quick Claim Deed instead of a lease

----

agreement while my father was in the hospital. Beatrice and Nick Armijo issued a quick claim deed to the notary for their signature.

When they went to Court for the Santa Fe hearing, my father became ill on the way. I immediately called the Judges' Office. We had a half-hour before the hearing, so I called to re-schedule but, there was no answer, so we left a message. Then I drove to the Courthouse, but no one was in the office. We called again fifteen minutes later but got the answering machine. I drove my father to the hospital. We never heard back from the Judge or his Office. We heard the Judge had granted and signed a Warranty Deed to their home to the Armijo's. My parents had lost the house my father had work hard.

The Armijo's immediately signed off the warranty deed to Ms. Wood, the Investors who lost their home to the bank. No one has paid property taxes since my father owned the house in Santa Fe, New Mexico. I had viewed it in the County Public Records. The people who took their home no longer are living. When my father got released from the Veterans Hospital, he bought two lots and a double-wide trailer in Albuquerque, New Mexico.

Trip to Dallas, Texas

My father got released from the hospital; I went to Dallas, Texas, on a business trip with the Albuquerque Job Corps Center. The director asks if I would be interested in educating the corporate office staff of my color-coded transportation monthly report. My Aunt Nina heard I was in Dallas; then she came to my hotel, then we both went to Mission, Texas, to visit my Abuelito. My Abuelito was well respected where ever we went. We met some of my father's side of the family that I would meet for the first time; they welcomed us when we went to the restaurant. With open arms, my Abuelito introduced me as Santiago daughter. We talked about things I never knew about my parents. When I last saw my Abuelito at his Birthday party, he asked that my children and I sit at his table. He introduced me to my cousins, aunts and, uncle. I couldn't believe it; there must have been over two hundred people, including my Abuelito grandchildren and great-grandchildren. There were four different bands, one of which was the mariachis, and there was family entertainment. My Abuelito's great-grandchildren, who were seven and eight years old, sang a Spanish song for my Abuelito. They had a big potluck—good old fashion cooking. Everyone brought a different dish they had prepared, and the men brought the drinks.

Three years later, I transferred to the Technical Vocational Institute as the Amnesty Program; Secretary. It was tough to get any office position in those days. First, you had to take a typing test. The requirement was you had to type at least 65 words per minute. Then you were given a spelling test. Everyone wanted to work in an office. I couldn't imagine why? After you get in, you have to work your way up to a higher position. Most of the time, you start as a clerk even if you type 65 words per minute. There was a lot of sabotage going on. My sister Felix worked at the courthouse as a file clerk. There was a girl who worked with her mix-up all her files and misplaced her work. She knew who it was, but you need to prove it before you can say anything. The best thing for my sister was to find another job. I knew how she felt it had happened to me. One day when I caught my co-worker red-handed, we worked side by side. She was in the process of break-into my desk. I asked her what are you doing and, she answered, oh, I was looking for a marker and, I said they should be in the cabinet with the supplies. On Monday morning, my supervisor's asked if I would go to his office. The girl stated I wasn't doing my job. I answered, what is it that I'm not doing he then said are all these reports done? I said yes and, when I finished my job, I helped the other girls in the office only if there behind and not coloring their nails or flirting with the teachers or students. The girl later tried to take my job. then called to the office to defend me; from this girl who was from Mexico. She lived with her aunt and graduated in Albuquerque; she wanted my position, being I worked with the immigrants who wanted to become citizens. Some of my student aids came in to help me with my filing and attend the information desk between their classes. They needed to work, so I tried to find them something to do in the office. We worked well; one of my student aids had a class at the University of New Mexico. I had him work after class. And if we weren't busy, I would let them do their homework. My husband was attending the University of

New Mexico then. A few years later, my husband finished college and had finally got a job. The school had provided a job for him at Honeywell, being he was on the honor roll three times in a row. He got the job three months later for some reason. He was fired from his job and decided to attend college again; after another year, he got hired at Intel. About a little over a year, Intel announced a lay-off. Jake immediately volunteered for the lay-off and started receiving unemployment and stayed home on the computer and wasn't getting ready for work, so I asked do you need to be at work and, he smiled and said he had gotten laid off. I said till when and, he answered till he could get another job or go back to school. I then said back to school for what? He said to learn another language how is that going to help you find a job. I then grabbed my purse and the kids and left to take them to school. Other than sitting on the computer all day. What was he planning to do all day at home? He was in his little world figuring out what he wanted, like take off camping without us; he just thought of himself. He would come home for dinner and back to his computer in the little house with a small window to the room's look. He could see us outside when we left the house or the neighbor's house; it was a part of the house when I bought it at the far end of the property. Jake put a desk, bed and, some of his stuff. The kid and I were not allowed except if he had something to show me. Then one day, after a long day at work. The kids and I walked into the house and, there stood Jake in the entrance room. With three boys standing around my drum set. I hoped one day my kids would want to have them. I had just taken them to a friend's house to have him adjust my drum set a week earlier. They were talking to my husband. I then said, what's going on? The boys didn't realize the drum set belonged to me. I sat behind my drum set and asked the boys, do any of you play the drums? after they heard me play wipe-out, one of the boys answered, yes, I do very little. Then, Jake, the snake, spoke up and said they came to buy the drum set. I said, What?

I wasn't aware they were for sale. The boys looked puzzled and didn't know what was going on. It was a done deal. The boy's faces lit up when they saw my drum set. I couldn't say, there not for sale. I refused the three thousand dollars they gave Jake. I went to my bedroom and cried. My drum set was the only memory I had of the girls. I never knew what Jake that damn snake did with the money as he spent every penny on himself. I remember once my son asked Jake if he could get some money to buy paper for school. I wondered why he would ask Jake as I always bought my kids what they needed. Jake answered, to a seven-year-old boy, I work hard for my money. It would be best if you got a job. I couldn't believe it when my son said his father refused to give him money to buy school paper. I said to my son; we brought into this world responsible for you until you graduate from school. I took my son and daughter to the store and bought them what they needed for school. Jake was not aware I had a Pearl White Drums set from Johnny, who taught me how to play the drums. I kept them at his mother's house. Johnny gave them to me when he joined the Air Force. My best friend Rosemary had died in a car accident. The rest of the girls started a family.

The Women who Worked
Ironing Clothes

When we finished their dinner, we cleared up the kitchen table and gathered around to hear my father tell us a story. My father started. There was this old lady who worked ironing clothes for her neighbors to pay her bills. She had a son who didn't want to work. The old lady was so tired she asked her son if he would go to the market to get some milk. She waited and waited, but her son didn't come home. She fell asleep waiting. Finally, when he got home with no milk and no money. The poor old lady asked where is the milk, her son answered. He spent it gambling, playing marbles with the boys. The poor old woman cried for her hard-earned money.

She again asked her son to get some flour to bake some bread; she was so tired to go to the market. He gambled all the money playing marbles but, this time, when he was rolling the marbles, the other boy said, let's double it, her son said, ok. He emptied his pockets. He lost all the money. Suddenly, her son noticed the other boy's feet as he was getting up to leave. The other boy had rooster feet. Her son ran all the way home. And never again gambled. I didn't know if this story was supposed to be funny or scary.

Then my father had another story that was similar to the story before. It was about another son who would take his mother's money. One day the poor old lady put her money in a can to hide it from her son. She knew he would spend it at the local bar and come home drunk. He yelled at his mother where the money Ms. Peters paid you for washing her clothes; she answered, I paid the rent with all the money; her son said, the landlord said, you hadn't paid the rent. She answered I didn't have any money. He yelled and gave me the money breaking all her dishes and cups, opening the drawers looking for the money. When he couldn't find the money, he grabbed his mother from my hair and dragged her around the kitchen. He yelled and yelled where the money was again and again until she finally gave him the money; she had to pay the rent. After drinking all of the money, he was drunk as a skunk when he got home. The following day he noticed his mother was still on the floor. She was dead. After his mother's died, they heard that he started to grow his mother's hair on the palm of his hand. And when he rode on his donkey around town, falling off the donkey crying, for his mother's forgiveness.

Matanza

My mother taught my father how to set up a Matanza we had once a year. When we had Matanzas, my mother made Empanadas (sweet pies) with meat and raisins. I also made Sopapillas (fried bread) with Frijoles (beans) and red Chile from the Rostra's we made. We had a Matanza once a year, mainly in the summer on the weekend because it was an all-day event; it started early in the morning till late at night. My father started to dig a big hole in the backyard and build a big fire with firewood. My mother boiled a massive pot of water ready for my Dad to clean and shave the hair off the pig, and put the ears, tail in another hot pot of water, then later put them in the fire to cook the skin was cut in long strips and, cut in cubes of fat thrown into a cast iron pot outside the fire. My father's favorite part of the pig was the chicharrones (pork rings). My mother got a tortilla and wrapped the chicharrones on a homemade tortilla—my father's favorite burrito. My mother made Empanaditas it's (sweet pies) with meat and raisins. I also made Sopapillas (fried bread) with Frijoles (beans) and red Chile from the Ristras we made. We had a Matanza once a year, mainly in the summer on the weekend because it was an all-day event; it started early in the morning till late at night. My father started to dig a big hole in the backyard and build a big fire with firewood. My mother boiled a massive pot of water ready for my Dad to clean and shave the hair off the pig, and put the ears, tail in another hot pot of water, then later put them in the fire to cook the skin was cut in long strips and, cut in cubes of fat thrown into a cast iron pot outside the fire. My father's favorite part of the pig was the chicharrones (pork rings).

My mother got a tortilla and wrapped the chicharrones on a homemade tortilla—my father's favorite burrito. My Mom made Meat Empanada. It was like a tiny pie. For dinner, we would eat Traditional New Mexico Enchiladas, Red or Green. We call it Christmas, which means both Red (Rojas) and Green Chile sauce. If you don't eat meat, you can make Chile Cheese Enchiladas. My mother used Pork, Onions, Chile, and Cheese, and used Corn Tortillas that she dipped in the oil to soften the tortillas and laid it out then she put part of the Pork and Onion stirred with red Chile then she would spread cheese across the top and, add another layer. I like making Green Chile Enchiladas with Chicken instead of Pork, and it is made the same way as the Red Chile Enchilada except for no Pork and Red Chile. New Mexico has the Best Chile in the World Hot or Mild. We used the Pork from the Matanza for different dishes. The oil that came from cooking the chicharrones used for cooking and baking for most of the year.

My parents never applied for food stamps or got help from anyone. When my father couldn't find a job, he would improvise by selling wood and digging out trees to transplant people's yards. One time they got a job cleaning bricks; my sister Felix was perfect and fast; I was so jealous as my sister piled up the bricks so perfectly stacked I could still see it. I miss my sister. Now that's for richer for poor they cared for each other.

My father worked odd jobs that no one else wanted. He was a dishwasher and, bus driver, and a Merchant Police at night watchman. He wore a uniform. Sometimes we watched our father work if they happened to be downtown selling our Newspapers. Curfew was at 10 pm all kids had to be home by 10 pm, besides most of the stores closed at 5 pm. My father would let my brothers take turns shining his shoes for work. If they did a good job, he would give them ten cents. My father worked as a Merchant Police. He drove a small white car with a blue light on top. He would check all the doors downtown to ensure they were locked and secure; he would put a business card on the doors to let them know they had checked. Once when my father was working as a Merchant Police, he said an old lady walked up to my father and asked him where the bus depot was. My father said I'll take you to where it's because it's a way up the street and dark. She was a short older woman dressed all in black with a black scarf on my head covering my face and, she spoke in a low voice and, walked very slow she followed my father to the bus station. My father walked her inside the bus station and directed her to the front desk to the ticket agent. Then my father started back to the building where he would have been checking before being distracted by the lady in black who he took to the bus station. My father looked down the street. There were Firetrucks, and the Police were down the road. My father asked the policeman what had happened; he said a big explosion the water heater exploded. After my father took the old lady, he decided to finish checking the buildings. Later before his shift was over, he decided to go back to the bus station to ask if the old lady was black; he wondered if I had gotten on the bus as scheduled. The ticket agent said, no, it's been a slow night. My father said he knew there was something about the lady in black. My father had a gut feeling about the lady in black. He said he thought it was his grandmother. She had saved my father's life. Could she have been his grandmother?

Family Holidays

Christmas is my favorite Holiday. When we were younger, we celebrated Thanksgiving and Christmas. Our birthdays were like another day. We didn't get any gifts for Christmas once in a while; if we did, it was always a coloring book and crayon for each one of us. We didn't have time to color, so we gave them to our sisters. We were too many children for any of their relatives to give all of them a Christmas gift. We wonder if they even knew our names. My parents couldn't afford gifts but, my mother always made sure the boys got new clothes. She did make us some from the material of the sack of flour. Once I didn't have another pair of clean underwear, I wore one of my older brothers' underwear. I used to think my mother disliked the girls. I did remember one exciting thing about Christmas, or I should say two things about Christmas.

One of them is the lights around the neighborhood. My father would drive us around the neighborhood and town to see the lights. It was like magic. I looked around with the happiest smile and said Thank you, God, for the people who decorated their homes for us to enjoy. God bless them. I would spin around and around, dancing outside, enjoying the lights and decorations at night. I love Luminaries (brown bags filled with dirt and a small candle lit up inside). Most candles are lit on the 24th of December, but most are lit every night for most of December until January after New Year Day.

Then there was the other part of Christmas that I remember. We got up early in the morning, put on our coats, and put socks on our hands because they couldn't afford gloves. On Christmas Day, we would go out with our neighbor and, all of the kids would be singing Christmas Carols. I would just stand there while the rest sang Christmas songs; I was too shy to sing. Besides, I didn't know any of the Christmas songs. It was like going trick or treating on Halloween, except we got Christmas candy and homemade cookies, fruit and, nuts.

Oh, I almost forgot, before Christmas, we went to the reservations for Oromos, Oromos, that was the most fun I ever had. The Natives in the nearby reservations celebrated the day of the dead. My parents would give each one of us kids a pillowcase and take us to the reservations. It would take my father about a half-hour drive from our house in Sant Fe, New Mexico, to Pueblos. It seemed like a long drive and, it was late at night. We could see the stars and watch the cars driving by. My brothers and I sat quietly in the back of the station wagon. On the front of the station wagon, my sisters always fought over the window seats. When we first got to the pueblo, we would go to the church and pray. Then we would go outside where the big bell was in front of the church. My parents would ring the bell for each one of their loved ones who had passed that year. The best part came when we would go to each house and pray The Lord Prayer. My father would pray the Lord Prayer Spanish.

The Lord Prayer
(In Spanish)

Padre maestro que estas en el cielo, santificado sea tú, nombre Venga tu hágase tu Voluntad en la tierra como el cielo, danos hoy damos hoy el pan nuestro pan de cada día. Perdona nuestras ofensas. Como también nosotros perdonamos a los que nos no ofenden. No nos dejes caer en tentación y libramos de todo mal.

I loved hearing my father pray the Lord's prayer in Spanish. They would all yell out Oromos, Oromos twice loud because most natives were still cooking and baking in the kitchen. Times have changed since I was a little girl. My son and my nephew went on Oromos but, the bread wasn't fresh and, they gave out popcorn. What happened to the pies and tamales? I was home sick with a bad cold so that I couldn't go hadn't gone since my mother died. I hope to go next year in honor of my parents. Hopefully, it will be better than this year. The best part was when the natives would invite us to their homes to eat homemade; they sat to eat. They didn't care how many kids my parents had; they welcomed all of them. After they finished eating, they then headed house to house, receiving Oromos, Oromos. We prayed at each house. They gave the adults homemade loaves of bread in different shapes; the bread was fresh, it lasted till we celebrated Thanksgiving. The Empanadas, and Biscochitos, Tamales were all homemade and fresh. The kid sometimes got what the grow-up got but, most of the time. The kids mostly got candy, nuts and, fruit, oranges and, apples, Cracker Jacks. I hated the popcorn. I didn't go this year because I was sick, but my son and sister and my sons were disappointed the bread went bad in two days, and he got lots of popcorn. I missed the good old days when they baked all day and night. I looked forward to the fresh bread to dip in hot red Chile to help with my cold and Green Chile soup. I loved going to the different homes in the Pueblos. They made you feel like family. That was the true meaning of MI Casa Es Su Casa. That's how I felt at the pueblos. The natives who live in the pueblos have the most beautiful home with dirt floors. The structure of the homes is magical, but most natives live in the city today.

Working Parents

When we went to work, we have good days and bad days but, do you ever hear what your child is going thru in school or at home? They deal with problems too. Life is not just about you. They need joy, happiness, love. Watch a good movie with your family with a good ending, laugh, cry, scream with your loved ones. When we finished our dinner, we cleared up the table and would gather around to hear my father tell us a story. My father started. There was this old lady who worked washing and ironing clothes for her neighbors to pay her bills. I had a son who didn't want to work; he gambles and hangs out with the boys. The old lady was so tired I asked her son if he would go to the market to get some milk. I waited and waited, but her son didn't come home. I fell asleep waiting. Finally, when he got home with no milk and no money. The poor old lady asked where is the milk, her son answered. He spent it all gambling, playing marbles with the boys. The poor old woman cried for her hard-earned money. She was so angry I had a piece of bread. I was too tired to argue, so I went to her room to bed. The poor old lady worked so hard and didn't feel like walking to the market. I asked her son again to go to call to get some flour to bake some bread, and, again, he gambled all the money playing marbles but, this time when he was rolling the marbles, the other boy said, let's double it, her son said ok. He emptied his pockets. He had played all his money and lost.

Suddenly, her son noticed the other boy's feet as he was getting up to leave. The boy had rooster feet. He then ran all the way home. After that, her son never again gambled. I didn't know if this story was supposed to be funny or scary. Then my father had another story to tell. It was similar to the story before. It was about another son who would take his mother's money. One day the poor old lady put her money in a can to hide it from her son. Her son asked her for the money. I knew he would spend it at the local bar and come home drunk. He yelled at his mother where the money Ms. Peters paid you for washing her clothes; she answered, I paid the rent with all the money I earned; her son said the landlord said, you hadn't paid the rent, she didn't have any money. He yelled and gave me the money breaking all her dishes and cups, opening the drawers looking for the money. Then grabbed his mother from her hair and dragged her around the kitchen. He yelled and yelled at her where the money was till she finally gave him the money. When he got home after drinking all of the money, he was drunk as a skunk. The following day he noticed his mother was still on the floor. I was dead. They say after his mother's died, he started to grow his mother's hair on the palm of his hand and rode on his donkey around town, falling off the donkey and crying for his mother's forgiveness.

Felling Safe

When we were young, the police would come and say it's almost curfew, pack it up in a friendly way. When you got speeding, they would say be safe and keep that pedal to the metal off and be safe. It felt good to see an Officer joke and respect you to be safe. We surround by State Police, the Sheriff, City Police and, the unmarked police. They say we need more police. We need protection and caring police, but when one of the police killed an innocent bystander.

The News Aire, a young girl, was killed, but they didn't say she ran away after her boyfriend dumped her and said he didn't want the baby or her in his life. When she told her parents they wanted her to get rid of the child, she packed a backpack and left home. It was getting late, and she was tired. When she noticed a car window open, she got in and fell asleep. Early the next day, The business owner reported her as a homeless bum and drunk. She heard all the commotion outside and got up when the police approached her. The police yelled, get out of the vehicle; she opened the door and ran down the street. She was three months pregnant. The police then pulled out his gun and shot her. Her parents now miss their daughter, who looked for help, not the death of her unborn child and herself. Both parents are responsible for the child but, for years, the female had to solve the pregnancy problem.

We have Amber Alert for mothers and fathers wanting to care for their children, but instead, the justice system will put them in prison. We have children in the system in foster care who will not be allowed to care for by their family members to adopt them. Why is it so hard to adopt a child? It's because we pay others to abuse our children? If you should die or get incarcerated, where will your children go? When it comes to our love, one God will give us the will to care for our children. Then there was a girl who was fighting with her boyfriend she wanted out of the relationship. Someone called the police when the police got a hold of her when taken to booking. After being released on her own reconnaissance, she had been beaten up by the police. When her sister picked her up, she had been beaten up non-recognizable. Her sister took her to the hospital to be seen.

We have investigators from Washington to see why our police are killing innocent people. We don't know what the outcome was. We blame the system you made them what they are. Police watch bad movies with killing shooting violence.

The police become heroes for killing instead of serving and protecting. Do you hate to call the police who may be trigger-happy? We give them the weapons to use against us. Why can't they come out with a less violent weapon? Police are killing innocent people—for example, the homeless man up in the Sandia Mountains. The Judge found the police clear for protecting the five or more police because the homeless had a pocket knife. How else can you open a can of Pork and Beans? Then the Latino girl was dragged by her hair, kicked around by the school police at the school grounds after being bullied by classmates.

I wonder where the police were when my daughter's friend and grandson's friend has dragged to the bone a pond his death on a dirt road in the South Valley and, there was no one to stand up for his death. Stand-up for all colors. We all have suffered the loss of our loved ones.

Fake News Again, the News announced what can we do to improve the city having better police; well, the answer to that is done they need more police and, training the answer is No. They need to use commonsense and, less killing, police who kill an innocent person should have to pay for their crime. We don't need more authority, are you kidding? It takes five police to pick up a drunk on the street. When you call 911, they transfer you to another person who is too busy picking up the phone and placed on hold. It's no joke as a volunteer; I think we could do a better job. Why can't we place the military on duty to protect us as they're on the payroll already and training we can also put them in the prisons? You'll read how I had seriously armed police who came to my house to check on my daughter's wellbeing. Outside there were police armed, ready to open fire for the safety of my daughter. The police are trigger primarily happy about domestic violence. When we cry for help, we call 911 because we need protection. My sister Felix feared going home knowing her husband would beat her up and was too ashamed to go to a battered women's home or call her family, but, for most women, it's the only place they have to go. Instead, end up in the hospital. I miss my sister Felix. May she rest in peace. These stories are happing all over the world to people of all colors. We matter.

We need more police who care about our safety and not just make their quota on traffic tickets and—other fines. What we need is training. When you interview for a police officer position, you need to know if they have issues and experience on how they deal with them. Do we have remorse for others and are not trigger happy we all have bad days, good days if we become stressed and can't work in the line of duty like our soldiers who need to stand up for the people, not like protesters. The News shows protesters who protest for the wrong reasons. There called Monkeys. They attack each other for food. We want to get it first, no matter who we takedown. All it takes is one person who makes you believe and don't care either way. How dare the person who took down the statue of Juan de Onate. How would the natives like it if all the Casinos were to be closed down? The city of evil is an addiction like drugs and alcohol and, worse of all, it takes away your hard-working money from not just the Casinos but also your families. How much did their government give to the reservation Corvid Virus hit? When most of the natives work and live in the city.

I'm not just talking about the natives; I'm talking about all races—Shame on all of you. I'm Hispanic, Latina, brown, whatever you want to call me and, I know how important the walls are. It's just not the Hispanic. It's different races throughout the world. We don't have enough funds to help their own and, we have to feed them. Mexico, Africa, and all over the world are beautiful countries that love it. We can make a difference in China or wherever and, make it work we have hands-on experience there are Mexican and, other countries who make things we enjoy having from their land and, not take it away from them. Ask God to help you, not their government. We need to help our own here and now. Stop Protecting against old traditions and the good police, but those of you don't know who you're protesting. Most of the men and women killed had a criminal record and, not for one or two crimes but several and, would have continued to do so we may have lived to kill you or. On government assistance, their families take them to court and become rich with their tax dollars. What did you, the protesters, get for putting your life in danger. It would help if you concentrated on your families and the care of the future of their children. We can't get a job after we finish college. Some can't afford college and go from graduation to work as my family did? Shame on you.

Karma is real. Most of their children, like my son, worked hard and have more experience than any other student and employee in his field. Private schools and students from other countries and colleges, pay-off to help their students get their certificates and leave the hard-working students behind. Please help support the people who deserve the credit, and those of you who come from another country to make it here in America look around you come from a beautiful country where your families live. I hope that God doesn't even have to leave my country to make a difference. Make your country something to be proud of. America is just as good as your homeland. God placed us here to live as his children. Trust in God was all of the same colors and, we all suffer like everyone else. Whether rich or poor, white, black, Hispanic, and natives were all the same. The blacks dye their hair blond, the blond dye their hair black to show off their blue eyes, and the Hispanics dye their hair red or blond. They're all beautiful in their way. If everyone looked the same, it would be boring and, if we didn't have history, what would we see and hear. The natives don't dress as their ancestors did, only during performing. When I was a little girl, I used to sell my tamales to the natives who sold their handmade pottery, silver and turquoise jewelry, and homemade rugs, one of the best artists who sold their work downtown, we dressed as their ancestors wore their jewelry that was handmade.

The tourist loves their culture and respects them for coming to the plaza from their Pueblo. Now, most of the turquoise jewelry is fake. I was born in the United States and loved to hear about my people in Spain, Mexico, Columbia and, other countries who speak Spanish. That's my history and language. Stand up, America. For our country, and all of the other countries as the world is a whole. Wake up see what you have, not what you don't have. We all want what's best for our children but, most of all, we want what's best for You.

Every country had its dilemmas. The USA has problems of its own their country has put most of its own in poverty. We need to help those who worked hard to take their business back and go to work. We don't need an increase in salary as then everything will go up on price, so we're still in the same shit hole. We need those educated and who worked hard for the job we have should get paid more, but then there are those of you who don't care and continue to stay at a low-paid job. There is no reason for education. There night classes video classes get up and, move to a better job but, know what's in your heart do you like to work alone or with others. Where do those protesters come from? Don't they work or have a family? How can they run around protesting? I'm guessing there on government assistance. The Monkey who get feed by us, the taxpayers. Hell, if we can protest so well. Run for president or join the military and help those who are out fighting in Afghanistan for us to have peace in their country. We see their children coming home in a body bag. Who fighting for us? Where are the protesters in Afghanistan?

We can protest from home, but when you have to fight for your life, who will be there for you, will you even be seen. Why are immigrants protesting in their country? Why not in their Countries with their families. Most countries are overpopulated and want to come to the USA to get government assistance. Stop overpopulating their country Sand-Up America for their families. The latest Protestors were at Acoma Pueblo here in New Mexico. The hate speech of The Native Americans and other non-natives tried to remove history an old statue of Juan de Onate from 1599 with a chain and an ax, which ended in the shooting of one of the protestors for removal.

The Onate is known for his brutal treatment of Natives. As we all have seen in TV movies where every schoolchild knows, Indians scalped their enemies and held dances and ceremonies over them. It served to satisfy a thirst for the glory and honor of the heads of the whites and Mexicans. They took the women and children as their own. The statue is entitled La Jornada, where the Onate leads a group of settlers, including soldiers, women, and children. The statue still stands in the heart of the history of their past life. The protesters who aren't Natives or Hispanics didn't suffer the pass their ancestors did. Believe in now, not the past. Believe in yourself. Your life is NOW. We need to hold on to their cultures for the good we can learn from what we stood for. Natives were well known for their home structures, handmade rugs, jewelry, pottery, the list goes on. Most of the Natives don't live on the reservation. They live in the city where they protested, not at the reservation where they call home.

The Hispanics before leaving the white house Obama policy "zero-tolerance" Before Trump became President, Hispanic families, children were separated from their parents and kept in shelters. The ICE Enforcement and Removal Operation thousands of immigrant children from their families called trafficking their children. The fear and anxiety their parents are going through traumatized Migrants children and parents who the government has forcibly separated children from their families. Where are the lost children now? There has been no News that took the 5,400 children from their families. The true stories transpire that 75% of immigrant children under the age of twelve had difficulty explaining they were sexually abused children, including fondling and kissing minors while in the shower they were raped, used if disobeyed detention center. I know while incarcerated, the guards sexually abuse the inmates. But, in this case, these are children. Can you imagine your three- and twelve-year-old child? Some are adapted to work as young as three years old here in their own country. Help those families who are unable to get their children back if they took your child from you. You would be hurting without your child. It's worse than death.

"White People Matters" look around. I said it before color is you and I are real? We of All Colors that Matter. Please, if you know of an immigrant child who is seeking their way home, Help them. It's wrong to take a child that's not yours. Most of them are taken and, molested, hurt. You can help those parents post a Wanted sign for their children to return to their families. We all matter be proud of who you are. Learn your culture, be the best you can be Shame on persons trying to take away the glory of their favorite Aunt Jemima Syrup, who doesn't love Aunt Jemima Syrup. Remember eating it as a child on your pancake.

In 1889, the first black plump woman wearing a headscarf became one of the first black woman models. Take a deep breath. What the heck do you mean, Black Lives Matter? I saw the black lives matter protest in a movie made in the 1970s. Was that a copycat's protest? It's just not the blacks. We of all colors matter; put ourselves in the place of the police. We fear you as you fear them. They're out there doing their job. Their families wonder if their loved ones will come home after a protest, car accident. A robbery, the list goes on. Protester, follow your heart, create peace, show gratitude enjoy the little things. When you have a terrible toothache, which can make it better? Yes, a dentist, you could die from an infection. As a patient in a Dental Office, you can hear and see most Dentists have the worse reputation to work for. And we also say most Dentists commit suicide. I wonder why? Those who choose not to be a donor for a person who could make a difference in their future lives. What good is your body parts if you are dead? Are you not saving the deceased person's body parts? It's for yourself. Funerals are for the living, not the dead. You can make a difference to someone suffering in pain and help them live their love those hoping for them to live. I may look good to you but, I'm hurting inside. Most people with cancer or being Dietetic or any other kind of illness live a painful life. It could happen to you any day, anytime, any age, even if you're as healthy as a horse, like we say. We are of the same colors but a different race. We matter stands by each other. You can make a difference. I heard commercials from different Attorneys stating most drugs cause cancer or smoking and food products. We don't even know what causes most of our illnesses or even know how to treat them. If what we stand for, we make it what it is.

I noticed police have a power trip and, the judges feel they have to blame someone for the Public to see Justices served. The committee has a significant crime rate because you will be caught if you come to New Mexico to commit a crime. We have a lot of Rats. A father called 911 when his daughter got bit by a dog. We don't see the whole picture. There were two girls. You can see them running and screaming in a video. Suddenly, the dog runs toward the girls attacking; simultaneously, the person who took this video. Who or why didn't the person taking the footage; intervene in helping the girls? The dog as they can't talk. The dogs feared the girls. They were screaming and running. The dog ran with fear and bit the girl to protect himself. Without any reason for the attack, the dog had to be put to sleep, sentenced to death. It's murder the dog owner, who is like family, was taken from his family and, now facing the end of their dog. The dog was defending himself from being hurt. They felt fear and sadness, and are who allowed a dog to put sleep is murdered end of the story. Karam is confirmed when you put a dog to sleep that is murder. How do you feel about having your pet put to death if they peed on the rug? Why couldn't the Judge order the owner and the girls to attend counseling a dog training class? Instead of killing the dog. Understand that one day your pet will be your only companion. You never know when you're left behind. God decides what will come to be Karma follows you for not standing up for the rights of allowing a dog to death.

We all share the same pain and happiness in our life.

By the sweat of your face, you shall eat bread till you return to the ground, for out of it took you, for you are dust and to dust, you shall return.

Move to Texas

My parents planned to sell their property. I took them to see some properties but my mother thought that she wanted to move to Texas a change in life but, then my mother got sick and, it never happened. After my mother died, I wanted my father to stay with me, even if it was only on the weekends, so he could get accustomed to being in my home. I wanted him to feel free to live in my home like it was his own home but, my sister, who lived in the house next door to my parent's home, wouldn't see that happening as she lived in my father's property next door. My father had put his property in my name. a few months later Felix and, I were served with a restraining order. My father called me and I said I can't see you; you filed a restraining order on me and he said what's that. We appeared in court I requested someone for my father that spoke Spanish so that he understood in English and Spanish my father told the judge all my children are welcome to visit me. The restraining order was dismissed. We had not been allowed to visit my father. When you get old, you want your children to visit or call as often as possible; trust me; they don't sit home and do nothing all day. Life has taken their ability to do the things they used to. Some are sad and, lonely others try to keep busy, life is strange for them. Don't wait till you get that last call goodbye. Thank God for all the good and bad blessings given to us.

Mother's Death

My father and my nephew George found my mother curled on fetus position behind the sofa. My father had asked my mother to see a doctor a month before her death. When she went to see the doctor, she was so angry with my father. She said we touched her in her private place and, the doctor put her hand in her butt.

She said to my father, I will never go to see a doctor again. After my mother died, we found out she had cancer. She died at the age of eight, five years old, with cancer. I had a dream of my mother not being able to talk. I never paid any attention to my dream. I heard my mother was in the hospital. I went to see my mother at the hospital.

I couldn't believe my mother just laid there looking around. As if someone had scared her, I sat beside my mother's hospital bed. All of a sudden, my mother grabbed my hand tight. I couldn't believe her strength. My mother just stared at me; she wanted to tell me something important, she was unable to speak like in my dream. I could see it in her eyes; my mother needed to say something to me, then my older sister said, leave her alone she needs her rest. I later thought to myself.

I wish I could have known what my mother wanted to say.

My father and I took turns staying in the hospital with my mother. I went every day after work but, on that one day, I had gone to work. I went to the five-star Hotel Resort to pick up my clients. I drove the Natives women attending a three-day convention for an educational training celebration with natives from all over the United States; suddenly, I got a call that the main speaker had canceled till tomorrow. I went to the Convention Center and picked up my clients and, I drove them back to the resort. I then went to the hospital to relieve my father; my father said waits and, I waited for about ten minutes, wondering what my father meant. My father looked at me and said, your mother has passed on. I couldn't believe it. My mother had waited for me before she died. I then called my oldest brother that my mother was gone to call the rest of the family. I had never experienced death of any kind, especially someone so close to me. After my mother had passed, I waited for one of my siblings to help my father with the funeral arrangements. Three days had gone by, and nothing. Then after work, I went to see how my father was doing. He said can you take me to make your mother's funeral arrangements. I said, didn't any of the other siblings call you? I expected one of my other sisters to call but not a one, not even my little sister who lived next door. Felix, who was closed to my parents, had her dilemmas with Jorge, her so-called husband. Who to this day doesn't know Felix has died? My father said no one had come to take him to the funeral home. I said, let's go. I didn't have a clue of what to do. My father gave most of the information to the Funeral Director, and then he asked us to select a casket. They went from room to room and, my father said to me. You pick one. I said, no, Dad, you should pick one. I knew it must have been hard for my father. I walked away, letting my father select the casket. I had a feeling that directed me towards a dark room; I put my head in but, the light was off, and I couldn't see anything. I thought it might be a private room. Suddenly, a man opened the lights, and we walked in as the man from the funeral home said, look around. I couldn't believe it. I had seen the casket. It was a Turquoise color casket with different beautiful Saints around it. I stated to the funeral director I had to find my father. he was at the same place I had left him. I said Dad, you have to see this casket. It's like the one my mother had described my cousin Carlos had; her father said that's the one. We then accompanied the funeral director back to his office. Oh my God, I couldn't believe there were so many things to consider, memorial prayer cards, my father was asked by the funeral director. My father did not seem to be paying attention to what was said. I repeated what was said to him. When I took my father home, he handed me the papers given to him by the funeral director. I read the paper they gave my father. I couldn't believe the bill; it would be so expensive for my mother's burial. The list went on forever; if my mother were alive, she would say I don't need all that I'm dead. The funeral director said to my father. Who is this person as he read the name to my father and, my father answered that's her and, my father pointed me out to the funeral director? The funeral director then proceeded to hand me an envelope. I opened the envelope, and there was a check from the insurance company. I looked at my father and, said Dad, it's a check for one thousand dollars from my mother's life insurance. I had no idea my mother had me as her beneficiary. I looked at the check and turned the check around signed it. I handed it back over to the funeral director; I said to add it to my mother's expenses for my father's bill for my mother's Services. My sister Felix came later with Jorge and picked up some clothes and jewelry for her funeral. With all the running around I had done, I forgot the casket's flower arrangement and got the food after the service. Thank God for my Aunt Gaby. She called me to arrange for us to go to her house in Santa Fe after the burial and provided the lunch, and now if my aunt should die, I will pay for her church service for her. My mother gave me a picture of herself. I had it enlarged to have it displayed in my mother's casket. After the funeral, my mother younger brother, who came with his wife from Santa Fe, New Mexico, asked my father if he could have his sister's picture that I had displayed beside my mother's casket. I couldn't believe my father had given my picture away, but it was ok. I had the original copy.

Who would have thought my mother would have died?

I had planned on going on a cruise with my co-workers and friends I had saved for almost three years. I was so excited to go. I couldn't wait. That's all we talked about for weeks. My best friend was able to sell my ticket to a girl who worked in a different department. I had to cancel to help my father with all the expenses that came up. The Priest, Church Services, flowers, and the flower arrangement for the casket, the musicians, the list went on and on. I used up all of the money, not including the thousand dollars my mother had left me. I used the money I had saved for the cruise and more to pay for my mother's funeral and burial. The oldest and youngest brother were the only ones that helped my father with the funeral expenses.

I was late to my mother's memorial service. I had gone to pick up my father's sister Nina who came to my mother's funeral. I had gone to the airport to pick her up. She came from Dallas, Texas, for my mother's funeral. My Aunt Nina stayed at my house when she came to visit my parents. I had her room ready for her when She came. My aunt asked me if I would take her to the church where my mother was and, I said ok. I waited outside for her. She wanted to ask my mother for forgiveness. When she returned to the car, I said, don't worry, my mother has already forgiven you, and she smiled. My aunt told me a story of her favorite son, who always made everyone laugh and loved everyone. He died in a motorcycle accident at a young age. My Aunt Nina died a year after my mother's death.

After the Church Service, that's when I felt my mother was gone when they wheeled my mother's casket from the church to the hearse to transport my mother to the cemetery. I knew then it was the end. I grabbed my mother's coffin. I refused to let them take my mother to the buried site in Santa Fe, New Mexico.

The man driving the hearse said to the other person beside him, standing by the hearse, said leave her alone, he backed off; I put my hands on top of my mother's coffin, rested my head on my mother's casket, and cried for the first time. Then my youngest sister stepped forward and, said let her go. Can't you see what you're doing to my Dad?

I later thought I needed my mother to come back. I was mad at God for taking my mother away. I needed closure; she took that away from me. My daughter stood beside me. Later my daughter said my brother called her and asked if she could pick him up on the way to the cemetery at his house to go with us to Santa Fe to my mother's burial; I didn't want my daughter to pick him up. I had a bad feeling. We left the church and went to pick up my brothers at his house in Rio Rancho, New Mexico. My brother was hesitating. We had to get to the cemetery. I looked at the time, and I said to my daughter we were going to be late. My brother had the nerve to keep us waiting till some guy came to get some marijuana from him. Then he had the nerve to ask my daughter while you're waiting to cut some roses from his garden for my mother. My daughter's hands were bleeding from the thorns. That damn idiot has the nerve to ask my daughter to cut some roses from his garden. For God's sake, why couldn't he have bought his mother flowers? My God, he was a millionaire, and he couldn't buy my mother flowers. It was a hot day. The flowers got ruined in the car with the heat, even with the air conditioner on. My brother did one good thing. He brought some Christian music to play on my daughter's CD while driving to the cemetery in Santa Fe, New Mexico. I knew my mother would be listening. It comforted me; she was at peace just thinking of my mother and my father. We had driven from Albuquerque to Santa Fe. It was about a forty-five-minute drive. One minute my father's car was in front of us as we followed behind; the next minute. We were lost at the cemetery. How could that have happened? I said, where is everyone. We were 'right behind my Dad. All of a sudden, I didn't see any of the other cars around us. Then unexpectedly, for no reason at all, the trunk of my daughter's car opened, my brother's wheelchair flew out of the trunk. We got out of the car to retrieve his wheelchair. The wind blew the wheelchair making it fly further down the hill it started rolling down the hill in route. We looked down the hill and, we could see where everyone was as they stood around my mother's coffin. We got my brother's chair back in the car's trunk and drove to where my mother was being laid to rest in the cemetery. The balloons were being released. The fourth of the girls, my sister Eva gave me three balloons to let free to my mother, but they refused to go up on the air. They just stood there and, I looked up and cried. My sister Eva said those three balloons my mother is holding on to for you and your kids. My mother wouldn't let them go up. It was a sign from my mother; we each got a message. My mother never told anyone I was blessed with God's love, the Angles, what? A Saint, or could it be an Alien. Life is filled with miracles. You have to believe and then let go.

After my mother had been placed to rest at the cemetery, I took my Father three weeks later to my mother's graveside. Then the funniest thing happened. My mother gravestone read Miquela Gabaldon. My father said, who is Gabaldon? Did your mother have another man? I said Dad, it's just a missed print lets go to the office to get it corrected Gabaldon happened to be the name of the Mortuary and, we laughed. Then a month later, I went with my Father to Santa Fe to see if they corrected my mother's headstone. That was the last time I had seen my father. My sister and I were not allowed to visit our father. My sister put a restraining order against us. When my mother died, everything went to the goodwill or city dump, including any pictures of my mother? My father had a strong box and the bibles he kept up in his closet. I was at my father's house when I looked in one of my mother's bibles. You wouldn't believe what I found. My mother had over four thousand dollars in a bible for a rainy day. There were hundred and twenty-dollar bills. Who would have thought? I said Dad; you need to take all this money to the bank. We planned to go to the bank in the morning to take the money but, my father told my younger sister, and the money was gone. About seven or eight months later, after my mother died, my father asked if I would go with him downtown to add my name to his house; the clerk sent us to get a notice of Deed to sign his property under my name. There was a court record of someone taking my parents to court. He tried to take my parent's property away from them. I got a copy of it and put it away. I then said, no, wait; my father should keep his name and add my sister Felix on the title. All three of us signed the Deed in front of the Notary at the County Clerk Office. She asked for our identifications. I said, Dad, the property is yours till you die, and my nephew could stay on your side as long as he wishes. I planned to sell part of the property, leaving my nephew's part as his own to stay and give all my brothers and sister the money equally divided, if it was ok with the rest of my siblings.

You do know a funeral is for the living, not the dead.

Ever since my mother died, I would find a dime in places I had either cleaned or moved and, there appeared a dime. I figured it was from my mother and, I would say to my mother, I hope something good will happens to me today. Thank You, Mom. When we went to the Community Center for my sister's funeral, family gathering only, she walked up to my nephew. When we talked to him, I said to George, "You know I keep finding a dime. I think it's from my Mom, and he said a dime would appear from nowhere and; he also thought it came from his grandmother to say she was looking after him like she always did. George was like her son. That was the last time I would see or talk to George.

My father missed my mother even if she gave him a hard time. I was so mad for many years at my mother for leaving my father behind for over twenty years. She died suddenly; it took my father a long time to let go of my mother. Life is short and, time is going by too fast. It would be best if you were happy for yourself first. Spend time with your loved ones, friends and, family. Live life, try everything once. When you get old you want your children to visit or call as often as possible trust me your parents don't sit home and, do noting some are sad and, lonely others try to keep busy, life is strange for them. They no longer have the ability to do what they enjoyed when they were young. The thought of thinking of retiring sounded great till you find out your retirement check is not enough and you sadly do what you can to survive. Would you please not wait till you get that last call when they say goodbye? Thank God for all the good and bad blessings given to you.

I think of all the things I could have had in life, like a real vacation a cruise. Even if I can't swim, my excuse is I live in New Mexico and, the Rio Grande is only ankle-high. But, I still want to travel and, I would of love to own a new car off the car lot, Not a used car which was all I could afford after saving for years and, a house I could call my own with a garden so, I could plant my flowers but, life is short and, money is not enough to make ends meet. My father always said all you need in life is a good home, a car, and food on the table.

My mother wanted to move to Texas. My parents planned to sell their property and start over in a new place. They needed a change in life but, then my mother got sick and, it never happened. After my mother died, I wanted my father to stay with me, even if it was only on the weekends, so he could get accustomed to being in my home. I wanted him to feel free to live in my home like it was his own home but, my sister, who lived in the house next door to my parent's home, wouldn't see that happening as she lived in my father's property next door. My sister put a restraining order on my sister Felix and me. We weren't allowed to visit my father. When my mother passed, my father left us his house after my mother died.

Our parents never expressed their love to us; they never embraced each other or said, I love you. I had gone to visit my brother at that Veterans Hospital. When I got home, I started to think, Wow, my brother is sick, he could die, and I couldn't say how I felt. It would be one reason for writing my story is for my oldest brother and my children. May our father God keep my brother with us for many years to come? And hopefully will receive a donor soon. My brother hoped the family would reunite but, it would take a big miracle to find each other after so many years lost and all the gossip told by the only person who could have started it all. My brother's wife got up and gave my son and me a hugged and, we hugged her back; I turned around, waved goodbye to my brother, and said I'd call tomorrow. Isn't that sad that I couldn't hug my brother? It's just the way our parents raised us. You won't find a family photograph of all of us together as a family. You may see school pictures of two or three of my brothers and sisters but none of me. I figured they couldn't afford it; besides, I didn't particularly appreciate taking my picture. I'm just not photogenic.

My father missed my mother even if she gave him a hard time. I was so mad for many years at my mother for leaving my father behind for over twenty years. She died suddenly. It took my father a long time to let go of my mother. Life is short and, time is going by too fast. It would be best if you were happy for yourself first. Spend time with your loved ones, friends and, family. Live life, try everything once. I think of all the things I could have had in life, like a real vacation a cruise. Even if I can't swim, my excuse for not knowing how to swim is I live in New Mexico and, the Rio Grande is only ankle-high. But, I still want to travel and, my other wish is to own a new car off the car lot, Not a used car which was all I could afford after saving for years and, a house I could call home to have my garden so, I could plant my flowers but, life is short and, money is not enough to make ends meet. My father always said all you need in life is a good home, a car, and food on the table.

Trip to Las Vegas

My father worked at home; he loved singing his Rancheras (Traditional Mexican Songs). Some of the songs I heard my father sing were El Rancho Grande, Hey Good Looking what you got cooking, I'm so Lonesome tonight by Hank Williams and many other Spanish songs. My father had a great voice, even though my mother wouldn't allow him to sing inside the house. I would go outside to hear my father sing. We visited my grandma Lucero, who had moved to Las Vegas, Nevada, with my uncle Fred. My cousin, husband played in a band. We decided to go to the park to have a cook-out. My cousin's husband and his friends started to singing then my father joined in. My cousin's husband was surprised and said to my father that he had a good voice. It had been a long time since I had gone to Las Vegas, Nevada. It had been over thirty years since I had seen my cousins.

I heard my niece was getting married in Las Vegas, Nevada. I was so happy I hadn't seen her since my sister Eva's funeral. I mentioned it to a friend and, he said go. I asked my son to go with me, but he said no and that I couldn't go either I felt so hurt I decided to ask a girlfriend to go with me because my other friend was with her boyfriend in France for three weeks. I ended up going with another friend I volunteered with; I drove to Las Vegas, Nevada and, all the way and back.

When we got to Las Vegas, the first thing I planned was to visit my cousins in Las Vegas, Nevada; my cousin said it had been 37 years since she last saw me. We talked about our parents, children, and husband; then, my friend said she was tired and needed to check-in at the hotel. I said goodbye to my cousins, and we left. Not more than ten minutes after we had checked in to the hotel and went up to our room, she asked if I wanted to go to the Stratosphere.

I didn't know what the Stratosphere was but, I went along with her. When we were at the Stratosphere, I said, let's stop at the Dunkin Donuts for coffee. I asked her if she wanted anything she said no; she then asked the clerk at the Dunkin Donuts about their breakfast egg muffin. I heard the girl say they were open 24 hours. Earl the following day, my so-called friend went on her own; to the Stratosphere to get her breakfast muffin. I couldn't understand why the hotel served breakfast. I waited an hour for her. I then went to look for her but after walking for an hour. I decided to stop buying my aunt from Santa Fe a postcard and then head back to the hotel and wait for my friend. She didn't want to wait for me to purchase the card the day before; she said the line was too long to wait to pay for just a postcard. I got back to the hotel. We had to move to another room. Because my friend found someone false teeth on the side of the dresser and, the bed she called the manager and, maids were in our room, my friend was crying. So, we moved to another room; I started to unpack. A few minutes later, my friend said she was going for a walk. It was getting late, and my friend had been gone for over two hours, so I started to get worried. I decided to go out and look for her again when she later showed up in the room. I asked my friend where she had been; she said I took the city bus and went all over Las Vegas site seeing. I said, isn't that dangerous' being alone in a big city? I then started to think of what my other friends had said to be careful with my friend. She liked to do a disappearing act and go off independently. They were right. It was almost time to get to the Chapel for my niece's wedding at 7:30 pm. The wedding was at 8:00 pm it was about ten minutes away from the hotel. When we got to the Chapel, it seemed as if they were the only ones there.

I asked the girl at the Chapel if we were the right place for the wedding, and I showed her the invitation. The girl answered yes. We were the first ones at the Chapel. Then all of a sudden, I felt my sister Felix present. I felt like crying but, then the groom's family started walking in and sat down. Then the groom turned around and, asked; have we met and I answered, no, I was from New Mexico. The bride is my niece. All of a sudden, a young girl across from us heard we were from New Mexico. She got up and turned to her father and, said that's my grandmother Felix's sister. My mother's Aunt Bryan got up and hugged me.

He was glad to see me and remembered me. I was surprised that my sister Felix's older daughter's family was there. Then I see my niece walking down the aisle with her little sister. I felt a cold wind behind her. I couldn't stop the tears as I felt her brother and my sister long side her and her sister walking her down the aisle with a smile. My sister's older daughter sat down. Then her older daughter said Mom look, it's your Aunt from New Mexico. She glances at me. Then after the service, we went outside. Her husband introduced me to his family for the first time. They were all grown up. When my sister Felix's older daughters got married, I had hers and the groom's wedding cake made. Thanked God I made the trip and thanked my friend for making it possible for me to go. I called my friend all during my trip to let him know I was ok. I hope to visit the rest of my cousins soon. When I got home again, I Thank You, God, for being my traveler.

The Story of Sasquatch (Big Foot)

My father tell us the story of Sasquatch. He said there was a young girl who was hanging clothes outside of her home in the wood. Then all of a sudden, a big bear grabbed the young girl and took her to his cave; he closed the cave where he kept her with a big rock. The bear cared for the girl. The young girl then became fond of the bear. The young girl had a son, who was born half man half bear. Who we call Sasquatch and, some people call him bigfoot, which could have been another story but, the story goes? The young girl and the bear stayed together in the cave and, their son Sasquatch roamed the woods. My father said he believe Sasquatch or Bigfoot will live forever.

Long Day at Work

I t was a busy day at work. I had decided to work late as the kids didn't have to attend cheerleading or football practice. I planned to pick up my kids from my mother's house, go home, make dinner. Then wash dishes, get the kids ready for school for the next day—same old stuff. The next day I got up like every other morning I drove the kids to school and headed to work. My daughter always seemed to be running late. We were in the car waiting when I had to go back and get my daughter, who couldn't decide what shoes to wear. When we finally all got in the car, I said to my daughter and son when I was young; we only had one pair of shoes. The only problem we had was to find the other pair. That had a long tongue, or should I say the soul was worn. I had to either sew it or try to glue my shoe, which we didn't have except Elmer's glue and, that only worked on paper. When I went to play for Reese's at the playground could only play on the swings or the monkey bars I couldn't run, because I would fall flat on my face. The kids laughed and, I wanted to cry.

The Affair

The other women and my husband would end my life as well as my children's. Just before going to my parents' house, I decided to stop at home to see what I had to make for dinner or if I needed to stop at the grocery store. When I noticed a vehicle on my driveway, I could see the light in the bedroom was on. I then drove up to the house. I rang the doorbell, but there was no answer, so I rang it again. I figured my husband was in the living room asleep and didn't hear the doorbell. I went to the side of the house to the bedroom. I looked inside through the window.

I couldn't believe what I was seeing. I banged on the window and yelled out to my husband. What's going on? My husband turned around with his pants down and looked at me with a puzzled look on his face. The other women ran to the bathroom and called 911. My heart dropped; I couldn't breathe; I was shaking.

My legs locked as I stood motionless. I heard someone slowly walking towards me on my right side. It was the police who asked what was going on. I said I was trying to get my husband's attention to let me in the house. The police quickly stopped me and said the man inside the house said he doesn't know you. I couldn't believe what he had said. Are you kidding me? Then the police said, Do you have a place to stay? I said yes, my sister lives around the corner. The police then said you need to stay at your sister's house till you appear in court. You and your husband are being charged for domestic violence. We were now facing our first domestic violence charges. I thought to myself, domestic violence. We had no contact?

Domestic Violence Hearing

When you go to court for domestic violence, most people don't need an Attorney. It's just a hearing with no witness. You just have to face the judge in court. There we were; my husband and I were written up for domestic violence. It was our first domestic violence. When I caught the other woman (Annie), and my husband was having sex in my home. I don't know about my husband, but I was dreading having to face the judge. The police said I could not go to my own house until after I appeared in court when I went to work with one of my co-workers who is well educated with legal knowledge. Has he passed on? Said police do not have the right to order you out of your own home; most of us don't know that police do not have the authority to do so. We trust that police would know what he can and cannot do by law. I had been ordered out of my own home over a love affair; The police may try to frighten you by searching your car or home without a warrant. In hopes of an arrest, but there is one thing on their side and, that would be if they have a probable cause like someone yelling out help. I was not too fond of the sound of appearing in front of a Judge. But, here I go. What is the judge going to say or do to me? I'd rather not have to face my husband and the judge, but I had a court order. I just had a bad feeling the morning I had court. I had to get my children and myself home. When I walked into the courtroom, I felt weak and sick.

There sat my husband and the other woman. As I walked into the courtroom, they both looked back at the same time as the court door opened and, I walked in.

I couldn't help noticing them both staring at me. I went to court alone. I did not want to involve my family and friends. In any of my dilemmas, I usually took care of my problems alone, like everything else in my life. I walked as far back to the far-right side of the benches and sat down at the end of the courtroom—the minute They both seen me walk in and sit down. Annie immediately started laughing, and she started rubbing my husband's back and kissing him. The other woman and my husband sat across from me on the left side about five benches up. Knowing I had a view of them together. I embraced myself and held my breath. I was going through the embarrassment as I hung my head down low and sat in the courtroom waiting for the judge to enter the courtroom after waiting for about ten minutes. There was an announcement that the judge was running late. I sat there calmly. I couldn't stop shaking. I decided to walk out of the courtroom to stop the tears from running down my face. I must have been in the bathroom for ten minutes. I couldn't stop crying. I washed my face as I looked straight at the bathroom mirror and said to myself, OK, I can do this. I took a deep breath and, said Oh, Dear God, give me strength. I didn't want to give them the satisfaction of seeing me cry. I walked back to the courtroom and waited for the judge. The judge finally got in as I sat in the courtroom wondering what he and. the other woman wanted from me; they couldn't leave me alone.

First called to the podium. The police testified to the judge that he did not witness the window being broken but noticed the motorcycle on the ground. There was no contact between the two of them other she was yelling when I approached her. She was standing by the window yelling open the door. What the heck is going on? Then called my husband to the podium. Then the judge asked my husband to describe the window as being broken. My husband answered it was the size of a quarter and, he put his hand up facing the judge and put his middle finger meeting with his thumb together up on the air showing the hole on the window to the judge. Jake the snake kept saying and, my wife, and my wife. I wanted to yell out, stop calling me your wife. Then I was called to the podium. I couldn't walk straight; I felt weak afraid, but mostly ashamed at the same time. I could feel Jake and Annie observing me. I was terrified I couldn't talk. I'd say something but, the words wouldn't come out. I looked up and tried again. I finally said, your honor.

I noticed the bedroom light was on, so I decided to ring the doorbell, but my husband didn't answer the door. I then went to the side of the house to the bedroom window, and I looked inside. When I saw that woman and I pointed her out to the judge and my so-called husband having sex, they were in a pig-style position. Annie, the other woman, sat there proud like it was a good thing. Your honor, it all started when that woman called 911 and told the police dispatcher she feared for her life. That's the reason we're here today. Your honor's there was no domestic violence; there was never any contact between us. I stood by my bedroom window when the police crept towards me.

I noticed the police standing on my right side when I was looking into my bedroom window. I had just witnessed. My husband with that woman is having sex. The police then asked me to stay at my sister's home until I appeared in court. The house is under my name, and all the utilities are on the kitchen wall, with my name and, the police answered, he couldn't do anything. Then he asked if I had a place I could go. The man inside the house said he didn't know me. I answered what. My sister lives around the corner. The police followed me to my sister's house and said to me.

Viola was at the house around the corner. The man in the house said he didn't know her. My sister answered, that's her house, the police answered. She should stay here till after the hearing. I then went to my parents to pick up my children and, we spent the night at my sister's house.

Your honor, I understand that the police officer did not have the authority to remove me from my own home; there was no violence or a reason I would be forced to stay at my sister's house with my children. Because that woman had called 911 stating she feared for my life. And, you're Honor about the motorcycle; it's been standing on blocks for months. The wind could have blown it down. My husband's motorcycle is sitting on bricks; the parts are in the garage, and as for his demonstration on the window cracked in quarter size. The judge then asked my husband, how long have you been married to this lady? Jake stood up proudly and answered twenty-three years and was still married. The judge then said this shouldn't have been a domestic violence hearing.

It should have been a murder trial. She should have killed you. Case Dismissed and left the courtroom. The charges were dropped. It had been enough just having to explain myself to the judge in front of other people hearing our testimony.

Domestics Violence Hearing

I had no criminal record. Annie had made me into a Monster in the eyes of people. The judge's eyes and Attorney Annie included me on the internet that I had become a statement of Pervasive fraud built into the way of hatred. There must be a way the justice system should find some way of stopping those who write stuff about others on websites, Facebook, or any gossip columns, primarily if it's written in anger as it was to my husband's lover Annie. Who sounds bipolar, disorder, a severe borderline personality disorder and, obsessive-compulsive features and, sadomasochism. That is hurtful to others' bullying.

Bullies are never around alone. There are three or more to stand by the main tormenter. We have caused suicide, killings; the list goes on. The ones who need to hear our voice are shut down. The facts are not on the News or Talk Shows headlines stories. That has made it worse, making it hard to be heard; you are marked for life once you are branded. Who is this person? Who my husband called Annie. That person should be charged for something and go to jail. Being human most people seem to like the wrong thing we hear about others on the News and not too much about the good we have accepted in life. When you turn on the News, what do you hear? The worse story headlines murders, robbery with that kind of News implanted in their brain we fear their own shadow.

Were quick to follow up on the stories behind the crime, but the News says who cares as good News is not suitable for the viewer's so if a person is found innocent, you'll never hear the outcome of the innocents of the person who was being accused.

My Husbands Catastrophe

My husband was a walking disaster every time I asked him to do something around the house. There are a couple of stories of what I mean by a walking disaster or the true meaning of Dennis the Menace. We'll here starts one of his disasters.

My husband had decided to clean the chain of his motorcycle.

I happened to walk outside to the laundry room. My husband was sitting outside the kitchen door, where he was sitting working on his motorcycle. He had a rag and a can of gasoline on his hand. He was dipping the rag in the can of gasoline to clean the chain of his motorcycle. I then told him that's not the way you clean the chain. You need to take the tire off and take out the chain. He said I had done it before. I said I knew what I was talking about as I had a Harley Davison motorcycle before I met him, so I went on with what I was doing in the laundry room. I went inside the house and, not more than a minute later, I heard my husband screaming. I ran outside, and there was blood all over. He tried to run the motorcycle with the rag running between the chain and, it got caught pulling his hand and caught his thumb, cutting it off. I grabbed a towel and wrapped it around his hand. Then I picked up his thumb from the floor and put it in a bag of ice. We could save his thumb. I gathered the kids, put them in the car, and took Jake to the emergency room. I gave the male nurse on duty the bag of ice with my husband's thumb.

When we got to the hospital room, he grabbed the bag from the nurse and threw the ice pack with his thumb in it down the hall. To this day, he has no thumb. Since he threw his thumb, it wasn't repairable. The doctor said he could place his thumb to heal; one is under your armpit, and the other is in your butt, where it would heal faster. I thought to myself, put it up to his butt. The doctor decided to place his thumb under his armpit or butt for a faster healing process. I thought to myself, put it up to his ass.

He was out of work for almost nine months without pay. He used up his unemployment. He got tired and, one day, he decided to take off his bandages and was out and about doing other stuff except finding a job. It had been over a year since his accident.

When he was working on his motorcycle, I had asked you not to leave the gasoline out. He still had another had he used and was on the computer all day. I said it's dangerous to keep the gas can out and, the house could catch on fire, or the kids may get into it. He left the gasoline out, so I decided to give him a hard time about it. I said to him, remember when I asked him not to leave the can of gas out. Well, the dog got into the gasoline and drank the gasoline. Then the dog started running in a circle and, the dog just dropped to the ground. He answered, what happened to the dog? Is he dead? I said no, he just ran out of gas. He didn't like my joke or any jokes and, he was mad at all of us for a week. I said to myself, oh my God, he can't even take a joke.

It was the weekend and, I decided to trim the vines growing on the chain-link fence in front of the house. It was getting hard to open the gate. I had blisters in my hand trimming the vines. I went inside to get a glass of water. It was a hot day outside. All of a sudden, my husband came outside to see what I was doing. He said, let me do it. He thought he could do it a better job and a lot faster and easier. He went and got the chainsaw and started to cut the vines. It worked well for him for a while, then all of a sudden, the chainsaw kicked back and almost took his eye out. Then we went again to the emergency room and, we stitched his eyebrow, where he has the scar to show for.

Then another emergency call, he was up in the attic. Hiding smoking marijuana, somehow he started a fire and was yelling fire, fire. I couldn't figure out where he was yelling from. I then noticed smoke coming from the attic. I ran and got the water hose, aimed at the top of the attic. I managed to stop the fire. Then here comes one of the Biggest disasters, not that the others weren't. The kids were looking out the kitchen window and, I said, what are you kids doing? We said watching; you need to see this. I looked out the window for a second; then I went to the kid's bedroom to clean up a little. Early Saturday, he went out and bought a big tractor tire and tied it to the bumper of his truck. He started driving his big truck around the yard gathering and, dragging all the tumbleweed in one big pile. When I went to the living room, I heard the kids screaming, Help, help. The kid ran to get me: mom fire, fire. I ran out, got the water hose pulled it as close to the fire as I could. I yelled out, get out and, I then got the water hose and hosed him down. I couldn't believe it. He had put all the tumbleweeds in a big pile like a mountain smashing the tumbleweeds down and stood in the middle as he poured gasoline around in a circle while he stood in the middle, then he got his lighter and lit it. He was then caught in the middle of the fire. I couldn't believe he only got his eyebrows and part of his hair. Then he had the nerve I was vacuuming the carpet. I noticed a wire alongside the wall, so I followed it to the attic. I walked up to my husband and, said what is this? I showed him the recorder, and all he said was, please don't break it. Besides, there wasn't anything nothing worth hearing. I said, what were you expecting to hear. He said he just wanted to hear what you and your mother had to say for hours. I said are you kidding me? You don't even understand Spanish.

He did so many things to us in the little time we spent together. I didn't think he was trying to look for work. I worked two jobs, and he stayed at home. He had a lot of free time on his hands. I picked up kids after work to go to football and cheerleading practice and sometimes they had practice on the weekends. On my second job, I worked from home as a medical transcriber till two in the morning.

It Could Happen to you
The beginning of the worse era of my life
I have the right to face my accusers. . .

Our Divorce

The ex-wife side of the story

A nnie attend my divorce with my husband when we attend our divorce hearing. My divorce was finalized, the judge granted me Spousal Support. I supported my husband while we were married and attended college. When the judge granted me spousal Support, Annie jumped up and yelled out to the judge; for how long does he have to pay Spousal Support? The judge answered till she dies or re-marries. After our divorce, Annie tried to hurt me, in the most horrifyingly, way anyone could ever imagine. The specifics of all charges brought against me by Annie, who started fabricating stories to the justice system, and whoever else Annie could drag into her approbation, would help destroy me, including the investigators and justice system. I was defenseless and confused; I didn't comprehend what was going on. I was subpoenaed to court numerous times; all I could do was show up to every court hearing.

I didn't want the judge to order a warrant for her arrest. If it meant having put me in prison for the rest of my life at the time. Annie continues to write her story about me on my web-site in her own words, mostly hearsay. Unbelievable story. I have the right to answer Annie's allegations written against me. Annie's web-site started with Their Divorce hearing (without children) scheduled before the district court judge and special commissioner. Annie started. The clerk told Annie that the judge had to recuse herself to be prosecuted; Annie stated that nothing ever happened.

The divorce case went before the District Court Judge the Presiding of Family Courts. Who granted me Spousal Support? Annie later stated once. The judge signed the divorce papers. I yanked the divorce papers from the judge's hand to get filed and added my comments, changing the amount of the spousal Support from $300.00 to $800.00, as the judge noted on the bottom of the divorce decree. Annie specified Viola admitted to doing so. I did not write any comments or changes regarding the spousal Support noted or alterations made. The judge handed me the divorce paper to take to the clerk to file. Annie and Jake shadowed me down the elevator to the clerk desk to seal and file as specified? The judge wrote the amount of three hundred dollars. Spousal Support a month on the divorce decree; the judge would have been very angry for tampering with legal documents. The judge wrote in her handwriting on the bottom of the divorce as noted.

SECOND JUDICIAL DISTRICT COURT
COUNTY OF BERNALILLO
STATE OF NEW MEXICO

Cause No. __DM__ '99

Viola █████████
_____
                    Petitioner

_____
                    Respondent

FILE
SECOND JUDICIAL

99 AUG 26 AM 9

Thomas G. K

THERESA L. KNIGHT

FINAL DECREE OF DISSOLUTION OF MARRIAGE.
(Without Children Involved)

THIS MATTER, HAVING COME BEFORE THE Court upon Petitioner's for Dissolution

of Marriage, the Court having considered the evidence presented before it and being full advised

in the premises, hereby enters its Findings of Fact, Conclusions of Law, and Final Decree as follows:

THE COURT FINDS:

A.   BACKGROUND.

     1.   Petitioner resides in the State of New Mexico and is resident of Bernalillo County,

and has resided in the State of New Mexico for more than six months immediately preceding the filing

of the petition herein.

     2.   Petitioner and Respondent were married on _____ at Bernalillo County, and

ever since their marriage have remained husband and wife.

B.   PROPERTY.

     1.   Petitioner and Respondent Community Property accumulated be grated to Petitioner

without contesting as agreed *any property between ___ J2 + Viola*

Di agrunted St)

C   DEBTS.

Petitioner and Respondent have no community debts.

D   NAME CHANGE.

Petitioner wishes to have her name restored to her former name <u>Viola Trevino</u>

E.   GROUNDS.

Petitioner and Respondent are of such inherently different temperaments that a state

of incompatibility arisen between them, making it impossible for reasonable expectation of

reconciliation.

WHERFORE, THE COURT CONSLUDES AS A MATTER OF LAW AS FOLLOWS:

Petitioner is entitled to a Decree of Dissolution of Marriage from Respondent, on the grounds of

incompatibility.

IT IS THEREFORE ORDERED, ADJUDGED AND DECREED AS FOLLOWS:

The bonds of matrimony existing between Petitioner and Respondent are dissolved, and Petitioner is

awarded a Decree of Dissolution of Marriage from Respondent on the grounds of incompatibility.

The community property shall be awarded to the Petitioner, without contesting as agreed.

The Petitioner and Respondent have no community debts between them.

The Petitioner is restored to the use of her former name Viola Trevino.

Paragraph II. Spousal Support of the Marital Settlement Agreement filed June 14, 1999 is amended to read as follows: Effective September 1, 1999, Respondent is to pay Petitioner $300.00 per month as spousal support. The MSA, as amended,

is approved and is adopted as an order of the Court. ___

Deborah Davish Walker

Viola ███████ , Petitioner

_____ , Respondent

Page 1 of 7 The other woman stated Jake had dinner with his wife and her children to tell them he was seeing the other women. When we had dinner, Annie said I told Jake the divorce degree was never filed, so we were not divorced. How could she say that when the other women attended our divorce hearing and escorted me to file the divorce papers with the clerk?

If we went out to dinner, I invited him to dinner with us, and paid for it. While he just sat there eating supremacy. Which is one of the reasons I regret inviting him to go with us to eat. My children couldn't believe his behavior. He had his diet where he ate seaweed, raw eggs, and all kinds of so-called healthy foods. While he trained for his Bicycle Tours, Running Marathons, Hiking, Swimming, and Martial Arts, you name it and, he did it. Oh and, he also bought himself an electric guitar with speakers he planned on joining a band. I can't say much for him now. New wife new life he now goes camping alone. No family to deal with but, then he never did have any family responsibilities. He can't even tell you when the kid's birthday was as I was the mother and father to my kid's life. On one occasion, he was caught eating out alone. The kids and I were going to the grocery store when the kids yelled out, isn't that his truck? He was at the Taco Bell eating down the road from the house. My children asked. Why was he at Taco Bell and he didn't invite them? I answered that's a good question. I thought he was going to work. Then there was the time I had to work on a weekend and called my mother if she could pick up the kids from the house. When I left to work, they were still sleeping. And, Jake was at home in his office a cross from the house. The kids didn't want to wake up early that Saturday. They didn't have school or practice, so they wanted to sleep in. I then called my mother, if she would watch the kids but, my father was busy. Although my sister Felix was at my mother's house visiting. She took my mother to my house. My mother doesn't drive. My sister took my mother to pick up my kids.

When my mother and my sister got there, they heard my kids crying. Jake was forcing them to eat raw eggs, they were yelling. We don't want to eat that.

When my sister and mother heard them shouting out, they were not hungry; he yelled back to eat it. My sister said to him they could take them to eat and later called me at work. My sister said they had my kid and that he was forcing them to eat gorse running eggs. My sister Felix said she couldn't bear to eat raw eggs herself; I said the kids have money take them out to get something to eat if they want anything.

Another sad story, or should I say, another one of the worse things he ever did. Jake asked if I could drive him to work out of the blue. I wondered why he had his truck, motorcycle, and the bicycle he rode to work while in training and, he usually didn't work on Saturdays, which would be the day when he had most of his marathons. My kids were in football and cheering practice for two hours. So, I decided it would be ok to drive him to work and make it back before my kids finished practice. I made sure the kids and the coach knew I would be right back.

I was going to take him to work and drive right back. Then he asked if he could stop at the Waffle House. Maybe he wanted to pick up lunch since he decided to go to work and the cafeteria may be closed on Saturday. Waited outside in the parking lot while he went into the Waffle House. I thought he was ordering his lunch. When all of a sudden noticed he had sat at the table and started eating alone. While sitting outside waiting for him, I couldn't believe what I had just witnessed. What a son of a bitch. I started up the car, backed up the car, and left him eating at the Waffle House. I cried to the middle school to pick up the kids from practice. Then they left for my parents' house and, I sat there, I didn't mention a thing about Jake behavior. You wouldn't believe what happened. My younger brother walked into my parent's house and, said guess who he had just seen and gave him a ride to work; damn it, what luck was that. Why does God help bad people?

My mother took care of the kids during the week for me. I paid her one hundred dollars a week for watching them from four o'clock when the bus dropped them off till five-thirty when I got to my parents' house. Once in a while, I had to work an hour or so late if needed, which wasn't often. Most of the time, I went in early, so I didn't have to work late. I dropped off the kids at school in the morning and, they took the bus to my parents after school. My son always took a nap after school, and my daughter played outside most of the time. My mother said I had good children. They were terrible, like the time my daughter broke the water faucet outside, and my son got in trouble for it.

The Power of Women

Most women fear divorcing their spouse but, what we don't realize is doing it independently. I didn't get a divorce sooner. For the same reason, most women and men continue to live in misery because they don't want to have to deal with their family, friends and, what they would say and what the family would think but, the truth was it's my life and, I need to live a better life in peace, and, be happy. I wanted a divorce because it's unpleasant to live with a man. I was not too fond of the sight of being with this man. Some men feel the same way with their wives. Being single most men say ugly things about their wife to their girlfriend. Like how terrible his wife looks, her boobs hang down to her knees, and her vertical vain on her legs look awful; she works out on the treadmill like it's going to help. Her kisses are sloppy and wet. They say that they can't imagine any other man looking at her.

I want him to work on his marriage and, he said it wouldn't happen. There is no love; the feelings are gone. It's too late. The ugliness of mistreating him for years left a scar. I believe you can't force a man to be with you. It's the worst thing you can do. Annie forced Jake to marry her so she could take control and file charges against his wife, but, as I always said, Karma will bite you on the ass.

Child Support

The investigator Annie hired reported word per word infused in the News. Annie had now listed me as a high profile. There was a great deal of discrepancy in the entire story it was difficult for me to figure out. The investigator and producer for the TV Station. Who couldn't hang on to her story, called "Where the Baby" piece aired on the Eyewitness News? Then Annie retained an Attorney who then filed a motion to reopen the case. After that, Annie received a letter from Children Youth and Family Department that we were closing the case without further investigation and wiping out all arrears. After Annie called CYFD to expose them to the News and talk shows, my ex-husband, a correctional officer, agreed to talk if he could wear a **mask** during his appearance with the News for security reasons. Jake stated he paid **$20,000** in child support. There was a great deal of discrepancy in the entire story. It wasn't easy to follow. The other women went down to CYFD to make sure this was, in fact, true and told her the case was set to close, but "since the News ran the story, Annie might have to re-think her decision. She tape-recorded the conversation. He reviewed the Child Support payment listed on the affidavit and stated that the amount was correct, a total of **$11,350** by Attorney II had Jake notarized in his own words. a different amount. Annie started the testimony was incorrect, being the **$1,800** of the garnishment wages included in the **$11,350** total child support payments.

As seen in 1999-2004. Starting 2000 to December 2003 Jake wrote, and signed that he paid the amount of $8,850.00?

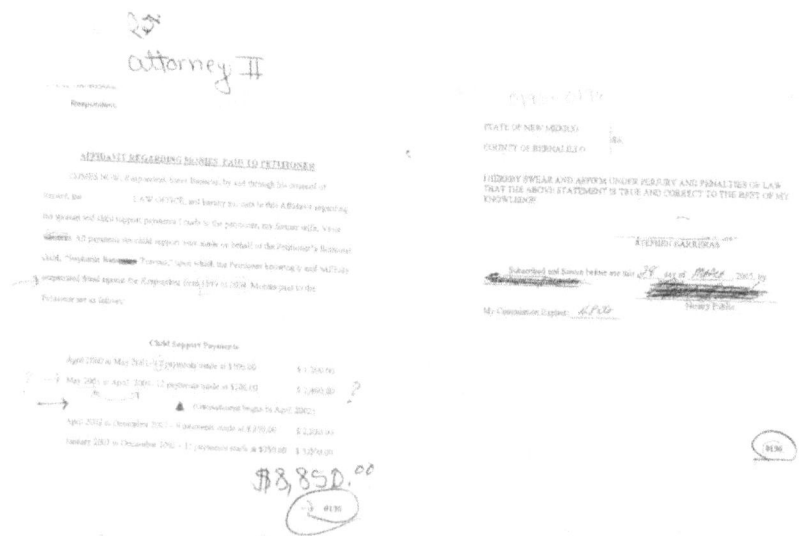

The Utmost News Aired
by T.V. Station

Annie called CYFD she stated she would expose them to the News and talk shows. After the story aired on the News, the investigator reported word per word infused in the News. I was now listed as a high profile. thereafter, Annie believed of herself as innovative of her creation. Annie, not Jake, stated she finally got a hit. Annie received an e-mail reply from the investigator producer for the T.V. Station, and he talked to his investigative reporter. He could not hang on to, Where the Baby piece aired on the Eyewitness News. We finally came out and interviewed them for the News spot that we planned to air in November in the interim. Annie retained Attorney II, who filed a motion to reopen the case. Then Annie received a letter from Children Youth and Family Department closing the case without further investigation and wiped out all arrears.

Annie wasn't satisfied with being on the News she then appearance; up on a billboard calling herself the Billboard Queen protesting a top of Highway I-25 on Thanksgiving Day perched atop a 75ft. Billboard against the Governor Annie was escorted by Channel 4 on top of a billboard, endangering herself and others.

The Billboard Queen

The billboard elucidated Governor alleged pledge to return the fraudulently obtained child support never materialized. Annie spread a white sheet writing Governor Keep Your Word the anger and hatred while writing such words Annie had against his ex-wife who had been terrorized, bullied that considered a hate crime. Only a mentally ill person could do such a dangerous stunt in that manner, to get noticed by the Public to help Annie's skepticism of losing her husband. Annie must have been out of her mind. For doing such a horrible thing to the ex-wife in such a dangerous and humiliating stunt. The hatred, anger and, rage to had written such a statement of retaliation. It was either Annie's way or no way. The embarrassing statement of Annie's words and movements on top of the billboard, she wrote on a sheet Governor Keeps Your Promise The Governor refused to get their money. Annie yelled out, if you don't do the right thing here, you won't make it in Washington either.

Only a psychosomatically person. Could have done such a dangerous stunt. Channel 4 staff should have known better than aired or accompanying Annie. The News reporters should have done their homework.

Annie thought of herself as a luminary woman.

Annie called herself the Billboard Queen. Look out, Queen Latifah. Annie, a woman who once worked at a gas station and later quit working to pursue filing charges against her newlywed husband's ex-wife, did nothing to manifest his new wife. Later Annie was encored by the Fire Department for endangerment. Annie should have been arrested. During the billboard protest and, News allowed such a protest. During the billboard protest, she said she can now safely say that she is wholly exonerated as far as Annie was concerned. My daughter would have been dismissed. What about her friend who did her job necessitated as the blood service compulsory did in a professional method?

handy for her, didn't they? So, with that bit of news I can safely say that Eve is completely exbonerated as far as I'm concerned. Now to prove it!

Harassment

There is no stalking law in New Mexico. I could only file if I got hurt by this woman or a family member. My son said, basically, what they mean is if she kills you. I said Yes. The harassment and stalking continue. The phone rang; it was another harassment call from the Rio Rancho police department. Annie called the police department that I was at her house harassing her. I said to the police I was at a Mother Day cookout with my friends.

My daughter had accompanied me. Then we went to a movie. When my daughter and I got home, my daughter said, you should hold on to the movie passes. It's a good thing I did as the police called that I had been harassing Annie at her home and asked if I could go down to the station. I said no, I wouldn't dare go. Are you kidding me? That sounds like entrapment and, it's a forty-minute drive from here. Why can't you call my friends?

I wondered why the Albuquerque Police wasn't calling instead of Rio Rancho, being they were in another district.

Then there was another encounter with Annie. I heard a voice yelling from outside." does she live here? Yes or no"? The landlord said; you need to leave your on private property. Then a couple of hours later, the Albuquerque Police woke up my son with a loud banging on the door. My son ran down the stairs, wondering what was going on. When my son answered the door, it was the police. The police asked if his mother was there. My son said no. The Albuquerque Police said we received a call for stolen computers. Then the police made their way in and started searching our apartment. When the police left, my son called me about the incident.

I called the police dispatch officer and asked who made the complaint and requested a police report. I then asked if the police officers had a warrant to search my apartment. The dispatcher said there was no report filed, being there was nothing to report. It didn't end there.

I then caught Annie red-handed with a can of red paint spray. Writing on my sister's garage door "bitch" the minute Annie comprehended me, she ran towards a brown and tan bronco, leaving her jacket behind on my sister's driveway with the bottle of the red spray paint behind. I allowed the police to pick it up from the driveway. The police put it in a plastic bag and took it with him. I never heard back from the police.

Then, the Worse harassment Annie ever illusory.

My grandson said, grandma, there someone outside; I looked up and saw someone passing by the living room window. Then there was a knock on the door. It was two policemen. The police asked if everything was alright.

I said yes; he then asked who was in the house. I said my grandson and my daughter (Stephanie) she was sleeping in the bedroom. The police asked if he could come in. I said yes, come in. The two police came in.

One of the policemen passed through us and started checking the inside of the house and, the other police kept us in the living room, asking my grandson and me questions. The police officer asked my grandson what we were doing. He said playing video games. While the other police looked around the house, he later returned and reported he had found a little girl in the back bedroom asleep he said he had uncovered the little girl and didn't find any sign of abuse. The police then said, have a goodnight and just left.

- -

When the police were leaving, my grandson ran out after them and, I followed behind my grandson. It was dark outside. When we looked down the street watching the two policemen walking towards their car, we saw there must have been seven or more police squad cars putting their rifles back in the trunk of their vehicles. I had never seen so many police cars in one place in my life. Not true there have been five or more police cars picking up a drunk in the street. The next day, I was puzzled by the whole thing; I called the police department and was transferred to dispatching. I asked for a police report again filed No police report; the dispatcher said there was no probable cause and did not report filed a report. I said are you kidding me? There were hundreds of rifles pulled out of the trunk of their cars, ready to outburst in my home. Later Jake said, are you ok? I heard Annie reporting you. I can't remember the exact words. But Jake said he listened to Annie calling to report a child being abused. I said to Jake are you kidding. They could have killed us, you know. They took out guns from their cars. Jake didn't say anything. All I could hear was heavy breathing and said nothing. The call ended.

He had the nerve to come to my house. I call it my house because I paid the down payment and most of the house payments. I had purchased the house with the money.

I received my royalties and would be taking a loss by selling my house. I found the house with my children as he said he was too busy to take time off to look for a house. We found the house and moved all our belonging out of the old house to the new house.

He moved the stuff that he had at the old house on his own time. We were living in a two-bedroom house, and the kids needed their bedroom. They were growing up and, soon teenagers, the house was too small for them. We had lived in the house for eight years.

Till the divorce, my daughter and I worked during the week. We fixed the house on the weekend or after work. My daughter helped me get the house ready to put up for sale while we were living with my sister at her house at the time. Till we found a new place to stay, that was the only time we had to work on the house. My daughter and I had finished painting most of the rooms inside the house, and we also put new tile, hoping the house would sell quicker, which it did. The place was more significant than needed.

My daughter's grandson got into the paint. He was all full of paint. He ran into the kitchen when we were laying out the tile. My grandson got into the big bucket of paint and was full of paint from head to toe. We had to take a break and clean my grandson and put things away. Then take a shower. And head back to my sister's house.

Suddenly my husband came to visit while in the middle of our divorce when he unexpectedly, walks into the house excited for some reason. I wondered what was going on. He answered that he just wanted to know how I was doing. I said they were tired and wanted to leave the house and go to my sisters where they were staying. When my daughter walked into the living room and, said what is he doing here. I couldn't believe what I overheard—the most horrifying story. My daughter yelled out I hate you, get out, get out of here. You know what you did to me, and I asked, what are you talking about? He just shrove his shoulders like, so what.

I couldn't believe what my daughter screamed out at him. I was sick to my stomach. I couldn't stand the side of him; what a bastard, how could he. I wanted him out of our lives. Jake had taken advantage of his flesh and blood, his little girl. She was just a baby, and she was only three (3) years old. Oh my God, how could I allow him to do that to my daughter? Where was I when my daughter needed me? I couldn't remember how he could have done that to me. I tried to imagine it in my mind how can a grown man do that to a child, not just any child. The worse thing is it was his daughter.

When it happened, I had been sick and on medication. When my daughter said, it started. I had been diagnosed with a Meningioma Brain Tumor. When he took advantage of the force of action with my daughter, she feared him and never said a word till my daughter confronted him that day. My daughter reported him to a counselor whose duty was to file a police report, but Shannon's office was downstairs at the Sheriff's Office Building downtown stairs. She refused to help us. My ex-husband had stated, who is going to believe you? He was right First of all, my daughter, counselor Shannon didn't have the right to talk to my husband about what my daughter said to me in confidence, what he had done to my daughter. He was right Shannon refused to see my daughter and help them, but my ex and Shannon didn't know that my daughter had a witness. I then asked Shannon what my daughter said happened. I said to my daughter, your mother was asking about your case. Shannon didn't even report it to the authorities. Instead, she said it would be best not to see us again; your case is closed. I went to Shannon's office and said I was responsible for my daughter's well-being and, you can't tell me what her father did to her. I can understand confidentiality, but, my God, her daughter needed help. She is a minor, for God's sake. He should be charged countable he hurt her. He told my daughter's counselor, whom he called by her name, that we made up the whole story because he had filed for a divorce and, I was angry.

I wanted the divorce, not him. The other woman and my ex-husband won the DNA blood service settlement. With the help of my helper, the other woman typed a confession note exemplified a contract offering his's daughter two thousand dollars to sign, stating, He never did anything to me. I became furious at the offer and refused to sign such a note. I would guess the e-mails to Mama Bear ended. Do you believe in Karma? Please, if someone is hurting your daughter, you need to report it. No matter whom it may damage, it's wrong for a child to live with the feeling of hurt.

My ex-husband and the other women articulated that he had become a Christian and believed God would forgive him for what he had done. You Can't buy God. My ex-husband and his wife gave the Church thousands of dollars after receiving the money from the Blood Service. God is a forgiving God. And, Yes, I believe in Karma; No one leaves this earth without his forgiveness. Yet my ex-husband gives to the Church to get forgiveness but, he can't ask forgiveness of the people he hurt. You can't buy God's forgiveness' trust and believe God saves those in his way. After all, I have been through. I had no confidence in the justice system. My faith is in God's hands. My father God was with me; he had to be.

Surgery

I tried to be strong. I had been sick, the sadness of having a brain tumor. I kept locked inside. I never had to deal with anything like this in my whole life. I was suffocating; I couldn't breathe. Whom could I turn to, I needed to talk to, someone I could trust? It had to be someone. I later knew my family was aware of my surgery. They didn't say a word to me, not even; when they could see my head was wrapped on bandages.

I got more sympathy from my friend and strangers. My car was at the shop, so a friend from work gave me a ride to my parents' house to pick up my kids. It was getting late, so; I asked my mother if my father could take us home and, my mother said no, so I stood up and put my kid's jacket on, and started to walk home. It was about three miles up the road. Then all of a sudden, it began to rain hard and, the road was muddy and flooded.

I tried to carry both my kids but; I couldn't. I had to stop every other block, trying to lift them both to each hip. I was wearing a beanie on my head and, underneath, I had bandages on my head; I had just had surgery on the brain tumor that had shaved off my hair. I felt empty without my hair. My children were too small to understand why I was crying. Besides, we couldn't tell that I was crying as the rain would wash away my tears, and my nose was red from the cold.

Suddenly, a car stopped; a couple about my age asked if they could give us a ride home. I said we live up the street, about a half-mile up the road we had already walked most of the way home. I didn't think of anything except getting my kids home safe and to bed. I couldn't feel the cold rain falling. I could only look forward, wondering how far it was to my house. All I could think of was getting home and getting to bed. I needed to rest. I was so tired and just hoped I wouldn't fall with my kids and wondered how I would get back up if I did fall. The road was muddy and slippery. A young couple stopped and asked if we needed a ride. I said we live a few blocks. We had walked most of the way. When we got in the car, the driver said he had never given a stranger a ride before. He had a feeling they should stop and help. We couldn't see the road with the rain pouring so hard. The young man said, we could see you struggling with your kids. When we decided to stop and give you a ride, he and his wife asked God if it would be ok to provide you and your two small children a ride. I wanted to cry.

I don't think my mother ever told my father; we needed a ride.

Domestic Violence

Annie website I appeared before the Judge in Rio Rancho, Municipal Court, for disorderly conduct, telephone harassment. The case has stayed; Annie stated Jakes wife had three more charges of the same, domestic violence against her scheduled for another hearing before the judge. Jake and Annie appeared in the hearing in Rio Rancho. I hated to attend the domestic violence charges. I received a subpoena to a domestic violence hearing.

Annie claimed she received many hang-ups calls from Jakes's ex-wife. Annie informed the police and kept excellent documentation. I was charged with four counts of telephone harassment and disorderly conduct. While waiting, he walked up to my daughter and asked if my daughter would be the other women's friend; she had no one. My daughter said I'm here with my mother to support her. You know she hasn't been calling and walked away. The judge asked Annie had do you have any proof it was her? Annie answered she had a list of times and dates of calls made to her ex on his private line from the room he was renting from her. The judge said to Annie that it shows an unlisted number. It could have been anyone. I was then court-ordered to appear with Special Commissioner. I thought to myself, that's just what

I needed; can't they leave me alone. His ex-wife appeared before the judge for another Domestic Violence charge. The hearing was in Sandoval County. Which was a mutual order but, I live out of Sandoval County.

I was sitting across from Jake and Annie. I couldn't help but notice my ex-husband just staring at me. I was not too fond of the sight of him. He looked at me as if he was a teenager in love. I was sure the judge noticed his behavior. It was as if all the domestic violence charges were made up just for him to have the opportunity to see his ex-wife—the third visit in Rio Rancho. Again, Annie said I was calling and hanging up. She didn't even know. My ex-husband gave me his phone number to call him; why won't that dumb idiot say something.

He gave me his landline phone number as if I would call him? He resided at Annie's house and was paying her $100.00 monthly to rent one of the bedrooms. I didn't have any reason to call him. she was tired of all the restraining orders filed against me. I then decided to file a restraining order on him and the other women hoping it would help keep them from harassing my children and me. The Courthouse said there is no such restraining order or stocking law in the State unless it's a family member. My son then said, so basically, I would have to kill you before they could do anything. I said yes. I was then ordered to a hearing and appeared for hang-up calls again. The judge told him it could have been anyone as we were unlisted numbers or blocked and were just hang-up calls and didn't say anything. The judge dismissed the charges. Suddenly Annie stood up and said to the judge that his ex-wife had requested his personal information via mail. I answered why I would need his personal information, being I was married to that man for several years.

The judge stood up and said to Annie the case was dismissed. Annie continued to say to the judge and, she had moved three times. I answered yes; I have been trying to run away from the two of you. Why can't you leave me alone? After the Divorce, he had asked me if I would please accompany him to the Motor Vehicle Department. That's when he wrote his phone number on the back a jeweler claim card when I met him at the Motor Vehicle Department to transfer her Sports car to his name. I never called him as he would come to my sister's house to visit her after work and stayed for several hours as if he didn't want to go home to the other women's house. He also went to my place of employment. My boss asked him to leave me alone.

I went through all the domestic violence in Rio Rancho, not knowing if I lived out of the area and the calls didn't originate from Rio Rancho. It was out of his district. Finally, there was a judge who knew the Jurisdiction Law. All the domestic violence the other women had been filing was in the wrong community. I had been dragged on over and over by the other women and my ex. I couldn't take it anymore, driving back and forth not once but several times. Now I find out after all charges Annie and Jake filed against me. I have subsequently dismissed due to a jurisdictional issue.

Page 3 of 7 Domestic Violence charges filed by the other women and, my ex the judge dismissed the charges. Annie ran out. From the courtroom towards me. Annie put her hand on my face as I came out of the courtroom. Jake was coming right behind me when Annie put her hand on my face showing me a ring on her finger that she was now engaged to marry my ex. I couldn't help but look. I then turned around and faced him and, said Oh my God, I said, couldn't you have gotten her a ring. That was my wedding ring. I gave it back to you to him when I decided to get a divorce. He just stood there and didn't say a word. I left without looking back or waiting to hear what he had to say. And to think he had written his phone number on the back of the jewelers' claim check for my wedding ring.

He had it enlarged to fit the other women's finger but, I didn't think anything of it at the time as the claim check did not say what it was. I then figured it had to be my wedding ring.

Then another domestic violence, Annie claimed she had received hang-up calls and, the police were informed, and I kept excellent documentation. Jake's ex-wife was charged with four counts of telephone harassment and disorderly conduct. While they were waiting, he walked up to my daughter and asked if I would be the other women's friend; I have no one. My daughter said I'm here with my mother to support me. You know I haven't been calling and walked away. They were asked whether you had any proof it was her. The other woman answered she had a list of times and dates of calls made to my ex on his private line from the room he was renting from me. It shows that an unlisted number could be anyone. Charges were dismissed. Then his wife was court-ordered to appear with the special commissioner. That's just what I needed; can't they leave me alone. Jake's ex-wife appeared before the judge for another domestic violence charge. The hearing was in Sandoval County. Which was a mutual order but, I live out of Sandoval County.

Page 3 of 7 The other women's website ex-wife appeared before the judge in the city of Rio Rancho Municipal Court for disorderly conduct, telephone harassment. The case has stayed; the other woman stated his wife had three more charges of the same, domestic violence against me scheduled for another hearing before the judge. The other women and my ex-husband were to appear in the hearing in Rio Rancho. I hated to attend the domestic violence charges. I sat across from Jake and the other women. Jake just sat there staring at me. I couldn't stand the sight of him. He looked at me as if he were a teenager in love. I was sure the judge noticed his behavior. It was as if all the domestic violence charges were made up just for him to have the opportunity to see his ex-wife. The third time in Rio Rancho, again, the other woman said I was calling her and hanging up again. I thought to myself, she doesn't even know my ex-husband gave me his phone number to call him; why won't that dumb idiot say something. He gave me his landline phone number as if I would call him? He resided at Annie's house and paid her $100.00 per month for occupying one of the bedrooms. I didn't have any reason to call him. I was tired of all the restraining orders filed against me. I then decided to file a restraining order on him and the other women hoping it would help keep t away from harassing myself and my children. The Courthouse said there is no such restraining order or stocking law in the State unless it's a family member. My son then said, so basically, I would have to kill you before they could do anything. I said yes. I was then ordered to a hearing and appeared for hang-up calls again. The judge said it could have been anyone as they were unlisted numbers or blocked and were just hang-up calls and didn't say anything. The judge dismissed the charges when the other woman suddenly stood up and said she had requested his personal information via mail. I answered why I would need his personal information, being I was married to that man for over twenty years. The judge got up and said to the other women the charges were dismissed. The other women continued and said to the judge and, I have moved three times. I answered yes; I have been trying to run away from the two of you. Why can't you leave me alone? After the Divorce, he had asked me if I would please accompany him to the Motor Vehicle Department. That's when he wrote his phone number on the back a jeweler claim card when I met him at the Motor Vehicle Department to transfer my Sports car to his name. I never called him as he would come to my sister's house to visit me after work and stayed for several hours as if he didn't want to go home to the other women's house. He also went to my place of employment. My boss asked him to leave me alone. I went through all the domestic violence in Rio Rancho, not knowing if I lived out of the area and the calls didn't originate from Rio Rancho. It was out of his district. Finally, there was a Judge who knew the Jurisdiction Law. All the domestic violence the other women had been filing was in the wrong district. I had been dragged on over and over by the other women and my ex. I couldn't take it anymore, driving back and forth not once but several times. Now I find out after all charges should have subsequently been dismissed due to a jurisdictional issue.

Spousal Support/ Child Support

T he other women's website read. I met him during Christmas of 1997, and we got married five years later. After hearing about the Child Support, Annie asked Jake to marry her to file charges against me. The other woman stated he paid court order child support for five years for a child that didn't exist. The Child Support Enforcement started garnishing his checks from work at the State Prison where Jake worked as a correctional officer. He refused to pay court-ordered Spousal Support but spent Child Support for a child he never associated or cared to.

Page 1 of 7 Annie hired an Attorney to get an immediate stopped on the Spousal Support. My husband had been paying the amount of **$600.00** a month, including Child Support? After that, the majority of his alimony receipts went missing. At the same time, he was residing at the other women's house. What Spousal Support was my ex-husband paying?

I received a court-ordered to have a deposition with my ex-husband and his first attorney. When I walked into the room, there sat Jake and Annie. Smiling, I walked in and sat down next to the court reporter. On my right side, her ex-husband and his wife sat across the table from her. The attorney stood up and started asking her question. Annie said about her husband. I just stared at Annie, taking over to hear what she had to say. I then stood up in front of the Court Reporter and his Attorney and, yelled out do you think. I would have gotten pregnant from him after what you did? With his flesh and, blood my God, I was a baby. I then ran out and said to his lawyer, how can you defend that sick man and that woman he calls his wife. After that, his attorney dropped Jake, Annie, as a client without any warning at all. Because he could not give his attorney more money, his attorney did not file for withdrawal, and he just dropped out completely.

Then Bingo Thanks for the information:

Page 5 of 7 The other woman stated on her website, held Spousal Support hearing before the Special Master for a hearing recommended an increase of **$723.00** per month owed Spousal Support of **$300.00** in Alimony. She was also added **$1,800.00** per month plus **8.75% interest** as arrears since, according to Jake, he missed several payments, which would have proved he never paid one penny in Alimony to his ex-wife.

The Child Support Enforcement Agency started garnishing his paychecks for **$253.61** bi-weekly; we included the Alimony as Child Support. Is that even allowed? The case had a lack of prosecution. Why would the Alimony be deducted as Child Support? That's impossible as the **Child Support Enforcement** was unaware of the unsettled Spousal Support due to his ex-wife. If there were an attorney that would have done pro bono on my Spousal Support, he would have investigated that Jake, Annie owed her back- Spousal Support.

I called the Child Support Enforcement Agency regarding copies of the garnished check by his employer in the amount **of $253.61** printout submitted to the Child Support Enforcement

Office and the District Attorney Office in person by Annie for child support evidence against her. Did either one of the attorneys and, Judge check the court records of her Spousal Support? His ex-wife called and wrote to Child Support Enforcement and the State Prison where his paycheck was supposedly had his wages garnished. The person in the Prison where her ex worked said I could only say the amount shown is incorrect. You need a Court Order to get that information. How the heck was I supposed to get a court order? My public defender was more like a Public Pretender who wouldn't request a court order to investigate the printouts submitted to the Prosecutor. my public defender declined to get a court order. I couldn't get a court order myself.

There was no way he could have paid the amount of **$14,198.00**; Jakes's attorney stated; Jake felt he felt forced to pay restitution to him when he owed me back Spousal Support. The figures changed with each Court hearing I recorded in the district court records. Later Annie hired Attorney II. Who had Jake sign and notarized the Affidavit regarding he paid Child Support in the total amount of **$8,850.00** from April 2000 to December?

ORDER/NOTICE TO WITHHOLD INCOME FOR CHILD SUPPORT

Paid

X Original Order/Notice
___ Amended Order/Notice
___ Terminate Order/Notice

State of _____ New Mexico
County of _____ Bernalilio
ate of Order/Notice 04/02/2002
ourt/Case Number DM-99-002039

'02 APR 4 PM 3:6

RE: Employee/Obligor's Name (Last, First, MI)
_____ Steve

Employer/Withholder's Federal EIN Number
856000565

Employer/Withholder's Name
NM Dept Of Finance & Admin

Employer/Withholder's Address
407 Galisteo Bataan , Memorial Bldg Rm 160
Santa Fe, NM 87501

770

Date of Birth incorrect

Employee/Obligor's Address
801 Coal # 25
Albuquerque, NM 87102

Employee/Obligor's Social Security Number
585-74-3970

Employee/Obligor's Case Identifier
000087157

Custodial Parent's Name (Last, First, MI)
Trevino, Viola

Child(ren)'s Name	DOB	Child(ren)'s Name	DOB
Stephanie Trevino	12/03/1999		

ORDER INFORMATION: This is an Order/Notice to Withhold Income for Child Support based upon an order for support from the State of New Mexico. By law, you are required to deduct these amounts from the above-named employee's/obligor's income until 12/03/2017even if the Order/Notice is not issued by your State.

[] If checked, you are required to enroll the child(ren) identified above in any health insurance coverage available through the employee's/obligor's employment.

$ 500.00 per month in current support

$ 50.00 per month in past due support Arrears 12 weeks or greater? [X] yes [] no and any interest, costs, fees

$ 0.00 per month in medical support

$ 0.00 Per month in other support

for a total of $ 550.00 Per month to be forwarded to the payee below.

The total amount of delinquency/arrearage, Including judgment interest is $ 7,047.54 as of 04/02/2002.

You do not have to vary your pay cycle to be in compliance with the support order. If your pay cycle does not match the ordered support payment cycle, use the following to determine how much to withhold:

$ 126.92 per weekly pay period $ 275.00 per semimonthly pay period
                                            (twice a month)
$ 253.85 per biweekly pay period $ 550.00 per monthly pay period
    (every two weeks)

REMITTANCE INFORMATION:
You shall deduct the amount designated herein no later than the next payment of income that is payable to the obligor following service of this notice and shall forward the amount withheld to the **CHILD SUPPORT ENFORCEMENT DIVISION** within seven business days of the employee's normal pay date. For each withholding you may deduct a $1.00 fee to be taken from the income to be paid to the obligor. The total withheld amount, including your fee, cannot exceed 50% of the employee's/obligor's aggregate disposable weekly earnings. For the purpose of the limitation on withholding, the following information is needed (see #9 on page 2).

When remitting payment provide the paydate/date of withholding and the case identifier .

If remitting by EFT/EDI, use this FIPS code: 3500000; Bank routing code: 107000275; Bank account number: 6016974237.

An employer may also arrange to electronically transfer withheld payments by contacting the Child Support Enforcement Division at 1-800-288-7207.

Make check payable to: Child Support Enforcement Division
    ad check to: P.O. BOX _____ SANTA FE, NEW MEXICO 87504 with the account number 000087157 on each payment.

Authorized by _____
Print Name: Cyndi Marquez

CSED Form 728

CSED Case ID 000087157

0180

782

24

DEPARTMENT OF THE TREASURY
FINANCIAL MANAGEMENT SERVICE
P.O. BOX 1686
BIRMINGHAM, ALABAMA 35201-1686

THIS IS NOT A BILL - PLEASE RETAIN FOR YOUR RECORDS

Dear :

As authorized by Federal law, we applied all or part of your Federal payment to a debt you owe. The government agency (or agencies) collecting your debt is listed below.

CHILD SUPPORT ENFORCEMENT DIVISION	TIN Num:
1015 TIJERAS, NW	TOP Trace
SUITE 100	Acct Num:
ALBUQUERQUE, NM 87102-2909	Amount Ti .00
	Creditor: U
(800) 288-7207 (800) 585-7631	
PURPOSE: Child Support	

The Agency has previously sent notice to you at the last address known to the Agency. That notice explained the amount and type of debt you owe, the rights available to you, and that the Agency intended to collect the debt by intercepting any Federal payments made to you, including tax refunds. If you believe your payment was reduced in error or if you have questions about this debt, you must contact the Agency at the address and telephone number shown above. The U. S. Department of the Treasury's Financial Management Service cannot resolve issues regarding debts with other agencies.

We will forward the money taken from your Federal payment to the Agency to be applied to your debt balance; however, the Agency may not receive the funds for several weeks after the payment date. If you intend to contact the Agency, please have this notice available.

Charles A. Wilson
Department of the Treasury, Financial Management Service
(800) 304-3107

PAYMENT SUM
PAYEE NAME: $
PAYMENT BEFORE REDUCTION: ($1048.00)
TOTAL AMOUNT OF THIS REDUCTION: $1048.00   → PAYMENT DATE: 02/06/04
PAYING FEDERAL AGENCY: Internal Revenue Service   PAYMENT TYPE: Check
(See Insert on Tax Refund Offsets for Additional Information)

$1048.00   12/6/04   IRS

FOR OFFICIAL USE ONLY:

 0179

Who are your Friends?

C o-worker, a family member who will betray you? Do you ever go to the break room and spill out your guts to a co-worker or your so-called best friend or a boyfriend, and even a family member?

Who would have thought my husband didn't lift a finger to help me? As did my co-worker, who I thought of as a friend? He had wanted to go out on a date with me. He was studying to be a lawyer one day; he met a woman in the grocery store. He told the men he had sex with her. Then one day, we were all hanging outside. I noticed a woman in the gas station watching us from across the street, seeing what my friend was doing at work. One of the other workers said it was a girl he went out with. Yet my friend had the nerve to make sexual advances towards me. I figured he had his dilemma in another relationship. A friend in need.

When I was on the News, my friend thought his shit didn't stink and thought the worse of me but, getting me in bed wouldn't have an issue for him.

One of the other co-workers right away thought of him and asked him. When he had seen me on the News, he asked if he had seen me on the News.

He had just started his Attorney practice, so he thought he should ask him to help me with the allegations against me. That my husband and his lover Annie had started announcing about me to whoever would hear her out.

He answered yes for twenty grand. If I had twenty grand, I wouldn't have needed him if I had the money to hire an attorney. Besides, he didn't work in the criminal field? He wasn't even a Criminal Lawyer. He was a Misdemeanor Defense Attorney and, he didn't have that many clients, yet he wanted to charge me for preparing a criminal case now that's worse than a Public Defender. Well, let see how his shit stinks. That was one reason you can't trust most attorneys. It was a career for him.

While in Law School, he could have used an Attorney on his behalf. Knowing he was already married, he married a woman when he was still married to his wife, who lived in Nevada or California. Before he graduated from law school, he looked for her to sign the divorce papers before graduating from Law School., he had to clean his record.

He had gotten married before finishing Law school, which he had married illegally. He was still married to his wife, knowing I had not gotten a divorce and was still married? He looked for his wife to get her to sign the divorce before he graduated from law school.

I couldn't believe it when my friend/co-worker, whatever you want to call him. Walked up to me in court while I was waiting for another domestic violence hearing. Had been battling for over a year with a restraining order hearing, dispute charges dismissed. I thought to myself, the new Attorney and I could have the same problem his wife may not be his wife and, my ex-husband could still be my husband, according to the catholic church downtown.

My friend or co-worker, a so-called Attorney, walked up to me and asked if he could visit me at MDC. I said, no, I don't think I want you to see me. I felt embarrassed and didn't have anything to say. All I could think of was how an attorney with no legal background offered to defend me and demanded twenty grand from me; I didn't have that kind of money. Unless he thought I got all that child support my ex-husband claimed he paid on the News.

Annie made sure the public eyes crucified me. I was sure most criminal lawyers have heard worse. I wish I could have had the money to hire an attorney. Is there even an attorney that would have taken my case in the criminal case pro bono? My public defender said, no, you can't get an attorney who does pro bono. What kind of a friend was he? He could have at least given me advice, but instead, he shut me out.

My old friend later called me; we met at a restaurant for lunch. He put his hand on my leg, making a pass. I pushed his hand; I wanted a friend, not some married asshole. But after I refused to have sex with him, he refused to help me. We needed to talk about my case; of course, he has said he thought his shit doesn't stink as most desperate people do. However, I did have a couple of co-workers who believed in me. One of them wasn't an attorney but had legal knowledge.

He never took the bar exam for his reason. My public defender refused to use the advice he gave me. I should not plead guilty. My public defender said if I didn't plead guilty, I would end up doing all the time the judge had sentenced me. Even if you say you're not guilty, the court system sees you as guilty. And most of those who judge you.

Internal Revenue Service

The Mystifying of Federal Marshalls

Annie called the IRS and wrote several times; That's all they would say to me. The IRS placed me on hardship. The IRS investigator got copies of my daughter's birth certificate without my permission and forged my name and then submitted to the federal court Judge to use against me. A letter from Sandia Health System states the allegations of my daughter's vital records from, IRS. It's hard to prove my incidents in the amount of time I had. I could get from different places; I had written letters and made phone calls. I had no idea what the IRS would be sending me and what I could use for my defense. I was then

Arrested: I was getting ready to go out. I always looked out the window from the top floor of my bedroom. I was getting ready. I noticed when I looked out of my bedroom window like I do every morning, but, this day, I felt sad inside. I noticed across the street a black SUV. It seemed as if they were staking out my house. I was so scared to go outside to my car I waited for a while then. I said to myself, I have to see what they're doing. I walked outside; I then noticed, across the street, there was another SUV. Then I thought to myself, they must be waiting for me to come outside. I finally got the courage to head downstairs. I was walking slowly towards my car. One of the black SUVs was blocking my car in front of my driveway. Annie had also called CNN News their Van had parked across the street. I knew it had to do with Jake and my taxes. The judge had ordered us to file our together the year of our divorce. But, he didn't do as the judge ordered. I then asked the CNN reports to check with the church downtown by the courthouse and ask for my marriage certificate. It was funny, but I never saw CNN News or heard from them. I often wondered why. I thought to myself, what's going on. The female and male Federal agents approached me; they walked towards my car. The female said, are you, Viola? I said yes. She asked me to get in the Van. So, I did, then she made two calls. We got her. The federal officers did not give me my rights. I said to the female sitting on the front passenger side of the black SUV, what's going on. She asked me, do you know a woman by the name of Annie? I aforementioned yes, she had an affair with my husband. I noticed on the back of their jackets read Federal Agents. They got off the SUV we had driven to some building. The two Federal Agents decided to make a quick stop at a facility where men and women were walking around and, sitting down looking at the computers; there must have been over twenty computers and a table with maps of places they were going to raid. On the back of their jack, It read the letters ICE. I didn't know what they were saying or what they were going to do. I was terrified. I thought they were there for me.

At the same time, I waited in the Federal vehicle. The Federal Agents rushed me to the Federal Holding Facility; they handed my paperwork to the clerk and ran out. The booking officer then put in an empty cell. I was in the cell for an hour when I saw the ICE agents I had seen in the building I was taken to by the federal agent. The ICE agents dropped off men and women. They put the woman in the same cell I was in and put the men across from us. The woman said the ICE police raided the manufacturing company they were working at and, they didn't visa some of the women who were arrested with their families and didn't have anyone to bond them out or call. The ICE officers gave the booking officers the paperwork and left. The booking officer started to search the immigrants. The booking officers began to empty their pockets and, putting their belonging on top of a large table, there were rolls of twenty and hundred-dollar bills the Mexican had for working in the factory. The booking officers, we're taking the Mexicans money. Thousands of dollars and put the money in their pockets, or I should say they were stealing their money. The booking officer must have known that most immigrants' families keep cash in their pocket. They don't have a Visa to open a bank account and pay most of their bills in cash. Did I wonder to myself, what good are the cameras? If they couldn't see this; The Booking Officers grabbed the money and put it in their pockets. When these people get incarcerated, they have no money to buy the hygiene they need while confined; it should have gone to the books or given back but, they were either put in prison or transported back to their country without any money. The immigrants feared to tell anyone or ask for their money when being booked. One correctional officer said the difference between the booking officers and the inmates is that they haven't gotten caught breaking the law like the booking officers who stole from their so-called illegals. These booking officers call them criminals whose criminals who should be locked up. I wondered if I would accidentally get deported, how would I survive?

Karma will bite the booking officer in the butt and all the rest of them.

Being incarcerated isn't cheap.

Karma, God sees everything.

Two weeks later, my public defender came to visit me at the federal holding facility and introduced himself as my public defender. He asked how I was doing and didn't say anything about my charges with the IRS; instead, he said he would see me at the federal courtroom.

The Prosecutor wanted to lock me up and throw the key away. I didn't know how to file my income tax Jake and, I had the income Tax Service to do our taxes.

I didn't have a copy of my income tax to view and explain to my public defender and the Judge.

The IRS arrested me with no warning of any kind; I wasn't given an agreement to pay the IRS the money owed or an unsettled IRS being charged for amount due. When I called I was told they had no record on file and gave three other numbers to call I couldn't get the IRS to send me copies of the income tax forms.

My public defender came to visit me, I was then sent to a halfway house.

The IRS Investigators got my daughters' information from vital records and scrutinized me after being sentenced. I thought it would only be for a few days, but the federal Judge sentenced me to a Camp in Arizona for fourteen months. The charges were for Improper filing of Income Tax. The truth was we wanted my daughter. I couldn't write to tell them how I was because I knew my ex-husband and Annie were interested in finding out my whereabouts. I only had a few people I could trust but, I didn't have money in my books to buy a calling card. I need to get stuff from the commissary to buy envelopes, stamps. A friend wrote to me when he found out I was in a Camp. We kept up with the News in the outside.

SANDIA
HEALTH SYSTEM

Quality healthcare where you need it most.

March 30, 2005

Department of the Treasury
Internal Revenue Service
5338 Montgomery Blvd. NE
MS 9000ALB
Albuquerque, NM 87109

Attn.:
      Special Agent

RE: Stephanie ███████
DOB: 9/3/99

Please be advised that we do not have any records pertaining to the above named individual. We are sorry
we could not be of assistance to you in this matter.

Sincerely,

Lead, Women's Hospital

Albuquerque Regional Medical Center • Northeast Heights Medical Center • Rehabilitation Hospital of New Mexico • West Mesa Medical Center

PO BOX 25555 • ALBUQUERQUE, NEW MEXICO 87125 • [P] 505.727.8000

184

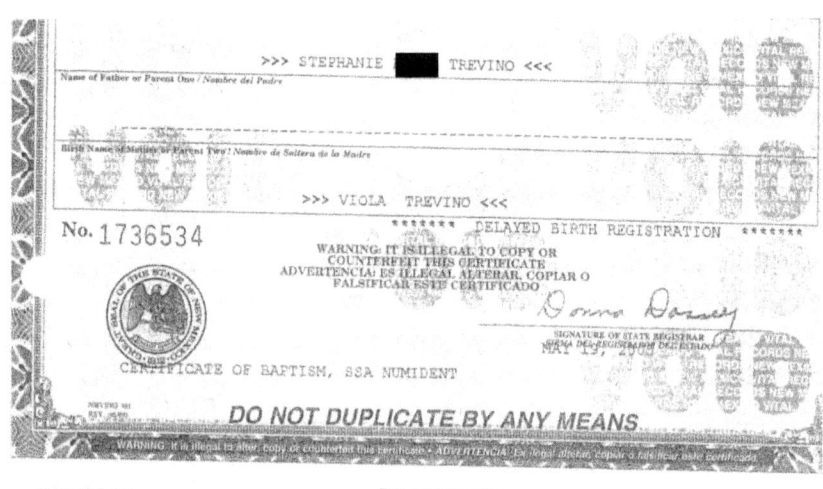

>>> STEPHANIE ███ TREVINO <<<

Name of Father or Parent One / Nombre del Padre

Birth Name at Motion or Parent Two / Nombre de Soltera de la Madre

>>> VIOLA TREVINO <<<

******* DELAYED BIRTH REGISTRATION *******

No. 1736534

WARNING: IT IS ILLEGAL TO COPY OR
COUNTERFEIT THIS CERTIFICATE
ADVERTENCIA: ES ILEGAL ALTERAR, COPIAR O
FALSIFICAR ESTE CERTIFICADO

SIGNATURE OF STATE REGISTRAR
FIRMA DEL REGISTRADOR DEL ESTADO

CERTIFICATE OF BAPTISM, SSA NUMIDENT

DO NOT DUPLICATE BY ANY MEANS

WARNING: It is illegal to alter, copy or counterfeit this certificate • ADVERTENCIA: Es ilegal alterar, copiar o falsificar este certificado.

This is your receipt.   Copy 01 of 01

FEE RECEIPT

New Mexico Vital Records and Health Statistics
Public Health Division
Post Office Box 26110
Santa Fe, NM 87502   Request No. 26401316900

SPECIAL AGENT
0.00 BIRTH SEARCH-NO FEE

Date of Issuance MAY 19, 2005

Amount Paid $

Reference:
STEPHANIE
TREVINO
01000002704-0903 1999-01

SPECIAL AGENT
INTERNAL REVENUE SERVICE
5338 MONTGOMERY BLVD, NE
ALBUQUERQUE, NM 87109

0198

NOTE: SUBMIT THIS RECEIPT ALONG WITH ANY INQUIRY

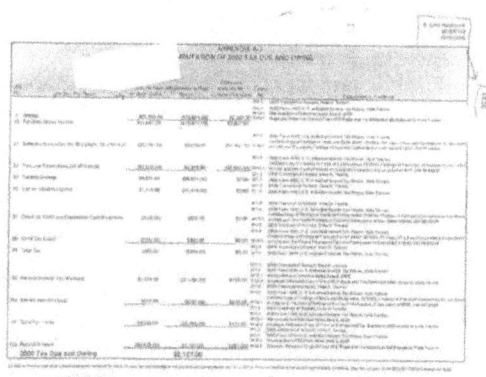

1999 Tax $1,730.00

Internal Revenue Service
United States Department of the Treasury

2000

This Product Contains Sensitive Taxpayer Data

Request Date: 06-17-2010
Response Date: 06-17-2010
Tracking Number: 100037769106

Wage and Income Transcript

SSN Provided:
Tax Period Requested: December,

Form W-2 Wage and Tax Statement

Employer:
Employer Identification Number (EIN): 850446198
TMC
ALBUQUERQUE, NM 87182-5919

Employee:
Employee's Social Security Number:

Submission Type: ....Original document
Wages, Tips and Other Compensation: $2,087.00
Federal Income Tax Withheld: $412.00
Social Security Wages: $2,087.00
Social Security Tax Withheld: $129.00
Medicare Wages and Tips: $2,087.00
Medicare Tax Withheld: $126.00
Social Security Tips: $29.00
Allocated Tips: 0.00
Advanced EIC Payment: 0.00
Dependent Care Benefits: 0.00
Deferred Compensation: 0.00
Code Military Pay: 0.00
Code Employer's Contribution to MSA: 0.00
Code Employer's Contribution to Simple Account: 0.00
Code Expenses Incurred for Qualified Adoptions: 0.00
Deceased Indicator: 0.00
Pension Plan Indicator: 0.00
Deferred Compensation: ....Unanswered
Statutory Employee: ....Unanswered
Not Statutory Employee

Form 1098 Mortgage Interest Statement

Recipient/Lender:
Recipient's Federal Identification Number (FIN): 210534340
CENTAR FEDERAL SAVINGS BANK
425 PHILLIPS BOULEVARD
EWING, NJ 08628-0809

Payer/Borrower:
Payer's Social Security Number: 585-68-4844
VIOLA TREVINO

Submission Type:
Account Number (Optional) ....Original document

2000 Tax $2,127.00

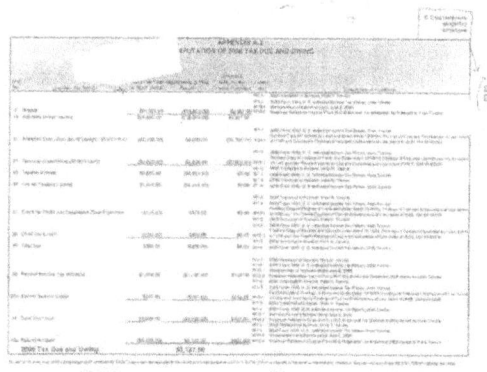

1999 Tax $1,730.00

Internal Revenue Service
United States Department of the Treasury

2000

This Product Contains Sensitive Taxpayer Data

Request Date: 06-17-2010
Response Date: 06-17-2010
Tracking Number: 100972769181

Wage and Income Transcript

SSN Provided:
Tax Period Requested: December, 2000

Form W-2 Wage and Tax Statement

Employer:
Employer Identification Number (EIN): 850448194
TMC
ALBUQUERQUE, NM 87182-5014

Employee:
Employee's Social Security Number:
VIOLA TREVINO

Submission Type:
Wages, Tips and Other Compensation:..................................Original document
Federal Income Tax Withheld:...$2,957.00
Social Security Wages:...$112.74
Social Security Tax Withheld:..$2,007.00
Medicare Wages and Tips:...$124.90
Medicare Tax Withheld:...$2,007.00
Social Security Tips:..$29.00
Allocated Tips:..
Advanced EIC Payment:..0.00
Dependent Care Benefits:...0.00
Deferred Compensation:...0.00
Code "D" Military Pay:...0.00
Code "G" Employer's Contribution to MSA:.............................0.00
Code "P" Employer's Contribution to Simple Account:..................0.00
Code "T" Expenses Incurred for Qualified Adoptions:..................0.00
Deceased Indicator:..0.00
Pension Plan Indicator:..
Deferred Compensation:...Unanswered
Statutory Employee:..Unanswered
                                                                     Not Statutory Employee

Form 1098 Mortgage Interest Statement

Recipient/Lender:
Recipient's Federal Identification Number (FIN): 219534340
CENLAR FEDERAL SAVINGS BANK
425 PHILLIPS BOULEVARD
EWING, NJ 08628-0000

Payer/Borrower:
Payer's Social Security Number: 545-68-4844
VIOLA TREVINO

Submission Type:
Account Number (Optional):...Original document
                                                                     M10601966/332

APPENDIX A-1
COMPUTATION OF 2000 TAX DUE AND OWING

2000 Tax $2,127.00

IT COULD HAPPEN TO YOU

....

Albuquerque, NM 87102

Investigation #: 860530142
Date: May 24, 2005
Time: 2:40pm - 3:00pm approx.
Participant(s): Payroll Coordinator
Special Agent
, Special Agent

On the above date and time, Special Agent (S/A)   ' and I arrived at the
above listed location to verify Viola Trevino's 2001 and 2002 Form W-2s that were
attached to her tax returns. Upon identifying   , S/A   and I
produced our credentials for her inspection and identified ourselves as Special Agents
with IRS Criminal Investigation. I explained to   that I wanted to verify wages of
an employee of Heart Institute.   ; provided the following information voluntarily
and in response to questioning:

1.   has been employed at the Heart Institute for approximately eight
years and has been in the payroll department for five years. She is currently
employed as the Payroll Coordinator.

2. I provided   the name of Viola Trevino and she conducted a search
on the company's computer records which resulted in no records. I then
provided   ' with the Social Security number   and she
conducted a search on the company's computer records, which also resulted in
no records.

3. Salazar stated that their computer software might have deleted the employee's
information after their termination.

4. At this time, I presented   with the 2001 Form W-2 made out to Viola
Trevino by NM Heart Institute, PA.   looked it over and stated that the
name did not sound familiar.   then retrieved the file containing the
employer's copy of all 2001 Forms W-2 issued by NM Heart Institute which are
maintained in alphabetical order by employee name   r searched for a
2001 Form W-2 with Viola Trevino's name, but no record was found.

0209

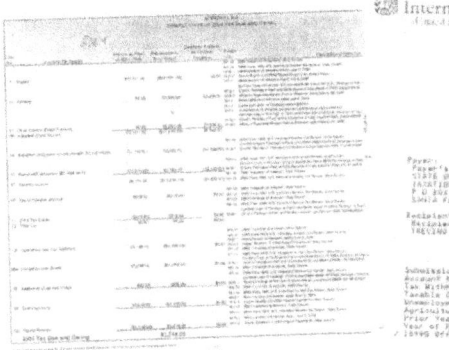

2004 Tax $3,518.00

Internal Revenue Service
United States Department of the Treasury

This Product Contains Sensitive Taxpayer Data

Request Date: 06-17-2010
Response Date: 06-17-2010
Tracking Number: 10057654910x

Wage and Income Transcript

SSN Provided:
Tax Period Requested: December, 2004

Form 1099-G

Payer:
Payer's Federal Identification Number (FIN): 850478248
STATE OF NEW MEXICO
TAXATION AND REVENUE DEPARTMENT
P O BOX 630
SANTA FE, NM 87509-0630

Recipient:
Recipient's Identification Number: 585-68-4064
TREVINO VIZOLA

Submission Type: Original document
Account Number (Optional):   184597858175175G5
Tax Withheld: 0.00
Taxable Grants: 0.00
Unemployment Compensation: 0.00
Agricultural Subsidies: 0.00
Prior Year Refund: 0.00
Year of Refund: $257.00
1099G Offset: Net Refund, Credit, or Offset for Trade or Business

This Product Contains Sensitive Taxpayer Data

Internal Revenue Service
United States Department of the Treasury

This Product Contains Sensitive Taxpayer Data

Request Date: 06-17-201
Response Date: 06-17-201
Tracking Number: 10057654910x

Wage and Income Transcript

SSN Provided:
Tax Period Requested: December, 2004

Form W-2 Wage and Tax Statement

Employer:
Employer Identification Number (EIN): 201411482

Employee:
Employee's Social Security Number: 585-68-4064
VIZOLA TREVINO
VIZOLA TREVINO

Submission Type: Original document
Wages, Tips and Other Compensation: $6,705.00
Federal Income Tax Withheld: $600.00
Social Security Wages: $6,705.00
Social Security Tax Withheld: $291.00
Medicare Wages and Tips: $6,705.00
Medicare Tax Withheld: $90.00
Social Security Tips: 0.00
Allocated Tips: $556.00
Advanced EIC Payment: 0.00
Dependent Care Benefits: 0.00
Deferred Compensation: 0.00
Code "Q" Nontaxable Combat Pay: 0.00
Code "W" Employer Contributions to a Health Savings Account: 0.00
Code "Y" Deferrals under a section 409A nonqualified Deferred Compensation plan: 0.00
Code "Z" Income under section 409A on a nonqualified Deferred Compensation plan: 0.00
Code "AA" Employer's Contribution to HSA: 0.00
Code "BB" Employee's Contribution to Simple Account: 0.00
Code "DD" Cost of Insurance for Qualified Adoptions: 0.00
Code "EE" Income from exercise of non-statutory stock options: 0.00
Third Party Sick Pay Indicator: Unanswered
Retirement Plan Indicator: Uncovered
Statutory Employee: Not Statutory Employee

Form 1099-G

Payer:
Payer's Federal Identification Number (FIN): 850478248
STATE OF NEW MEXICO
TAXATION AND REVENUE DEPARTMENT
P O BOX 630
SANTA FE, NM 87509-0630

Recipient:
Recipient's Identification Number: 585-68-4064

Federal Holding

T he IRS refused to answer my letters. All I had was the statement of 2000- 2005, the IRS Special Agent reported my findings I didn't have a voice. I was crucified and punished with no remorse. I wondered if the federal officer's promotions were worth my life? The federal office investigator of the IRS made up stories. I couldn't get a straight answer— fabricated copies of my income tax and those shown in court, the Investigators couldn't get a straight answer from the IRS office or federal court. I requested for the IRS to send me anything a copy of her W-2 form. I had nothing for my defense. The judge ordered me to pay restitution and was placed on hardship by the IRS and said: "Don't worry." I got sentenced for Improper filing of Income Tax the Judge directed me to a Federal Camp, where I completed it successfully.

Annie wrote on her website that I was trying to get the judge for a lesser sentence. I ordered to have an evaluation. Why wasn't this letter submitted to the court? What lesser sentence I received the maximum amount and, yet, Annie was still not satisfied. After I was released, I received a letter from the Honorable U.S. District Court Judge.

1.   In support of this request for a sentence outside of the guidelines, attached is a psychological evaluation. Stating

I was well in a structured environment as it is evident is employable based upon employment history. And is employed should not have difficulty to begin restitution to the IRS if the court is not inclined to grant the request to place the court be set either in a correction program or Electronic monitoring after serving my sentence. And may receive counseling so that nothing like this would ever happing in the future.

Halfway House

I was escorted to the halfway house the next day. Till the Federal Judge put me on her agenda for my court hearing. The halfway house was a coed boarding house. I shared the room with seven girls. The first rule was finding a job to pay for room and board, including our meals. With my office experience, I got a job the first week I arrived. I began working in a flooring company as an assistant bookkeeper. The halfway house gave me a bus pass that got deducted from my check. I had to show the halfway house manager my check subs every payday. I was required to dressed professionally and wore high heels that matched my suit. I wondered if he thought I was a prostitute because I dress up for work, but that was part of my dress code. I went to work on the bus every day to work. The bus driver asked where I worked and, I said up the street from here. He then asked me out to dinner, but I couldn't go because I lived at a halfway house, and I had a curfew and, I wasn't going to ask for a pass to go out with anyone. I had been working for about seven weeks. When the IRS Marshall found out where I was working. During my lunch break, she presented herself as the investigator for the IRS and that I was under federal investigation for Improper filing of Income Tax. I was immediately fired. My supervisor felt terrible and didn't want to let me go, but she couldn't risk working there. I went back to the halfway house and told them what had happened.

I was not charged room and board after that. I could go out till five o'clock and had to return to the halfway house. I used most of my time figuring out what my charges were about my public defender was out most of the time. I finally caught him around eleven o'clock and, the first thing my public defender said was where Stephine had nothing to do with my case. He said all this could go away if you produce her whereabout. I told him; you need to leave her out of this. I thought it was about my income tax. My public defender said he had to be in court.

My public defender said we would talk later. I was never my public defender till I had to face the federal Judge. We met with a counselor at the halfway house who came once a week to talk to us, but no one was facing IRS charges. I sat in the meeting listen to the others talk. My public defender never came but, the halfway informed the public defender of my performances in the halfway house. The office manager at the halfway house I had court. I called my public defender's office. He was in court. I decided to go to his office and wait. On my way to see my public defender, or should I say my Public Pretender. I had no idea what was going on in my case. He was concerned about his daughter, who was going to have surgery. On my way, the federal agent trapped in the parking lot asked Stephine. I said, why do you want to know where or if she exists? My Public Defender was late, and the federal court Judge had already ruled me guilty for Improper filing of Income Tax and would be transported to a Camp in Arizona for fourteen months. What was going on? They didn't give me a chance to pay the so-called overpayment of my taxes for the year in question after my divorce. Annie provided the IRS and prosecutor; a copy of my income taxes. My Public Defender's only interest was Stephine's whereabouts. The Sheriff escorted me to the camp. I was terrified.

If any Public Official (plus millions of citizens) is alleging that federal police operations are sending. Innocent people to prison, one would think this at least a matter for discussion, if not an investigation especially an agency that acknowledges its operations are "way out of balance.

The Grandmother

During the IRS hearing, other charges would develop the grandmother's set-up. I had been driving slow enough not to splash as the puddles were enormous, not wanting to splash the old lady and the little girl on the road. There stood a lady holding a little girl's hand, standing by multiple mailboxes belonging to the apartments. When the lady flagged me down, I stopped. The old lady asked if I could take her to the Salvation Army to get a fifty-dollar gift certificate for her granddaughter. Her son had received one for his other kids. I answered I needed to go downtown first. I parked my car in front of the old lady's apartment while she went inside her apartment.

She was waiting for the grandmother to come out. Her neighbor came outside and sat on his doorstep to smoking a cigarette. When the grandmother started to head out to my car, she stuck her head in the door and yelled out to someone inside her apartment. I'll be right back and, we drove away. Not more than ten minutes later, the little girl started crying; I asked what was wrong with me. The grandmother said I was hungry, so I stopped at McDonald's to get her granddaughter something to eat. The grandmother then asked if I could have something too. I got both of them something to eat. When I arrived at the courthouse parking, I said it wouldn't take me long to re-schedule my Court date. The grandmother asked me if I could take her granddaughter inside with her while she finished her breakfast and catch up to us in the courthouse. I said, are you sure she'll come with me. I'm a stranger, and she doesn't know me. I will only be gone a minute.

I need to go to the office to re-schedule my appointment with the Judge's secretary. I needed time; I wasn't sure what would happen and who I could trust. I needed time to think. Why was it so crucial for Annie and her ex-husband to have my daughter? They wanted me to take her to court? I thought to myself. Who would hire an attorney to do something to take my daughter from me? How was the News reports, and federal agents, the Sheriff? We're waiting for me, hoping to charge for kidnapping or any other charges. The grandmother knew where we were. Later, fabricated stories came out by the investigators. Where did the story come from that I took the little girl to see Santa Claus at the mall at nine in the morning?

The Grandmother

When I walked into the courthouse, I informed the guard that if an old lady would be looking for her granddaughter, she should be direct to the Judge's secretary's office. I was on my way judges office to see if I could change my court date. When I got to the courthouse? Not just were the Federal Agents right there but, the News reports came running in front of them. The Sheriff immediately handcuffed me.

I was escorted to the Judge's chambers. The only person I told about my visit was her sister. They plan to have me charged for kidnapping by the IRS investigators; and the IRS Special Agents and the Sheriff accompanied me to the Judge's chambers.

Then the IRS Special Agents produced credentials for inspection to the Judge.

The investigators immediately said I was the subject of a criminal investigation for filing a fraudulent tax return. I never got to see the Judge's Secretary to re-schedule my appointment.

The grandmother walked into the Judge's Chamber and sat in the back watching what was going on. The grandmother stood up and yelled out to the Judge she didn't kidnap her granddaughter. The judge asked the grandmother to come forward and the judged questioned her. The Judge immediately ordered the Sheriff to un-cuff me. Then grandmother and child were taken home by the Sheriff.

It's wasn't until the two special agents escorted me to my car. They started to searching my car, right away, I noticed the grandmother had ransacked my car.

The Special Agents checked around my car without a warrant; when they finished they left without saying anything. When we got to my car, I looked inside. The agents had ransacked my vehicle. When the grandmother stayed behind in my car to finish eating her breakfast, I must have noticed when I had grabbed my wallet.

I had over thirty dollars' worth of silver dollar pieces in a black sock. I kept it in her glove compartment. I had been collecting for her grandsons; why is it when you try to vhelp someone, we end up stabbing you in the back? I wouldn't have noticed them missing except that the IRS agents dumped everything from her glove box to her car seat.

The Forfeiture of my Daughter

My child's voice was all I had. Knowing my daughter would have to leave, we both cried and held on to each other tight. The Investigator and the IRS Special Agent were following me. The first chance I had; I called my friend to meet me at a specific place. I needed her to take my daughter and would explain as much as I could to my daughter; I hoped she would understand, I said we were in danger and, I needed to deal with Annie, and a man named Jake the federal agents were following me. We both cried and, held on to each other. I couldn't imagine letting my daughter go but, I had to protect her. I feared what may happen to her. I had to think fast. I sent her to a place no one would ever hurt her. I said to my daughter as I held her. Remember, our hearts will always join together as one.

Each beat will be the love I will always have for you with all my passion. May God protect my friends family, my daughter and me. your father will go visit you when he can. You have to go with my friend and her family. I whispered to my daughter, you need to stay with them till I can come and pick you up. I said to be good. I will miss all the little things we did together, your father will call once a week to see how you're doing. I cried all the way home, wondering when I would see my daughter again. The courts had three different dates of birth on my daughter legal papers submitted in court 09/09/98, 09/03/99 and, 12/03/99.

POWER OF ATTORNEY

THE STATE OF NEW MEXICO ⟩
⟩   KNOW ALL MEN THAT:
COUNTY OF BERNALILLO ⟩

Date: May 16, 2008   (MDC,)

I,   querque, Bernalillo County, State of New Mexico.
I do hereby commit and dispose the custody, support, education and all other matters
concerning the general health and welfare of my 1 minor child/children,

Stephanie Trevino DOB 9/9/1998

To   at
City o.   County of Bernalillo
State of ___ New Mexico ___ , and hereby appoint   a guardian of the
above named child/children.

This appointment is temporary and shall take effect immediately and shall
continue in force while I am incarcerated, and revoke this Power of Attorney in writing
and or finished with my incarceration.

IN WITNESS WHEREOF, I have executed this instrument at Albuquerque, New Mexico
on the _____ day of _____ 20_____ .

Signature

Subscribed and sworn to me this _16th_ day of _May_ 2008
My Commission Expires on the _31st_ day of _August_ 2009

Notary Public

Metropolitan Detention Center

After completing my sentencing with the IRS. The Camp received a subpoena from the Second Judicial District Court Judge. To this day, I don't know what the charges were against me. They were, all the same, wanting to know where my daughter was. I would be charged for child support. My counselor advised me to sign up for a public defender. My public defender said I was facing the Forty-one exact charges (41) in prison for exact charges with the IRS. But the District Court Judge gave me probation. It was almost like being incarcerated for five years of probation: the same commands and her daughter's whereabouts, the force of being interrogated again. The list goes on. I blame the Justices Systems, the Federal and District Court Judges, for being subpoenaed to court in honor of my ex and wife. I'd rather stay locked up than give up my daughter to any of them. It was the courts responsibility to seek the truth. Jake wife continually charged her repeatedly with the exact charges and, now comes a new Attorney II who, after airing on the News, took Annie and Jake's case. How is it possible to continue to charge her again and, again now, this is a DNA hearing?

Attorney II did not enter the whole story of the DNA finding, making it difficult for me to figure out what had happened. Attorney II. Had my file sealed. I suffered false Imprisonment, placed on probation for five years I was dragged to court several times. My life had taken a turn; I now lived in fear. My life I had a Power of Attorney drawn up at the Metropolitan Detention Center

The notary signed and dated while I was held at the Metropolitan Detention Center by the District Court Judge ordered for a hearing. My public defender was no help to me. He said his workload was too much for him; what about me? I had charges for something that I didn't do. What was going on? I continued fighting a lost battle. Very little was said to me regarding my case, then I was escorted in front of the district court judge; who didn't know me?

Annie and Jake had acknowledged that my daughter did Not Exist. Then why did Annie call Child Protective Services and the police department in the middle of the night, stating my daughter's endangerment? I refused to materialize my daughter to anyone except her father.

He wasn't able to care for her physically. But supported her and had a phone conference, visitation with my daughter as I hoped I would be home with my daughter soon but, it took several years to do so, hoping Annie would not file any more charges and we would be safe. I was also worried; Jake said Annie could not have children and wanted my daughter; I told Jake, " Are you kidding. I couldn't trust you with her after what you did to your daughter. What makes you think I would let you have my daughter leave us alone and? I drove off crying. I couldn't allow the father of my daughter to get entangled with my dilemma.

DNA Charges/Testing's

You will find the testimony written on Annie's website

What information was presented to the judge and, jury. What was missing? It was written on Annie's website? Annie hired Attorney II to file a civil suit against me. I stated, how did that happen; they didn't have the money to pay their first attorney? But they could hire Attorney II. Who was hired right after airing on the News? Yes, that sounded like the perfect case. Ambulance Chaser Attorney II. Immediately filed a motion to re-open my case, the Honorable Federal Court Judge granted to re-open my case?

And, it made it possible for Annie and Jake have the judge, and jury grant them 1.2 million dollars without viewing alternatives. There were other tests done other than the Blood Service, which may not be accountable in the lawsuit Annie claimed Jake got tested. Annie and Jake aired on the News regarding fraudulent DNA samples from his adult daughter, and then there was the state fair and other DNA Services; he included an employee at the Blood Service who was also her daughter's friend. There were other possibilities. Which were all included on Annie's website? For the whole world to read including, the legal system.

Attorney II had information from the judge, including the Jury; Why was I kept out of the courtroom; who was the most critical person in the DNA hearing who mattered?

I couldn't get any information on the DNA hearing as Annie Attorney II sealed my file. I received most of the data from different sources, including Annie's website.

I entered what I felt would help.

Continuation of the DNA: The history of all the other DNA testing posted on Annie's website. I researched Annie's website, the prosecutor, Annie Attorney II.

I was not assigned a public defender or was aware that I would not appear in The DNA hearing The DNA.

The Transportation Clerk called me at the Camp that I would be leaving to Albuquerque. in the morning. I had been subpoenaed to court for DNA charges.

I had a few months to complete my sentencing for the IRS.

Annie disclosed on her website.

Page 1 of 7 UPDATE: **First DNA Testing:** Annie said Jake got tested at the Blood Service on **January 12, 2000**. Jake went to his ex-wife's sister's house to me. He got tested and, I'd better go. I aforementioned him why; should I get tested, leave us alone. Go home to your crazy wife. You know damn well she's, not yours, besides. Why didn't I get a call from your Attorney's Office, being he made the appointment? He said, just go, it's at and, he gave me the address of the Blood Service he had gotten tested.

Page 5 of 7 **Second DNA Testing:** On **April 13, 2001**, his attorney requested another paternity test. The DNA test was scheduled at the same Blood Service again.

Page 4 of 7 His ex-wife was then informed by the Blood Service that I had an appointment for a DNA test per Jakes Attorney. Jake then called me to get tested.

I said I didn't have the money to pay for another DNA test and, besides, I had a cold and couldn't go.

He aforementioned if I don't go, you will be in contempt of Court and go to jail. So, then he suggested we could get tested at my home. In **January 2000**, a girl from the Blood Service came to my house and said her boss sent her to do a DNA test. It would only take a minute. The girl who came to do the DNA test turned out to be my daughter's friend.

I didn't know it until my daughter walked in the house and her friend said, so here where you live and, my daughter asked, what are you doing here. She answered I had a DNA my boss had me do. My daughter usually went to her friend's house when they went out. Annie accused me of tampering with the DNA testing. Jake had seen. My daughter and her friend at the Club where he worked as a bodyguard. How did Jake and Annie know my daughter's friend had done the DNA test is still a mystery? My daughter's friend came and did her job. She took a swab, tested both my daughter, and I then requested a picture of my daughter. I had a picture of my daughter, but she had to take it and brought the office camera and took a photo of my daughter. She took my daughter's picture for the DNA file. She said it would be ready for pick-up in two weeks. Full payment would be due at the time of pick-up. A little over two weeks later, I got a call from the Blood Services that the DNA results were ready. I went on my lunch break to pick up the results of my DNA.

When I got to the blood services office, they didn't have the DNA results Annie and Jake had picked them up. I said to the owner I was court-ordered by the judge to bring the outcomes of the DNA. I was ordered to call the Judge's Office to let the judge I had the DNA results and schedule an appointment to appear in court. When I went to pick up the DNA results, the owner told Annie that he could not give her the DNA results. He could only release the DNA results to either the ex-wife or her husband.

Annie became difficult. The owner said Annie returned later, accompanied by Jake, and paid the remaining balance of the DNA test results showing a 99.97% probability. How was that possible?

When my daughter's friend returned to the office with the DNA samples, Annie was in the Blood Service office and, she started a diversion yelling and screaming at the Blood Service staff. Was Annie planting her evidence? When the judge asked his attorney if they acknowledged the paternity test, he told Jake to sit down and be quiet. Jake attorney said I would be getting child support from Jake I said I don't want it and he said by law you have to take it. I said by law he should have been paying me spousal support, and has he but, he'll pay child support for a child he doesn't know. The DNA "was never entered into the court records and, he never signed anything to that effect. I investigated the file in the court records to see what they had on my file. When I asked for copies of my file I was told my file was sealed. I came out with nothing to help explain what was entered. Later Jake would take more than the two DNA tests taken other than with the Blood Service.

Third, DNA Testing Annie stated the *New Mexico State Fair*, and I gave away DNA testing kits where his wife got several swabbed. I took my older daughter's DNA which could add up to another DNA testing. When her children were three and five years old, they performed at the State Fair for several years. The State Fair never gave out DNA Testing kits. There was no such kit that we were aware of, as Annie indicated.

Fourth DNA Testing Jake Attorney referred Jake to Dr. Henderson, M.D., Jake complied **July 19, 2000**. I disobeyed the order; again, after stalling for several months, I decided to call Dr. Henderson, M.D., regarding the DNA testing. I asked who set the appointment and when I could get a DNA test.

Dr. Henderson specified, he didn't do DNA testing and practiced for over (20) twenty years. His office did not schedule a DNA for me or my ex-husband as he had claimed he complied with being tested on **July 19, 2000**. The investigator mentioned it on his report and his attorney. That Dr. Henderson had tested, Jake. It was not possible and never contacted the doctor again.

Pages 7of 7 **Fifth DNA Test April 26, 2007**; Jake then tested for another DNA test at Enchantment Examination Service, Jake got tested on **February 23,2001**. That would make it a total of Five test DNA testing possibilities. Then, Annie mentioned another DNA testing, Not including the following DNA stories that Annie wrote on her website.

UPDATE: Annie's DNA Speculations we now know how she used her **older daughter's DNA.** Then Later, Annie tried to say to her daughter had nothing do with the DNA test Attorney II also specified her ex-husband paid Child Support for a child that didn't exist and her daughter's whereabouts. Annie wrote about seven DNA possibilities? The stories said and written by Jake and Annie made up unbelievable stories. Many of my friends said I should write this story. It's Not just about Annie but the court system and how Jake and Anne won the DNA hearing and why her daughter's friend was accused of wrongdoing? When she did what she was supposed to do. She took the samples requested and took a picture of my daughter, and sealed everything; she then grabbed all her stuff, said goodbye, and went back to work. Who would have thought Annie would have blamed her. The Blood Service wasn't the only DNA Supplier. As written on Annie's website word per word, it had to have been Annie's idea to entrap the blood service. At the time, she was my husband's lover and her first controversy with the Blood Service. Annie made a point of letting the owner of the Blood Service repeatedly know of his ex-wife's propensity toward deception and forgery; the owner's exact words were, "Do you think I would risk my business for a DNA test?" Annie's second bad encounter with the Blood Service was when they refused to hand over the DNA test results to Annie. For the second time, Annie started a diversion. The third time, Annie disliked how the owner handled his staff and the management of his office. At the time, her husband noticed her daughter's friend was working in his office, and Annie found it a good excuse to continue her plan. After Annie and her conspiracy helped her get information to get her story or evidence against me.

I wondered what she would do next to help destroy a stranger to her, but she notified the News reporters and whoever else could procure.

Who didn't know me? Annie wanted to destroy me. I was in the Camp in Arizona, when one of the inmates came running to me and, said you're on the TV, your ex-husband, and that woman who introduced herself as his wife. They're talking about you. Then the inmate said to me, believe me, there is no comparison. They both deserve each other. Annie and Jake appeared on the talk shows; that aired about, The DNA God only knows what else they said about me I couldn't get to the TV room on time. Annie and Jake were aired on.

The Montel William Show on Thursday, **July 12, 2007**. Then Annie and Jake appeared on Maury Povich Show on **August 16, 2007**. Shame on all of you, how dare you. How could you have done the Show without me being there to defend myself.? It's not like Maury and Montel to have done the Show without listening to both sides. How could Annie and Jake that snake accomplish this without having both parties on the Show? After the Show aired. How could they allow me to be humiliate like that? While I was in Camp, I wrote to both talk Show Host, but they never answered my letters. Montel Williams and Maury Povich aired Annie and Jake on their Show but refused to hear my side of the story. While

I was being transported to MDC in Albuquerque, New Mexico, from a Camp in Arizona for the Internal Revenue Service charges of Improper filing of Income Tax, I was summoned to court for DNA charges against me one month before being released from the Camp. The Transportation Office said I was being transported to New Mexico early in the morning. The transporter picked me up in a white van and drove me to California to pick up other inmates transferred to another Prison.

At first, I was terrified but, then the Inmates mentioned to the transporter to change the rated movie, there was a lady aboard. I was surprised they were gentlemen.

I was the only female aboard at the time; I was the only female on the van on the first day.

I spent two days on the road, with hard-core prisoners for murder with a lifetime sentencing. There were others who had a few years. I was supposed to attend the DNA hearing. They had railroaded me all over. We ended up spending the night in Texas. When we got back on the van early the following day, the inmates said to the driver, hey, this lady needs to get to New Mexico. She has to be in court.

One of the inmates I rode with asked me what a lady like you was in prison I said I was in a Camp. I said my ex-husband and his wife were constantly filing charges against me. He said, oh yeah, I heard about you on the News and the Talk Show.

He said I'd like to meet those two and kick there ass and we laughed. I said I couldn't believe my husband would do such a thing to me. The men who were transported with me weren't as bad as I thought; although their stories were scary, they told me how they murdered and committed their crimes. Wow, I thought to myself, I wouldn't want to be their enemies. I finally got to MDC, where they held me till I was called to court for a DNA hearing I would be seeing Jake, the snake and, his so-called wife for another one of their charges against me. I was kept at the **Metropolitan** **Detention** **Center** for three (3) days and then returned to the Camp in Arizona to complete the duration of my sentencing. They did not call me the District Court hearing for the DNA charges against me. The court had to have known I was being transported to New Mexico for the hearing as the transportation clerk had the orders, and I was the main suspect, as the Courts would call it. Then Annie wrote on her website DNA shocking story that made Annie and that snake her ex-husband a Millionaire.

I pieced together to prove the lie told by Annie and my ex-husband they aren't educated and would not confront his ex-wife with misleading information to the courts independently. Jake can't lie as well as Annie; The whole hearing was coerced, being her ex-husband can't lie well and held back the evidence. Jake and Annie were told, promised Jakes, the snake's ex-wife, would not appear in court. Jake would have frozen and yelled out the truth. I know he followed the attorney's advice step by step instructions as to what to say. Most of the time, Attorney II does all the talking and, you sit there. My ex-husband had to have been coached and assured his ex-wife wouldn't be in the courtroom, nor did she have anyone representing her; in court, no Public Defender, it was easy in and out of court the hearing for Annie and Jake the snake to win the DNA case. Before going to court his Attorney advised Jake to grow back his eyebrows as he had shaved his head and eyebrows. He looked like Casper, the ghost. Why wasn't I appointed a public defender or allowed in court to defend myself? It was a set-up.

Don't Stop-go directly back to Camp and finish your IRS sentencing.

I was not informed to attend the DNA hearing in court; I would have been the main witness. I was NOT allowed to say a word; I had no voice.

The Judge and, Jury must have thought I had something to hide or was guilty.

I thought the judge would have put a warrant for my arrest for not appearing in court, but they didn't question why I wasn't in court? I didn't appear for the hearing to defend myself, the Blood Service and his employees. Did they know I was at MDC waiting to voice my incents in court? Jake and Annie's case with their Attorney II. At the same time, I stayed at the Metropolitan Detention Center clear across town. For three days before the hearing. When Jake won, I was transported back to the Camp the following day. I got back to the Camp, the transportation clerk asked how did court go. I said they never called me to court. He said your ex-husband and Annie filed charges against you for DNA fraud. You were subpoenaed to court for a hearing—that why we transported you to Albuquerque, New Mexico.

They took me to California, Texas, and God only knows where else. Then I stayed at MDC for three days; I was, transported back to the here to Camp to finish my sentencing. The judge in the DNA hearing I never knew as my files were closed.

I had very little information about the hearing except what Annie had written on her website. After the DNA hearing, Annie's Attorney had my file sealed.

I went to the courthouse and, they gave me some forms to fill out for Jake the snake, and, his Attorney to unseal my file but, I never heard from either one.

I had to get information from another source.

I was marked by the media as a Monster, a Blood-Sucking Bitch.

After that, Annie's Attorney II sealed my file. I don't know why after all; they had won the DNA case? What did they have to hide? Isn't that against my rights?

Not to be able to defend and read my charges. I questioned how a District Court Judge and Jury could have awarded 1.2 Million Dollars to them and, the court did not consider all the other possibilities other than the Blood Service being at fault.

Annie had all of this information on her website. Why didn't we demand that I appear in court or re-schedule the hearing? They must have known I was in a Camp in Arizona?

After he received 1.2 Million Dollars, Jake had become a millionaire or should say Annie. Seven months later, my son asked Jake for help with his college tuition and, he would repay him. He needed to pay his tuition before he could register for college. Jake said to my son; you have to ask Annie she said we gave most of the money to the church and friends. I thought to myself, why couldn't the Jake the snake; give my son the money for college? It was his for college. What happened to the college fund we had saved for the kid's college? It's not like we were asking for money from him. I worked hard to put the money on their college trust fund. Annie must have cashed it out to hire the investigator and their Attorneys.

It belonged to both of the kids. Her son continued college with his own money. With the help of his hard work and his mother's, help. He needs to finish college.

The student loan will cost my son forever to pay. We didn't need Jakes money.

Just what belongs to my children? Karma.

The money we had saved for the kid's education, Jake and Annie cashed in. Jake, and Annie no longer have a penny left from the Million Dollars, including her new business of being her own boss business as a Pooper Scooper. After they were awarded to them, when they sued the Blood Service who just did their job. The Attorney who coached her ex-husband and Annie win the case that was slandered and wrong. Karma has taken place; you've all heard. I was the foremost person being in that courtroom charged for DNA fraud? What was the outcome of Annie and Jake won the battle.

Was I now facing a new charge? What happened? No, it was as if it wasn't a part of the DNA scandal. What evidence did they have for the DNA? Why would Jake bring up his wife having a tabulation? He was not allowed in the hospital room. When his wife gave birth to her daughter, I asked the nurse not to allow Jake in the room. I was not too fond of the sight of him. He had just confessed to me in the hospital. He had an affair with a woman while he was overseas. His story was the woman he had sex with reminded him of me. Jake said the only difference was that the woman had terrible teeth. How is it that Jake could have even known whether or not his wife had a tabulation?

Annie was trying to get information about me having a tabulation.

She accomplished to looking at my hospital medical records as Annie was pretentious as me to view my medical records. They had broken into my apartment and taken mine and my children's credentials that Annie had used to get information on me.

There couldn't have been anything on my file that Annie could have used. What did they get from my medical file she took copies of my surgery of my brain tumor? Annie had taken my medical record to the District Attorney's Office.

Later it was submitted it to the prosecutor, and they requested to have me evaluate. Who knew we would be having a DNA hearing with Jurors and the witness?

How strange would you think that with all the effort we had made, why wouldn't the main suspect, who was me be a part of it all. I fear being in front of a judge and in the courtroom with the judge, and Jury, and whoever else I would have had to face. How would I have answered their question, and what would they ask me.

There were **(12) twelve jurors**. Eleven were men and one female juror. That seems unfair, and it didn't make sense, another set-up. Why didn't the judge and the jurors question the fact that I was not in the courtroom? Annie Attorney later became the chief administrative officer, who has retired from such a great position.

Thanks to Annie for winning the DNA case against me, Annie made him her benefit, Attorney II. Jake quit his job at the state prison. He was never good at keeping a job anyway.

He claimed that he feared for his life. Are you kidding me? With years of Martial Arts, he should be able to protect himself. He was kicked out of the martial arts class as he went to his martial arts instructor's home and fought with him and was told never to go to his studio. Jake's supervisor asked my husband to go to counseling for his temper with other co-workers. Jake has always been a loner. He was always alone. Jake never helped me tell the courts what Annie was doing. Jake only appeared in court for the DNA and domestic violence's Jake just wanted to see me, or should I say lust over me; I hated him. Karm will come out of their wrongdoing.

What Do you Think? You know life is short and, the clock is running out, things are changing, and we have no control. The days are rushing by. We follow the road till we find the Dead-End sign and, you look back and say, why didn't I take the chance? Why didn't I do anything but, then when you realize you've gotten older and you can't do what you used to do or didn't do. You'll get to the point where you don't care about what others think or say. Who the heck are you to have mistreated me?

We are all human beans, but you allow others to make your life a living hell. Then we have those who put you down or show off what you don't have. Wake up; the materialistic things are not accurate when you die; you came to this world naked and, you're going back naked that's life. We were here to do what we make of it. If you're a store clerk, that's all you'll be if you're a doctor. Will you treat every patient the way you would want them to treat you? Even if we're all a different color, we compare ourselves instead of working together to make it a better place. There were times I had such a bad feeling about going to work just hated everything about it and couldn't change it. The girls would show off when their boyfriends or husbands sent them flowers, candy, balloons, and calling to say how much they love them and couldn't wait to see them.

When the clock hits 4:45 pm, all the desks are clean and, they have one foot out the door. The worse thing at work is gossiping; believe me, they will find something wrong with you. Gossiping is usually bad. That's why it's called gossip. Then you have a boss who thinks he owns you. And will make your day worse than it already is. Or family and friends who you trust put you down. I had lost the ability to continue writing again. Wouldn't you believe it. This manuscript should have been an easy process but, it wasn't; instead, it was another nightmare. I tried the replacement key to change names and, it tore up my whole story. The words changed and, it didn't make sense. I hope my manuscript will finally get published and, my story will help others because I was badly treated and Crucified in the most horrifying way you could ever imagine. Not just the justice's system but my own husband's wife, who got away with filing charges against me over a love affair

I feared those who were accountable might want to replica my story because it may incriminate them. Then there the rich and famous who write books and, have no idea what life is like on breast Cancer or Dietetics is like on less you live it or write children books when we don't know what's it like to raise a child. It's not easy we have problems too, with kids in school or the babysitter or with family. My kid did with their family members. Believe it, when I heard anyone mistreated my child, I would front them. Who is gave them the right to hurt your child verbally of physically?

I lost both of my daughters and, I don't know how to fix it. My older daughter is still not talking to my Annie made sure my daughter; knew I called my **Mama Bear** a replacement mother who received e-mails pictures and, notifying Mama Bear she would be in town to visit her. I cried to hear Annie and my daughter collaborate as if she were her daughter. My sisters did the same thing to me. Instead of helping, she made things worse for me. I was suffering; I had no voice. The stories went on as if I didn't matter. Was I wrong for trying to stop him from taking my little girl. I knew the other woman would have mistreated her as she was a part of me. I would not allow it. My ex-husband wanted me and would have used my daughter to get it his way. When my brother heard I had not spoken to my oldest daughter, he said she was a grown woman and should know better. I heard Annie and my daughter no longer write to each other after being released from Camp.

Annie conspiracies were shocked when I was released; they thought I would be sentenced to life in prison. My younger sister told my children to forget that I would be facing forty-one years in prison; that's what my Public Defender said I would be facing. How weird is that Annie and my younger sister wondered how I could have gotten off from being incarcerated for a life sentence. It's a miracle from God. That's what it was he freed me from the chains you put me in for life. When I was released Annie heard and my younger sister were afraid of me. I don't know if it's out of fear of my getting revenge or guilt. It's known to be a fact we couldn't believe I was free. I was in shock too. I couldn't figure how it could happen to me. The first time in years, my sister walked up to me in person at my sister Eva funeral and gave my Eva cremation necklace which hopes to go on a vacation and, I hope I could take Eva to a different place where I would have made a trip and, say I was able to make my dreams come true. When incarcerated, I wanted to make Annie and everyone who took my life and made them suffer as I had but, when I got out, for some reason I couldn't find myself taking revenge on them.

Then my friends said to me, write your story. It's an incredible story and true. It could happen or to just anyone. When I wrote this book, I wanted to write about a Court System gone wrong but was afraid the attorney who sealed my court file and everyone I wrote about who sentenced me would figure out a way to fabricate my evidence or try to keep the truth from resurfacing. I had a friend make copies of whatever we could find. If in the case would erase my file. Remember, money talks it's an actual fact in life. We need to fight back on pay-off in education, jobs, etc., etc.

I suffered from being locked up and poorly treated. It was horrible for me. The court system doesn't allow you to get your life in order before you go to jail. It's like dying. You don't take anything with you and, if incarcerated for an extended period, your stuff is gone, your own family will sell everything you own. And the correction officers, not all of them will take whatever you have when you get incarcerated, you would need someone on the outside to bring you clothes, or you'll have nothing to wear when you get out. Most people like myself didn't want to bother my family or friends or didn't have anyone on the outside. Hopefully, you'll find something that may fit when taken to—the clothing room where clothes were left behind when another female left behind, another girl lost their wedding ring and other expensive stuff. My son and the second to the oldest sister put money in my books to get hygiene's or what I needed but, I never got it. For what reason did they want me incarcerated, but I know about having to defend myself in court, nor did my son and Felix.

I did learn one thing I never forget when the judge said to me never to give out too much information. Wow, I get it now. You know that more than half of the people in prison are here because someone called the police.

We call them Rats, Snitches. Hate to say it, but we have terrible habits on telling our darkest secrets to our families, friend, and, worse of all, your children and your most trusted husband. Because when the time comes to pass. They will use it against you. Who would have thought a mother put my daughter in jail for using her credit card to buy pampers for her child?

No one keeps a secret, I know, as I worked in a counseling office. I did everything, plus my job as office manager. I worked mainly with the doctors and counselors. They say everything about their patients that should have been confidential. Trust me, if you have a problem, work it out on your own, start with soft music, then take it one step at a time. When I went to counseling for the first time in my life, the first thing they wanted to talk about should be what brought you to counseling: Are you feeling suicidal, angry, or want to hurt yourself. No, they throw you to the wolves. If you're a criminal, you're scared you can't trust anyone. While working at the counseling office, I learned how to cope with my problems. You can do to overcome it, being incarcerated, you know to watch your back.

The tears, and so I wrote this book, the daughter who was my best friend and, a part of me is now with my converter Annie who didn't know me, and, Jake whom I was married to for over twenty-three years, helped crucify me. I wanted to die but, God wouldn't let me die? I had nothing to live for except my children. All I had were old friends who had a family and, I had lost hers. I wrote this book for my family and friends and primarily for myself to have a piece of mind.

I start to write about a court system gone wrong. Then I began to write about my life and the life of those who meant a lot to me. It would be a miracle to finish writing this book; I will miss writing. I'm a living miracle.

Exodus 23:20 I am sending an angel ahead of you to guide you along. The way. His eye is on the sparrow, and, know he watches over me.

John 3:17 If anyone has the world's goods and sees his brother in need yet closes his heart against him, how does God's love bear in him? How often have you seen a News story about a person who was obviously in trouble, yet people, not wanting to get involved, walked right on?

Ask God to help you become more familiar with his voice. Is there someone he wants you to reach out today, as his angel on earth, with a message of love and hope? Is there a way you can use the exceptional talents he has given you to serve his purpose? Trust and, Believe in God, and his Angles and, Saints there for real.

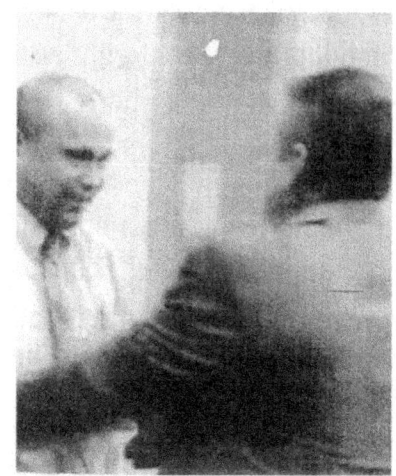

KOB TV 4 - 'Dad' Wins a Round

District Court Judge

After released from Federal Camp, where I had completed my sentencing for Improper Filing of Income Tax, I was subpoenaed to court by the District Court Judge for the fifth time. Again, Annie took it upon herself to file the exact damn charges against me that's called double jeopardy. No, it's more like a quintuplets?

I headed to court as ordered. I had a wearying feeling and didn't want to be there.

I walked up to the courtroom door to looked for my name on the court roster. Annie stood there with the News Reporter. I then called my public defender.

He wasn't in the courthouse to defend me. I got a hold of my public defender, he said go home. He had rescheduled my hearing. Go home; since it was walking distance from the courthouse to my public defender office, I went to his office. I wanted to find out what was going on. My public defender was not in, and I could leave him a message, I waited to hear from my public defender. He didn't call for weeks, so I went to his office. He seemed to be in a hurry, like he didn't have time to talk to me. He said, you see all those boxes on the window. That's the evidence against you. I thought to myself, what could they have as evidence and, most of all, what kind of charge they had that would incriminate me? Weeks later, I was ordered to court to appear in front of the judge had sent for a warrant for my arrest for not appearing in court. Right away, my public defender said to the judge it was his fault, and then the prosecutor said to the judge I was a flight risk. Flight risk? My soulmate managed to say that he had an airplane. The prosecutor used it to keep me from getting out of jail on bond. The judge did not grant me the opportunity to post bond, yet a woman was in jail facing murder charges was released on bond from jail. I waited to be put on the judge's docket for the judge to decided what was going to happen to me. It was my Public Defender's fault; the prosecutor said Your Honor; this woman is a flight risk. How could I be a flight risk? I've lived in New Mexico all of my life; my family lives here. I couldn't afford to hire a criminal attorney and, that's what I needed. I didn't understand the court system. I was confused and mortified as Annie sat in the courtroom waiting to have me incarcerated. The district court judge had me incarcerated. I asked my public defender what happened he said, don't worry, I'll see you after court. What could I do for myself? Whom could I call? Could I have gotten bailed out with a flight risk?

Whom can I call someone who can view my case to find out what's going on?

I cried. I felt like a criminal, and the people who judge others say that if you're in jail, they're all considered innocent till proven guilty, but that is not true. You are never innocent when you're in front of a judge. There stood Annie next to all my supporters who didn't know me and, Annie wanted to make sure I never got out to see daylight again. My public defender came a few days later and said he was facing forty-one years in prison. I was hoping he would say I would be acquitted. What could I have done to be charged a sentence for forty-one years? Forty-one years that a life sentence. I could have killed my ex-husband and his wife and all the conspirators. I waited for my hearing at the Metropolitan Detention Center for my public defender to come to see me. My public defender came to see me once when I was incarcerated, waiting for the judge to put me on his docket. And, even then, we hadn't gone over my case.

The one thing I noticed was that my date of Birth was wrong on my court file case? I was assigned a counselor by the District Court, who came to visit me twice a week. We talked about my public defender and when he was coming to go over my case. But she couldn't give me any information on my case. I wondered what was in those boxes in his office on the public defender's office window seal.

I needed him to tell me something. But that just didn't happen. The next time I would finally see my public defender would be when I was ordered to court by the district court judge. My public defender asked me to tell him where Stephanie was and, it would all be over? I thought to myself, what the heck is going on. She had nothing to do with my case.

My visitors were my son, sister Felix, and my friend, who is also my soulmate and; I could have had my co-worker visit me, but I refused to see him. Everyone, including my son and my sister and my soulmate who wanted to help me, my public defender, said to them the same thing. You see all those boxes against the window seal that was full of evidence against me. Why wouldn't he show them what we had against me? He never showed any of them what was in the boxes. He just pointed them out.

My public defender just sat there and said nothing about my case, and, of course, they left not knowing what he had to say to defend me. I called one of my friends, a co-worker, to inform him that the public defender wanted me to plead guilty; he said I could plead no contest and, I said, isn't that the same thing. My public defender said, No, you can't plead No contest. My friend wasn't an attorney, but he was all I had and was very resourceful. My public defender pleaded guilty on my behalf. I was not allowed to speak on my behalf to the News reporter in my defense. My public defender aforementioned reporters weren't allowed in the detention center. I had no voice; I held back from saving my own life. I didn't know what was going on; I didn't understand. I couldn't stop crying. They kept me away from my family, and I couldn't call my friends. I was alone. I cried with anger that Annie sat in the courtroom staring at me with the News reporter by her side. I sat in the courtroom, sucking up whatever my public defender said; I couldn't help but cry. My two public defenders sandwiched me out of the courtroom from the News reporters. I had no one whom I could speak up for me.

I stood there like a loser.

I could only pray. That's the one thing no one could take away from or control me from doing. You do experience the love of God. He won't leave you or forsake you. The judge never questioned why my ex-husband wasn't in the courtroom after all the charges were about him and his ex-wife Annie had married my ex-husband to give me the power to file charges against his ex-wife. What the hell was my ex-husband thinking? What did he want? Is that even possible can an outsider to file charges against a stranger? That's what Annie was to me. She didn't know me. What did my public defender have planned on my defense? I stood there, not knowing anything. My mind was blank. What will happen to me? Will the judge put me in prison? What kind of game is she playing? Oh God, help me. When Annie suddenly stood up in front of the judge and said she feared for Jake, my ex-husband, and her life Annie pleaded you keep Viola incarcerated. She and Jack felt safe.

I can't imagine how I could believe he said to stay away from them when Annie was stalking me if you fear someone. Not Annie kept finding ways to pursue me;

I had my house ransacked by Annie and my sister when my nephew lived in my apartment. That woman even followed me to the store when I lived clear across town.

The list goes on forever. Annie and her co-conspirator were collecting evidence against me. Jake said to be careful'. He didn't have anything to do with it. Which is somewhat believable? Jake cannot stand in front of the judge and jury to say anything without being coerced. I knew they manufactured most of the evidence but, I couldn't prove it and, my public defender wouldn't help me. Whom could I call? My Public Defender was overwhelmed with other clients and, he didn't research the boxes in his Office. Annie had the News reporters in and out of the courtroom. A gag ordered was requested but, my public defender had denied my request. Annie made my court hearing a sideshow. I wondered what my public defender was thinking, whose side he was on. I never questioned my public defender. I figured he would go over my file with me and try to make some kind sense in my defense. I heard most of my charges when the prosecutor stood in front of the judges as I heard I superannuated for the exact charges. My public defender's excuse was that he was overwhelmed with other clients that needed his assistance. I wondered if my public defender was no public defender even though

I was facing forty-one years in prison. That was a reason to help someone; it wasn't some misdemeanor charge I was facing. I was facing forty-one years that's more than a sentence for murder. After being incarcerated, I felt like going to prison for whatever charges my ex-husband did not stand up for me. Please, Jake, tell the truth. Karma will be your sentence, trust me and all the others who deceived me.

I could only pray I had no more tears left to cry. If you were in my situation, what would you do; believe me I tried to write letters, make phone calls; there was nothing else I could do. I wrote to my public defender and pleaded with him to help me, but I never heard from him. All I had was a pencil and paper that the lady from the church would bring for the inmates.

My public defender neglected me, he said he was overloaded with work that wasn't good enough for me, who needed his help. I didn't think the judge identified that they had judged me for all of the above charges with the federal court judge and now district court judge. Annie was not happy my ex-husband owed me back Spousal Support given to me during my divorce hearing. The court could have followed up on those charges and may have dismissed them. The judge was not given all the information needed and couldn't say anything on my behalf. The judge asked if I had anything to say after he had sentenced me to probation for five years. How is it imaginable? I couldn't say a word; it didn't matter anymore.

Mishap: Second Judicial District Court Judge had ordered me to five years' probation, but the district court judge paper got screwed up.

The Sherriff then transported me to the Grants Prison is about seventy-seven-point miles away from where I should have been. After I was booked, I called my counselor that I had been transferred to Grants Prison. I had been placed on five years' probation but was sent to prison instead. My counselor got right on it and called me back to let me know what was going on as the Booking Officer said that it doesn't sound like the Courts could make that kind of mistake. It wasn't till my counselor called the prison and explained the whole thing, but I had to stay there until the correction was made and signed by the Judge, Public Defender, and the Prosecutor. They had a hard time getting the prosecutor to sign. I had to wait till the prison got the paperwork. It took months to mark the Amended forms from **November 07, 2008, to January 23, 2009**. Then I had to wait till the Grants Prison received the documents from the judge.

I was then transferred to MDC till I could get another apartment or a place to stay.

I had lost my apartment when sent to a Camp. I waited almost two weeks before I could get released. Annie made me a high profile? After the entire dilemma with getting released; everything I owned was gone. Then my son came to see me.

I almost cried. I asked him how he found me, and he said I have my way and asked if I needed anything. I answered right away said, yes, I need a change of clothes. The guy next door gave me a pair of his jogging pants—my first pair of jeans and, T-shirt. I worked in an office most of my life. Being in the office workforce, I never wore jeans. I only had dress clothes and heels in most of my career life. When we went camping, I wore a pair of jogging pants. I hit rock bottom. Then my soulmate came to see if I was ok and acquired some things I needed at my shared apartment.

Times had changed. I didn't have a chance to explain to my children or say goodbye to those in my life. Suddenly, I was placed in a camp far from home without knowing I would not be going home. They took my life from me. Some inmates don't have a chance to get their pets to a safe place, or their children maybe call a friend or family member someone who could care for them.

I can't selfishly forgive those who hurt me and made me suffer; I ask God to forgive them for me. I am still dealing with my ex-husband and, Annie wondering what's next. I feared for my own life. I couldn't say or do anything till after I completed my probation. I didn't want to give Annie another reason to have me sent to prison as soon as my probation had ended. I went to the District Courthouse to read my file when I got to the office. The file clerk said the file you requested was sealed you need to fill out paperwork and send it to Jake's Attorney to un-seal my file, but I never heard from him, so I called his office and tried to get Attorney II to re-open my court file but, I never received an answer. I went to his office and was told he was no longer working there. He got promoted to a higher position.

It cost a hundred dollars a week on commissary for snacks, hygiene's, coffee, sugar, Being incarcerated at any facility is very expensive. The inmates buy envelopes, stamps, paper, and phone cards; the list goes on. If you don't have commissary, you're basically hurting in every way possible you need the help of friends, family anyone on the outside. I had no one except the inmates who helped me. Can you imagine I had nine brothers and sisters and only one went to visit me? If your ever incarcerate or know of anyone, help them. It will come back to your goodwill always dose. Some inmates are innocent or just made a mistake. when you get incarcerated, you need to help each other, but, in most cases, we lookout for ourselves. When you're placed at MDC and have no money in your books to buy hygiene, you did what I had to do. I never really wanted to accept the fact that you had a gift with Empathy. It worked with others but not for myself. If you're not accurate, you could get beat up in jail for accepting commissary if you're a fake. I thank God most of the girls trusted my prayers and would ask me if I would pray with them for some reason. We had faith in my prayers and readings. I could tell people about their lives, but I can't read my upcoming gift from God and how I got commissary at the Metropolitan Detention Center. One day a young girl came to me and, asked can you read my hands I could read it by the weight of their hand and, I said ok but, I'm not sure if what I tell you is true so please bear with me, you can't expect what I may or may not say will come about. I told her everything would go well for me in court, and I would be released, but you need to be careful. Someone you trust and care for a lot will betray you and, you will be serving three or more years in prison. Be careful. A month later, she came running to me and said, you were right. My boyfriend got me to help him with transporting his drugs and, he told the judge I was accountable. She said I wish I had paid attention to your prediction. I then mentioned my ability to foretell to the correction officers at the detention center. The correction officer came to visit me in my cell and asked if I could read her hands. I then said to her; there are two men in your life. She said yes, she needed to decide which one of her boyfriends was the right one. she believed her current boyfriend would propose to her on Thanksgiving. When I read her hands, I said it couldn't be. She didn't believe my reading. I said what I'm telling you may or may not be; let me know the outcome? She said she had gotten the day off for Thanksgiving and would be having dinner with her current boyfriend's family; she believed he would propose to her. I said, no, you'll be working here. And you'll be going back to your old boyfriend. he canceled the thanksgiving dinner. She then received a call asking if she could come to work. Someone had called in. It was just as I had predicted. She went back to her old boyfriend. I couldn't believe it came true I had a gift God gave to me; it was a miracle. I always had but refused to accept it. I prayed with the inmates for some reason; my prayers were powerful to them. I had been victimized and didn't think I would ever see my children; I was facing life in prison. While the snake, my ex-husband's wife, was on the outside fabricating my case against me. I had nothing to live for I couldn't defend myself. I decided life wasn't worth living. I stopped eating, hoping I would die. The girls got worried and spoke to the correction officer. They were worried about me and, the correction officer called a counselor and told the counselor there was nothing wrong with fasting. The next day in the late afternoon, I heard what I thought was a shakedown, but they came rushing to my room when suddenly, the girls started yelling from her cells leave her alone, banging on their cell door. Then the MDC supervisor opened my cell and came in. He asked me what was wrong, why won't I eat, and I said, I'm just tired of my life; it's worthless. He then said would you eat for me and, I said, Ok. Two days later, the Supervisor ordered me to his Office. I sat down in his office, and I said to him. I had eaten my food as I promised. He reached into his shirt pocket and gave me a calling card. I said to him have you heard anything on my case; he said no? I said ok and was escorted back to my cell. I met a woman at MDC. Who didn't have anyone to visitors or send her money to put in my books. Just like her but, I helped her out as some of the girls gave her commissary. Her son and girlfriend disagreed, and her son's girlfriend took their child to her house. Then suddenly, early the next morning, the Police and Child Protective Service knocked on her door and took my grandchild and, then the police arrested her for kidnapping her grandchild. she got charged for endangerment by Child Protective Services. Because she had given my grandchild cough medicine. She brought her granddaughter to her with a fever and running nose. The baby had been crying. That was the reason the girlfriend the girlfriend brought the granddaughter to her.

After being incarcerated for almost one year without talking to her public defender, they said, you're released; pack your stuff. There was no court hearing. Her public defender never called regarding she would be released. That was the strange release I have ever seen but, I was happy for her. After all, she was the grandmother.

Then there was a young girl who got caught stealing sandwich meat not worth more than a couple of dollars to feed her two children who were with a friend till

she got back from the store. I had a phone card given to me; she called her friend to tell her she was downtown at MDC for stealing. She waited a little less than a year to see the judge. She had no one to pay her bond to bail her out. Child Protective Service had taken her children away from her. She would have to go to court to get her children back. Instead of child protective service helping her get on her feet. They gave her bad News she needed a job and an apartment, your require a deposit and the first month's rent. So, she had to stay on the street till she saved enough money from work to get her children back. I was so proud of myself. Sometimes that's what it takes—the love of your children. Life isn't easy and worth living without having—someone to love and love you back.

The other story I heard was when I was in medical, we all had to go to medical.

I listened to a guy talking. He had been there for five months. He was at a baseball game with his son and, he didn't want to leave his son alone too long but, he had to pee. The line was long. He looked around and had decided no one would see him if he went behind the building and, take a leak. When an off-duty police officer followed him and said he had seen him peeing, called for back-up, was handcuffed, and arrested him, and put in the squad car. The police called the children's youth and family to take his son. The little boy was kept in child protective service children's custody for days till the mother called the Police Department and reported her son and her ex-husband missing. Two days later, she found out child protective services were holding her son and, her ex-husband was in jail. After that, his ex-wife filed for full custody of his son and was confident the courts would give her full custody. Child Protective Services never tried to contact the mother. Her son cried and asked to call his mother but, he wasn't allowed.

When he got out, he would have lost everything visitation right to his son, his apartment, the stuff he owned, and his job. That's how the system works? He could be scared as a child molester. You don't realize after being held in a Detention Center waiting to be put on the s docket. Then you're found not guilty and released. You have nowhere to go. Most inmates wait for a year to get the Judge on the docket heard when the judge says you're free to go.

You ended up homeless, and you've lost your job; most lose their families and everything you owned. You have no choice but to apply for food stamps but, first, you need to find a place to live, then you can get approved for food stamps which is not much.

It's only enough for two weeks you get money to spend $184.00 a month for a single person, even if you buy beans, rice, macaroni, and cheese. Most people who get food stamps sell some of their stamps to buy hygiene because you can't use them except for food; it's embracing to pay with food stamps, but what can you do. Now about recertification. You won't receive a notice for recertification. Your food stamps get canceled if you get them on a Friday, you can't reapply till Monday and, it's a holiday; you end up losing three days of your food stamps after recertifying you've lost three days till you get them. You end up with seventy dollars till the next month. After you requested a hearing for not receiving the 40 %, the President gave the elderly and low-income. Your food stamps got canceled until the hearing; then, we said you needed to recertify. Then you received eight different letters for a fair hearing request, a notice of appointment, a schedule of fair hearing, and information of case action. Then you can't recertify till after the hearing in three weeks, or you can recertify over the phone if you withdraw your request for a hearing. You have no choice but, to reapply or your food stamps for next month would be less to add the 40% from $187.00 a month even if your income had not changed. You'll end up with very little. So, if you look down at people who are forced to get food stamps, we aren't lazy bums there like you and those who worked hard most of their lives, and when things happens. I was fortunate that my counselor helped me get my birth certificate, driver's license. Then I had no choice but to apply for a food stamp. After receiving food stamps for a month, I ordered to appear at the Human Service Office. I went to the hearing with my counselor. We sat in her Office for 37 minutes while waiting for the Supervisor at the Human Service Department to find my file.

She then made a phone call to someone regarding my file. At the same time, we sat in my Office. The person on the other side of the phone said we didn't know where it was, so the Supervisor went over her notes. Still, found no file at the end of the meeting. Were told I could not receive food stamps for one year and could reapply then. Later I received a letter from Human Services. Enclosed is a copy of my criminal charges. Annie had given them. FRAUD (over $2,500) third-degree felony. Human Service. I was issued a Medicaid card for my daughter and my grandson that was never used. They then denied my food stamp; I asked a friend to take me to the storehouse. That is a food bank to get some groceries, but I felt embarrassed and couldn't go in when we got there.

I couldn't get the nerve to go in, so I asked him to take me home. Days later, I had no choice but to asked my counselor to take me to the storehouse to get food. All they had was expired can food, and lots of bread and cakes stuff I couldn't eat sweets. It would kick in my sugar. It was already in the 400 and, that could cause me to die. It was embarrassing; I couldn't believe it. I had worked all my life and, now this I couldn't handle it. I didn't know how to go from everyday life to losing everything I owned, sold even my car. It's was the worse feeling ever. I couldn't retrieve some of my stuff; I would have to go to court and, I had enough of court, so I just let it go. The craziest thing was that I helped others but, now that I needed their help, there was no one to help me. I had been abandoned by those whom I would have thought would have been there for me.

I thought to myself for those who hurt me and made me suffer; I could never find it in my heart to forgive them. They had selfishly crucified me. I ask God to forgive them for me. I feared for my own life. I couldn't say or do anything till after I completed probation. I didn't want to give Annie and the Judge a reason to have me sent to prison.

The judge gave me probation. What else was left for the judge to do? I was crucified by the only person who knew me and those who didn't know me who followed Annie and believed what they heard. Gossiping is a sin and is mostly lies. My Public Defender did not allow me to say a word but, that didn't matter. The judge had sentenced me Unsympathetically.

Five years later the District Court Judge was now facing his own dilemma and, was taken off the bench. Even though he used my as an example; in Court. The Judge was charged with Rape by a Prostitute. She was a prostitute not an innocent victim. My saying is You can't rape the willing. The person who brought in the evidences to the district attorney office was the Prostitutes' boyfriend. It sounds like a set-up he had tape recorded everything and, the crazy thing about it was the Judge wrote here a check. What prostitute excepts a check they usually want cash. The judge was known to be a fair judge. The he was arrested on rape charges and, placed in jail. The Judge was on life support crutches and, about four feet tall and could barely get up how could the Judge had raped a healthy woman. I heard her boyfriend took the pictures and, recorded the sex act. The set-up costed the Judge his job. As a Judge now he knows how felt. There had to be someone that wanted him out of the court bench and, had him set-up. It's funny how karma works. He could have done a lot for the Second Judicial District Court system for a lot of people.

Other judges under microscope

Here are some of the judicial misconduct cases that have damaged careers and reputations over the years:

- Appeals Court Judge Robert Robles resigned this year after a drunken driving arrest.
- Bernalillo County Metro Court Judge Victoria Grant retired in 2010, ending an investigation into allegations of judicial misconduct.
- District Judge Bob Schwartz of Albuquerque last year was reprimanded.
- Bernalillo County Metro Judge J. Wayne Griego was removed from the bench in 2008 for fixing traffic tickets.
- Appeals Judge Ira Robinson retired in 2008 rather than face misconduct allegations.
- Third Judicial District Judge Larry Ramirez of Las Cruces resigned in 2006 amid accusations of sexual harassment.
- District Judge Thomas Fitch of Socorro pleaded guilty to drunken driving in 2005 and resigned.
- W. John Brennan, former 2nd Judicial District Court chief judge, resigned in 2004 after he was arrested on drunken-driving and drug (cocaine) possession charges. He had been chief judge for almost two decades. Brennan later resigned and pleaded guilty.

NEWS ALERT:Judge Pat Murdoch Arrested On Rape Charges

www.nmnewsandviews.com/2011/07/19/news-alertjudge-pat-murdoch...
Albuquerque police have arrested criminal **judge Pat Murdoch** who is in the Second Judicial District Court in Bernalillo County on charges of rape.

Albert S. "Pat" Murdoch - Judgepedia

judgepedia.org/index.php/Albert_S._"Pat"_Murdoch
Albert S. **"Pat" Murdoch** was a District Court **judge** in the Second Judicial District of New Mexico. He retired from the court on July 29, 2011. Allegations of rape

Murdoch's lawyers say the judge is the victim — read their ...

newmexico.watchdog.org/8427/murdochs-lawyers-say-the-judge-is-the...
Attorneys for **Judge** Albert "Pat" **Murdoch** say the district court **judge** is the real victim in an arrest that saw one of the most well-known **judges** in the state ...

Probation

The judge sentenced me to five years probation; they would help me get back on my feet. I lost everything. I went on probation with only the clothes on my back, I had no food, my car was sold. I couldn't get a job till my probation officer met with me. My probation became a living hell. It was bad enough dealing with life on the outside. I feared someone would recognize me from the News or Annie and Jakes appearances on the talk shows. I felt undemonstrative. I didn't know what to do. I thought being on probation would help me get back on my feet. It was bad enough dealing with life on the outside.

I feared leaving my apartment. I couldn't get an apartment, they did a background check, so the only place I could get is an apartment where all the felonious lived. The apartment I had applied at had refused me. A month later the apartment complex had blown up someone had a meth lab. Some background check. There shouldn't be a wait to get into an apartment I remember when my sister had an emergency move in problem, she had the money and needed an apartment to move away from her abusive husband. There should be a law against not being able to get an apartment. Most of the people with a clean record are worse than a felon. The difference is they haven't gotten caught. I feared going to the grocery store and riding the bus to report to my probation officer, hoping my probation officer wasn't in a bad mood, and transport me to metropolitan detention center for whatever reason, or they didn't need an explanation. Whenever I reported to my probation officer, even if my charges had nothing to do with drugs, I didn't drink alcohol or take illegal drugs or smoke. Can you imagine how much a drug test is costing the city or the state of New Mexico? The probation officer gave me a drug test every time I had to meet with the probation officer, but she was in court another probation officer Kim asked for a drug test right away but, I couldn't pee. It was hard for me to pee. Especially when you have someone watching you. The embarrassment of exposing your body while the probation officer stared at my pussy as she called it, with a smirk on her face. I couldn't pee. My body froze and, I felt deprived of my rights to my body. I kept drinking water but, I couldn't pee. I tried for half-hour.

I peed a little bit; the probation officer said it wasn't enough and tossed it in the toilet and, then Kim, the probation officer, came back in a furious mood and said I need to go home soon. If you don't pee in five minutes, I'm going to have you transported to the detention center. I tried again and, I sat on the toilet seat and prayed. Oh God, please help me pee. Please, please, God helps me pee, but I couldn't I got up and went to the hall to drink more water. Oh no, my stomach couldn't take it anymore more; I felt ill. I thought to myself. Oh my God, I think I'm going to explode. I felt sick from drinking Sooo much water. Kim said she would send me to jail for disobeying an order and, I said I'll try again. I went for the third time to the bathroom and tried again. I did pee a little bit; Kim said it wasn't enough and dumped it in the toilet again. Then my probation officer walked in. She had been in court. She asked how I was doing and, I said I was having a hard time trying to pee and, Kim said she was going to send me to jail for disobeying an order.

My probation officer then said can you try now. I said yes. We both went to the bathroom and, I sat down and could only pee a little again. My probation officer looked at it and said, that's enough and labeled it. I said I had peed more for Kim and, she dumped it in the toilet. My probation officer then said on your next appointment. I need you to keep a record of all visitors and scheduled visits with my probation officers starting in February 2011. I didn't have any visitors. Except for my counselors and my probation officer came unexpectedly; whenever they wanted to come check-up on me? I wrote every meeting with my probation officers and made copies for my probation officers, counselors, and the district court judge file.

I feared being left alone when I knew Annie was still out.

The judge would be putting me in prison for the entire term of the **forty-one years for not complying with my probation.**

The bad behavior of my probation officers and her supervisor while on probation. Annie was part of calling and informing the probation officers of insufficient information against me. I continued to see my counselor on my own for two years. On a one-to-one basics, every Wednesday night, counseling classes mainly were for drugs and alcohol abusers and, I didn't drink, smoke, or take drugs but, I feel as if I was now taking all kinds of medicines and insulin-like shooting up. I thought the class was interesting. At first, my counselor couldn't believe my story, so he called the district court counselor to whom I was assigned after talking with her, he was surprised. I didn't know what my counselor said to him but, he wanted to help me and, he wrote out a check for $100.00 to buy what I needed. We met for three years. He then moved out of town; his wife had heart problems and needed to see a specialist in a different state.

Five years later, the District Court Judge was now facing his own dilemma and taken off the bench. However, he used me as an example in court. Karma is an authentic the district judge was charged with rape. She was a prostitute, not an innocent victim. You can't rape the willing. The person who brought the evidence to the district attorney's office was the prostitutes' boyfriend, sounds like a set-up. She had tape-recorded everything and, the crazy thing about it was the judge wrote her a check. What prostitute excepts a check they usually want cash. The judge was known to be a fair judge. Then he was arrested on rape charges and placed in jail. The judge was on life support crutches and, about four feet tall, he could barely get up; how could the judge have raped a healthy woman. I heard her boyfriend took the pictures and recorded the sex act. The set-up cost the judge his job. As the judge who sentenced me as an example now, he knows how I felt. There had to be someone that wanted him out of the court bench and had him set up. It's funny how Karma works. He could have done a lot for the Second Judicial District Court system for many people.

February 07, 2011   I had an Ear Infection My immune system was at risk of complications. Can be life threatening. The Infection may spread and, affect other parts of my body.

February 10, 2011   Reported to see Probation Officer Kim not

in checked in with Dan male Probation Officer went ok.

February 14, 201   Swimmer's Ear Infection I couldn't get out of bed.

February 17, 2011   Met again with Probation Office Dan. I was very sick with **Swimmer's Ear Infection** I couldn't hear. He said go Home everything looks ok.

February 24, 2011   I went to the Hospital ER I called my Probation Officer Kim.
I waited for several hours and, couldn't stand the pain.
I decided to go home and, left the ER and, went home to bed.

March 01, 2011   Went to the First Nation Community Clinic the next day I had lost my hearing.

March 02, 2011   I was in counseling probation officer Kim left a message that I had a warrant for My arrest.

March 03, 2011   Surprise home visit Kim requested I see her on Monday at her office at 1:45 pm

March 6, 7, 8 2011   Went to see Kim at 1:37 pm Kim sent me to MDC for three days for being a liar, that I was sick with swimmers ear infection. I couldn't hear and, was sent to the MDC. When being booked the Transportation Clerk Maggie said to the Booking Officer laughing poor Drama Queen she lost my hearing ha ha.

March 09, 2011   I was still sick with Swimmer's Ear Infection. After being released from MDC Probation Officer Kim said to me. You may have Completed Federal Probation but, you won't get away with it here. One of the inmates overheard Kim.

March 10, 2011
Probation Officer Kim was not in. I was seen by Pete I gave him my Medical Record and, visit with the Doctor as requested by Kim

March 17, 2011
Reported to Kim I had seen my Probation Officer sitting in the lobby While I was waiting to be seen I waited over a half hour till Karen was ready to see me Kim was talking and, talking about her personal life with the Receptionist till she was ready to see me. she then walked up to the window and, said you can go now.

March 23, 2011
Called Kim that I had a Doctor appointment. tomorrow at 2:15 pm. Can I see you before or after my Doctor appointment. Kim said after

March 23, 2011
I went to see Kim at 3:42 for my 4 o'clock appointment. Kim passes by after waiting for 45 min. Kim said you know what It's getting late just come back tomorrow.

March 24, 2011
I was the first one in the office waited to see Kim I waited for a half hour till Kim felt ready to see me, five people came and, went, and there I sat waiting. The other probation officers volunteered to see me but, Kim said I needed to talk to her.

April 07, 2011   Kim wasn't in seen by Sam. Ok go home

April 14, 2011   Kim said O.k. You can go home.

April 20, 2011   Surprise home visit from Kim at 7:35am.

April 21, 2011   Kim had me arrested. My Neighbor told the
                      probation officer.
                      I had a visitor. Who she claimed was an
                      X-felon, hearsay.
                      I wasn't even home. I was at counseling till
                      8pm when the bus dropped me off by my
                      home. I asked how long was I going to be at
                      MDC Kim said she was going to teach me a
                      lesson.

Note: While waiting for Kim to Transported me to MDC. I sat in the CCU Office. When Kim Supervisor sat down on her chair and, looked at me. Like she had all the power in the world and, said I'm going to call the Judge to have you put in prison. She said you have a long probation ahead of you. You won't make it. The Supervisor had several calls from Annie. Annie said, I had been charged with perjury. Do not trust her. Annie wanted her restitution. Restitution really everything I owned was taken from me. I had no car, food, money or a job, and they were millionaires.

April 24, 2011   I was released from MDC Easter Sunday at
                      5:35pm,

April 25, 2011   Kim my Probation Officer then placed me
                      on-curfew Kim said, you can't go out before
                      8am and, be home by 6pm and, see my twice
                      a week Monday and, Thursday between 2:30

----

and 3:30pm I had counseling at 6pm I had to cancel.

May 05, 2011   Met with Kim went ok.

May 09, 2011   Kim requested I do Community Service.

May 12, 2011   Reported to Kim after completion of Community Service.

May 16, 2011   Met with Probation Officer Kim went Ok.

May 17, 2011   Surprise Home Visit 5:28 am, Kim said come in on she said come in Friday will be busy on Thursday

May 20, 2011   Went to see Kim it went Ok.

May 23, 2011   " " " "

May 26, 2011   Kim came to the window and, said sign in and, I did Kim then said you can go.

May 30, 2011   Kim said go home.

June 02, 2011   Met with Agnes Kim Supervisor said Annie called did she make her restitution. I thought to myself how could my ex-husband need restitution when he just won over a Million Dollars from the DNA hearing.

June 03, 2011   Surprise home visit 7:28 am Kim was hoping I wasn't home I wasn't allowed out till eight in the morning Kim had been watching me. My counselors came to see me at home. She took me to see my other counselor at his office.

June 06, 2011	Kim wasn't in seen by Art he said everything seem ok go home.
June 09, 2011	Seen by Lesly she asked if I was ok. I said no she let me go home
June 13, 2013	Kim requested counseling report.
June 16, 2011	Seen by Pat he said it looks good.
June 20, 2011	Seen by Kim ok received progress report nothing to report
June 22, 2011	Surprise home visit 9:53 pm by Kim
June 23, 2011	Seen Kim ok
June 27, 2011	Kim requested update Diabetic Medication list.
June 30, 2011	Assigned to new Probation Officer. Who requested to write list of anyone visiting me.
July 07, 2011	Frist meeting with New Probation Officer went well.
July 14, 2011	Probation Officer was not in met with Les.

July 28, 2011   Kim surprise visit 7:39am per Supervisor Agnes take me to MDC for Associating with x-felon. Her supervisor said you're going to Prison.

August 03, 2011   Met with both Kim and, Jacky I wasn't allow to talk to any of my friends Kim claimed I was talking to an X-felon who came from out of town both Probation Officer. Did a background check on my friend who had the same name on the office Computer. It was the Wrong person he wasn't a felon. Then they said you can go home and, continue your visitation list.

August 11, 2011   Seen Jacky ok

August 18, 2011   My Probation Officer Jacky said my Supervisor received a letter from Annie she wants her restitution money ASAP.

August 25, 2011   Then my probation officer said I needed to log in where ever you go and, if I disobey her she would put me on an ankle bracelet and, if she does a home and, I don't answer the door she will call the police to open my door.

September 01, 2011   I was sick when I went to see my probation officer she said go home.

September 08, 2011   Still sick Jacky said ok go home.

September 22, 2011 " " " " "

September 29, 2011 Sill sick went to see Janet sent home

October 06, 13, 2011 Met with Jacky she said Annie called. she wanted her restitution money Jacky said to her supervisor. The money order hadn't been log in and, mailed. My neighbors gave me some stuff and, I had a yard sale and, I was able to make restitution.

October 14, 2011 Home visit Jacky my probation officer came at 10:30pm. I lived alone in a bad Neighborhood I feared for my life. I answered the door wondering who was there. Make sure you get the restitution on your next visit.

November 03, 09, 23, 30, 2011 Annie continued to check in with the Supervisor she wanted her restitution; And, continued to say I was a bad person.

December 01, 08, 15 22, 2011 Went to see Jacky everything was ok and, then I went home.

December 29, 2011 My next check in appointment with Jacky was at the end of December
My Probation ended on December 22, 2011. I waited before I met with Jacky
After my probation so they wouldn't find an excuse to keep me on probation.
When I said my probation ended on December 22, she said **go**, home.

I feared being left alone when I knew Annie
was still out there. but, the Judge would not
be putting my in prison for the full term to be
served of **forty-one years for not complying
to Probation. . .**

The bad behavior of my probation officers and, her supervisor
while on probation. Was part of Annie calling and, informing the
probation officers of bad information against me. I continued
to see my counselor on my own for two years. On a one-to-one
basics every Wednesday night counseling classes were mostly for
drugs and, alcohol abusers and, I didn't drink smoke or take drugs
but, I feels as if I is now taking all kinds of drugs and, insulin
like shotting up. I felt that the class was interesting. At first my
counselor couldn't believe my story so he called the district court
counselor who I assigned for myself to and, he was surprised. I
didn't know what my counselor said to him but, he wanted to help
me and, he wrote out a check for $100.00 to buy what I needed.
We met for three years. He then moved out of town; his wife was
having heart problems and, needed to see a doctor in a different
state.

Charges Filed Against Me

FINDING OF FACT: My main concern; Is why they would transport me to a hearing from a camp in Arizona when I had one month before the ended of my sentencing. The court sent a subpoenaed to the camp for me to attend. I had no defense Attorney for the DNA hearing after returning to the Camp. I realized someone had sabotaged the transporter to stop me from getting to court. How and who had that kind of authorization?

a. The courts determined there was no child. Why then did Annie call the police that my daughter was being mistreated?

b. Jake testified child support payments to the petitioner? Jake lied on the Affidavit ordered by attorney II signed and notarized, paying a total of **$8,850.00**. Had Jake stated garnishment of his paycheck for **$14,198.00**? It was fake my public defender would not investigate— Jake's employer as given to the courts as evidence.

c. The IRS records never claimed a false claim of my non-extent child, as the Investigators reported. There were three different dates of the birth of my daughter as were of mine. Other discrepancies were in their finding to the court. It should have been a miss-trail or investigated.

d.   Five judges took the cases for the exact charges; I was placed on probation by the district court Judge. Not including all the domestic violence hearings in the city of Rio Rancho and Albuquerque. The domestic violence wasn't probable. They were all dismissed. I was confused from attending all the court hearings; I didn't know what was going on. I kept wondering what each judge had to say but, they all wanted to know the whereabouts of my daughter; I felt confused and ashamed as Annie waited to hear the judge say lock her up and throw the key away. As I held my head down low and, I cried, not knowing what would happen next. The judge sentenced me to five years' probation. Life on probation can only make your life worse. What probation officer helps an ex-con make it in the outside. I made it with the help of my counselors. I had no change of clothes, no job, money. My probation officer had their hands tied. The probation supervisor was on a power trip. I was lucky. I had three counselors' who helped me.

e.   Released: I feared going out. I was afraid that someone would recognize me from all the publicizes Annie broadcasting against me. I had no voice. I lost so much in my life I didn't care if life went on or not. How could I reach out to those who didn't know me, the judge, jurors, and probation officers, talk show, radio announcers, the list goes on? Who cared enough to help a poor old soul like me. My Counselors understood my needs. As my soulmate did Annie made me look like the greedy person taking money for a child that didn't exist, I will never give my daughter to the hand of the court or my ex-husband. I would rather go to prison for forty-one years if needed. But losing my daughter was not an option. I put my ex-husband through college and supported him for years.

Including his thousand-dollar bike and the uniform he used to run marathons, karate; the list goes on, not including the money he took we had saved for the children's education.

Those were the Days

W hen we were young, the police would come and say it's almost curfew, pack it up in a friendly way, when we were teenagers. If you were caught speeding, the police would say, you know why you were stopped? You were over the speed limit, and would give you a warning ticket and ask you to be safe. And keep the pedal off the metal. They weren't on a power trip. It felt good to see a police joke and respect you and care for your safety.

We are surrounded by state police, the sheriff, city police, and the unmarked police. How could they say we need more police after the officers have killed innocent bystanders. How do we know how our children were killed. The police need a camera on their car or wear one on their lapel. It's for their own safety. We blame the system you made them what they are power trip.

Police and children watch bad movies with killing shooting violence. The police become heroes for killing instead of serving and protecting our community, as do the children and adults who want to act like they were in a movie. We need to talk with our children. Stop making, and seeing movies with violence and showing more color. We need to teach our children that we all matter. Do you fear to call the police? Who may be trigger happy? We give them the weapons to use against us. Why can't they come out with a less violent weapon? When you have power you miss use it. A power trip can kill you. I know a police officer who ran into an old school mate who made fun of him in high school. He figured its time for a pay back her planted narcotics, and a gun in his car enough to put him in prison for nine years. The man had a wife, and three children who moved on, and left him to stay in prison instead of helping him their had to be a way of finding his innocents. Years later the police was dismissed from the police force for disorderly conduct as he had been reported using violence against others he had arrested. Karma is real.

For example, the homeless man up in the Sandia Mountains was shot by several police officers. A bystander citizen took the footage. Called the police because the homeless man was yelling to get out his frustrations, not till later in court, they claim he had a pocket knife for their defense of the police's responsible. How else can a homeless man open a can of Pork and, Beans? Besides, it was in his pocket. Then there was a school police who dragged a girl—she was taken by the police down the hall by her hair outside the school to be transported to the detention center. The teacher reported the little girl disobeying her teacher and refused to do her work-study with the other children. The poor girl was having a bad day.

Then, we have the teenage runaway. Who was found sleeping in a car? The owner called of a drunk or drug addict in a vehicle. When she saw the police coming towards her. She feared the police. Got up quickly and ran knowing the police would arrested her, and be sent to MDC; the police grabbed his gun, she ran till she dropped dead on the ground. Instead of the police could have run after her and trying to talk to her but chose not to as most police are overweight, and, not physically fit. We need police who understand our needs. She was unarmed and, pregnant on the street homeless confused a first-time runaway in the streets. You need to know what to do and where to go. What was not told by the News was that the girl wasn't just a runaway but, pregnant?

Fake News Again, the News announced what can be done to have better police; the answer is that we need more police and training. They need to use commonsense and training with people's problems that why we call 911 were in need, it's an emergency number which never gets answered call, and time it I did it took them 23 minutes to tell me I had to talk to someone else then after waiting and finally got someone on the line they said you can't report your car stolen I need more information that was in my car. But, I could get it from my insurance company. Another half hour wait by now there on their way to California with my car. Police who kill an innocent people should have to pay for their crime. Trust me, life is strange and, you may be at the wrong place at the wrong time. We don't need more police. Are you kidding? It takes five police to pick up a drunk on the street. That's what you'll see in the Land of Entrapment. You'll read how I had a line of dangerously armed police who came to my house to check on my daughter's wellbeing. So how do you figure the police were armed, ready to open fire for the safety of my daughter.

My sister Felix feared calling the police. When her husband abused her, she was afraid to go to her own home because she knew she would get beaten up by her husband and end up in the hospital. When you call 911 on domestic violence, there usually armed police. Who will either take you to jail or kill you? I miss my sister Felix. May she rest in peace. Most women don't want to end up at a battered women's home. It's the worse place to be. But, for most women, it's the only place they have.

Why can't there be apartments to go to not like a hotel but, a place you can call home. Till you can get on your feet. Most apartment complex get government money to rent you an apartment but, when you leave to go to work or just out they come into your apartment and search I know my dog was kicked by maintenance workers, and broke his ribs. When they went in my dog who is small barked at them as they were strangers. My dog was traumatized, I couldn't get him to eat or come to me till he felt safe.

We do have more than a few good police and, they have the right to protect themselves. Anything can happen. Most of us notice, the judges feel they have to blame someone for the public to see justice has been served. They say that we have the most considerable crime rate here in the land of entrapment. We have a neighborhood watch here in my area. With technology, we have cameras, cells phones, and so on.

Prison should be for people who cannot be helped, like murders and sex offenders who rape women they don't know and continue to rape, not on a one-time basis. Some women allow men to have sex with them, but if the sex goes wrong. Women have a way of hating a man. Who just wanted to have sex or didn't love her anymore for their use; women show off their boobs, legs, and whatever else to get a man's attention. They look for opportunities. The attorney looks for the prospect to sentence the sex offender, especially if they have money. The court system should not mark a man as a Sex offender on a one-time sex mishap. Women will make a one-night stand or mistake that looks and sound like rape. The attorneys are trained to make it sound worse than a one-night stand or a sugar daddy point of view.

Have you ever had sex, and it just didn't feel right, or you just wanted to have sex? It's called horny, not rape. Young girls change from little girls to women and have no idea what happened. They get Horney, at twelve-year-old girl who then becomes a mother. Life has changed for them. It's not a joke; becoming a woman, it's not just growing up but facing life. You're old enough to know what you're doing.

Men with money are usually a good target. Until the woman changes either because she falls in love or has gotten her fame and doesn't need her so-called Sugar Daddy. They will write books and fantasies the story to make you feel sorry for them. It should go both ways. I know from experience how a young girl screamed rape because her boyfriend was with another woman. She calls 911.

The attention she received was unbelievable. Years later, I ran into her. She had gained weight and looked terrible. Karma will get you.

Why can't you watch a good movie with your family? Where are the good old movies like the Pretender, Mash, Perry Mason, J. Leno talk show? When he did street smart, how is it that a college student didn't know what a yellow light meant? Then their NCIS, The Good Doctor, only comes out once a week. Now you've got to see Providence with Frank Caprio, a brilliant Court Judge. Can you imagine going to court and being heard and recognized like that? We need more caring judges like him in every courtroom as we all make mistakes and should be heard. I'm sure they wouldn't want to face the judge again, as he gave them a break. I like to watch La Rosa de Guadalupe, the Mask Singer, and, most of all, hallmark Christmas movies. Oh, and you can't forget Steve Harvey on Family Feud. The sad thing about the family feud is that most contestants are wealthy and have great jobs and, their kids are in a good college, and a future. It should be for ordinary people who work at a minimum wage job and can't afford a vacation.

The worse TV show I've seen is REPO they show the repo man working out in a ring boxing then they call the person and tell them their car is being repo of course there wait for someone to come out mad with fear of losing their car the one lady starts pushing a man and her brother get into it with them it's so sad why can't they boot the tire or take the car quietly it's all about fighting and taken their anger out on the person who didn't or couldn't pay for their car, and gets repo these men, and women have anger issues and take it out on others. It's a power trip. The shame of being shown on TV is a crime. Find something to show that is good like the other repo guy who tries to give them a chance to get there car by answering some questions. Like a game show. God Bless you for trying.

Then there's music; I'm glad there the TV show the Voice. It gives others to show their talent. I believe that the best music ever made was the fifties and early sixties and, most of all, Country Music will live forever as well. It's the best music to listen to; it's spiritual. I met a man from Cuba who learned to speak English by listening to the oldies and, country music because he could understand the song.

I like to see celebrity dress up and look good like. It gives young girls ideas on what to were on their prom or a wedding. The celebrities are more than they know the girls from the Real dress nice.

Women have become sloppy and don't dress up as I did in my days. If you had a professional job, you had to look the part. I went to the city hall before the coronavirus. The lady who helped me was wearing her pajamas to work. How weird is that? Believe it or not when you dress up you feel good when you look and dress sloppy you feel lazy and don't care. Wake-up and smell the coffee life is worth living only you can make a differentness. Look good feel-good dress up to go grocery shopping or visit a friend. You'll feel the difference trust me.

You need to see the show What Would You Do? With John Quinones, My soulmate always said to me; you have a place in heaven. For example, when I went to the grocery store and was behind a woman who didn't have enough to pay for her groceries, I said, wait, I'll pay for it. The Clerk said that was nice of you. Don't get me wrong; I had a young man pay for my stuff for no reason at all. The strangest thing I had ever witnessed was that my soulmate has more money than I do and never thought of helping a person in need. Except his own, how sad is that? Then there was a young girl with her three children who had overspent. She told her kids they had to put some of it back. I again said add it to my stuff. The mother asked if she could pay me back; I said no, it's ok. The woman insisted that I give her my address a week later; I got a Thank you card and the money I had paid for her stuff. I have given my last two dollars literally to a person who is really in need. That's one reason my soulmate says you have a place in heaven all the time. I think he should try it, but his money is his to spend. Trust me; God will provide. Pay Forward I even help; when someone has car trouble, I carry cables in my car. So when I watch the show with John Quinones, I cry on every show.

I said to my self Be there, done that. Hey, when you get to be my age, you don't have anything to do. Except for watching TV, it becomes your best friend, and so does Volunteering. I did for over fifteen years for different organizations. I had my great-grandchildren with me. We were looking for a good cartoon movie to watch. I couldn't believe who was making those children's movie. You call that person a superhero. The movies I grew up with were funny, not scary or killings. The Disney movies have bad storytelling like Bambi, his mother gets killed, and snow-white, the witch is evil, giving poison to a girl. The language is terrible. I would like to see a true Christmas story of a struggling family at Christmas who finally had a wonderful Christmas. Christmas should be the ultimate family being together. Thanksgiving has always been the time of family fights but, the truth is it's your family. You need one another. Sure they may have a great job or a big house, but what is in your heart When you were young you all were best friends; things have changed. When my grandson was young, We would buy our grandson all the Disney movies. Now that he's older, I pack most of the movies and noticed when my son said Mom did you know Mickey Mouse never had suspenders. I said what.

My great-granddaughters started watching the new version of the Disney movies like Mickey Mouse, Snow White. I questioned myself and, friends did Micky Mouse have suspenders. What happened to Mickey Mouse's Suspenders? They said Micky's shorts were going to fall off and, we laughed. Mickey Mouse suspenders have been taking way. However, they did leave the two buttons on his shorts where Micky used to have his Suspenders hooked up to Micky Mouse indeed had Suspenders. If you buy a Mickey Mouse T-shirt or anything with Mickey Mouse on it. He doesn't have suspenders anymore. Then another Disney movie my great-grandchildren like is Snow White. Ask your parents or grandparents about the movie Snow White. You may be surprised to know that your memory of the Evil Queen says to the Magic Mirror. Was it? "Mirror, Mirror, on the wall" Who is the fairest of them all? "The Mirror, Mirror" the lines have changed to "Magic Mirror" on the Wall who the fairest of them all." My son asked me how do you spell Folders Coffee and, I answered Folders that also changed to Folgers. If your grandparents have an old Tin can of Folders Coffee, you'll see it's spelled Folders Coffee, Not Folgers. The other thing they noticed was the Cereals and, Chocolates don't have the same taste. They taste like some residue of toxic chemicals. It's been said that glyphosate and arsenic are without consumers' knowledge or consent. Glyphosate arsenic has been tentatively linked to cancer. There have been traces of weed-killer in their Cereals. Then their soda I never cared for Diet Soda. What chemical was added to that??? Energy drinks kill people. My sister drank a couple of energy drinks; to help her make it. through the day, her heart started pounding hard. She ended up having a heart attack. What I can't understand is why these things have changed and, for what reason? Is it a mind control thing? Are they getting in too deep by not questioning these changes? The soil to grow their fruits, vegetable, and feed for animals all have chemicals. Why did they need to change these things? God help us in making this a better world. Bring us a leader who knows it's wrong to hold back information to the people and allow us to have freedom of choice. Who let the protesters in the white house? as seen on video, the police were waving them to go inside. The Talk shows are no longer fun to watch or hear they have become gossip and hurtful. I heard a person say him against the death penalty but, they should put President Trump on 5X8 cell. Be careful karma, a bitch. Are they making fun of our President? Trump has a hard job. Do you think you can do better? They elected him to be their President. You don't see other Countries making fun of their President. They respect their President whether or not they like their President. Are we trying to make our Vote count? Most people know that our votes don't count. Why do we have to hide in a booth to Vote? Show us our Vote it counts. We've taken the time to vote. Why not show us where you added my Vote. Put it up on the board; we have the right to vote for who we choose were grown-ups, not some kid that needs to be told what to do. Do you ever have someone ask you who you are voting for? Yeah, most people won't say. It's my Vote you can choose who you prefer. I voted for the first time for Trump. What do I care what you think. You can't vote for me. I went to the pole to make my Vote count. Don't let others tell you who you should vote for. 2021 Isn't about decimation but asking to show us our vote counts. Ever since Trump became President, he was dragged by the Democrats who accused Trump of everything they could. Who is Biden? Does he have something to hide? The people have the right to know all they hear is Trump did it. Biden, what's your plan. Biden, are you taking votes for Kamala Harris in hopes you expire to take over the presidential seat. As the people would not have voted for her. Biden, you won't make it in office for four years. You look like death is near. You are too old to become our President, and Pelosi, who is old too, is called the Queen of Social Media. She talks about a wall being put up. Have you seen her home? She has the biggest Wall around her home. What is she protecting? The fear of Mexicans camping out on her property. The house has already voted for Biden because they want to teach us that they don't give in to protesters but do to puppets. Did we ever have a President? No, what I can see or hear and, I don't have any politician background 97% of us don't. Why can't they see the protester's side? They just wanted to have a voice. Is it possible that it was a trap that the police were ordered to let them in the white house to blame President Trump? It's called a frame-up. I don't care who becomes President as long as they help our country and the people. So they vote against the rights of their people. What is wrong with these people. Don't protest in anger. It won't get you anywhere. Don't live other people's lives. You don't know what they're feeling. did not take Pelosi computer; they just wanted the people to believe it had been taken to let them believe we were in trouble. Mis-Leading information by the News, talk shows, and anyone else who wants points to be heard. We shouldn't be the Politician puppets. Why do people hide their race, religion, and who they voted for? That's your right F them all that want to judge you for voting for Trump. You now have Biden and this shadow Pelosi, Kamala Harris. Like most of you, I wonder how Kamala got her position. Most women pay the price and step on a lot of toes to get where thereat. I know how that works as I was left behind when irresponsible women wanted the higher position that I knew for a fact that I had the hands-on and education training for the job. I cared for my children, but she could not provide the reports needed in the office after she got them. It took three girls to figure out what she had done. She was later fired and, she then went to the executive director. She reports her old boss for firing her and, put him on suspension without pay. He never did come back, and, as for the woman, I'm sure she found her next victim. You can do anything you want. All it takes is a little hard work. Sometimes, most college students are held back by the universities and won't help them complete that last test to continue their work.

They did it to my son, who has more than enough experience than his boss. Why do people with authority have a power trip instead of working with an employee who makes him look good? They don't live their life, so butt out.

The Mayor bought new ART buses, 60-foot, able to carry up to 42 seated passengers, Mr. Mayor, have you ever been on a bus in Albuquerque?

How do we, the taxpayers, benefit from getting this bus? The only people who ride are homeless who get free bus passes; students have student discounts. Where are we getting the money for a fancy bus like that? We're one of the top poorest States; why would we need this bus. Why weren't we allowed to vote on the important thing in our state? Social Media and the judge's representatives refused to see the big picture when the other women posted the evidence. Why didn't anyone step up? They could have freed me, but instead, they crucified me. We, the people, don't have a Voice. I refuse to vote now; my vote doesn't count do you believe yours dose? Let us stand for what we believe in we count.

Church and Life

My brothers and I first headed up to the church to thank
God for protecting us when we went to work to shine
shoes and, of course, for blessing my homemade burrito
and tamales. I sold to make my share of the money. Each of us
gave tithes of a quarter each Sunday. which was a lot of money
for us but worth it. We could have used it to buy candy but, God
comes first. We figured the church needed the money to pay the
electric and gas bill to be warm and comfortable while the priest
gave service.

We were the first ones in church for Mass every Sunday. In
those days, females were not allowed to enter the catholic church
unless they had a hat or a vail on the top of their head. We always
sat on the third row on the right-hand side in front of the church.
Where we could see and hear what the priest was saying and,
every Sunday, that small short chubby bald man who was the usher
would come up to us in the middle of the service and ask us to give
up our seats for the elders who came in late and, stand in the back
of the church as there was no more seat left. We were small and
couldn't hear the priest from the back of the church. One Sunday,
I finally stood up to the short bald man, and I said, No, we won't
give up our seats. We were here first; we've been here since 6:30
in the morning. Why can't they get up early and get their seats?

Everyone looked at me, and I ran outside crying, and my brothers followed me.

None of the Catholics ever spoke their mind in the church. They all just sat there and stared at us but said nothing. When we went outside to sell our Newspapers. an old man padded me on the top of my head. Like he was sorry.

I remember once my brother decided to go to the Loretto Chapel. My brother and I were bored, so we decided to go to the cathedral church downtown. Where the Spiral Staircase (the "Miraculous Stair"). When we were halfway up the Spiral Staircase, we heard the priests yell out. Hey, get down from there; we turned around and ran down the stairs.

My brother ran past me and, the priest was right behind me; he was ready to punish me for going up on the staircase. I would have gotten a good whipping if he caught me, but I got away. I asked my brother why the priest was so mad. The nuns go up there all the time. There were about thirteen nuns who sang on top of the staircase they had just finished choir practice. Nuns sat down on each step till they got up and down to the top of the staircase to the five benches that were up there. The staircase was spiral-shaped and very narrow; the nuns could only go up the stairs one at a time.

The people in the catholic church, including the priest, made up the stories like when you got married. They say when you get married to death, do you part. God never said that in the bible. Does that mean you would have to kill your spouse to end your marriage? People fall in love, then things happen. I got married in the catholic church. Will I go to hell when my husband was the one who dishonored their marriage? The Catholic believes that it's a sin if you're living with your boyfriend before you get married.

My mother said to me when I was a little girl. You weren't allowed to get married in white. If you had sex before you got married because you're not concerned pure in the house of God

I believed her then, when I got married in the catholic church in white and, was a virgin; look what happened to me but, I also got married at the courthouse which wasn't real to me. When Jake and, I married we both went home as if it never happened—he left for the Navy. I stayed home with my family. Then we planned our wedding in the catholic church. And I left with him to Chicago.

When I was eight or nine years old, I overheard my father talking to my mother about girls becoming sexually active when they start their period. She needed to talk to us. Three girls were growing up in their home. But that never happened.

My sister got pregnant at the age of seventeen after she graduated from high school. She didn't know about birth control like other girls that had been sexually active for the first time. Most girls are sexually active at the age of 13 or even ten and start motherhood. I met a young girl who had a baby girl. The father had abandoned them when she got pregnant. This little girl just had a baby being a baby herself. Her first worry was how she was going to take care of herself and her baby. She needed to find work to support herself and her daughter and someone to watch her daughter while she worked. She could cook, clean and, do other duties but, she wasn't old enough to get hired as she was underage. Her dream was to finish high school. That was important to her.

I was volunteering at a place where we help unwed mothers; they could help her get baby clothes, diapers, and a stroller. It was helpful to her but, that wasn't enough. She needs a place to stay. She couldn't stay on the streets with a baby.

I was out with my friends, one of them was my neighbor. She said her son was moving out, and she needed some help. She lived in a three-bedroom home. I then mentioned my little friend to her and, I took her and her daughter to meet my friend. She said she could help her but needed a place to take her and her daughter while she went to work. She said, "Oh no, dear, you can bring your daughter while you work. She started to work for my neighbor part-time and attended night school. You would be so proud of her. She got her GED at the age of fifteen. She had a high school diploma and was able to care for her daughter later. My neighbor later asked if she would move in with her. She didn't want to live alone; it worked out for both of them. God does provide.

What do you think of abortions? Most people call it murder, but why would you want to have a child after being raped or don't want the pregnancy? The worse story is when she had been forced to have her child, and she didn't like the baby. I heard that she had abused the child, killed it, and ended up in prison; I know she could have given it to a new home. It's not easy to take care of a child, especially when they're sick or hungry. These mothers need a time out. Who will help them look out for their baby? They need time for themself they miss their friends, going out. They're trapped with a child there, forced to raise on their own. It was just the one time she had sex. We need an after-care place for these girls whose family and the baby's father have abandoned them and have moved on to their next victim.

Some kids are in prison for murder for killing a child they did not care for. The child has taken away their liberty; would you take the child into your home and care for it? The answer is no. you're too busy and can't take the time to help our children. They need a place called home for new mothers to help them get on their feet and get a job and a place of their own, and, most of all, have no one to teach them to be a parent. Would you protest on finding them hope?

Instead of protesting against a young confused girl who fears having an abortion because of her religion, she can't get an abortion.

I wondered, if you were to see a Nun pregnant, what would you do? Would the good Catholics stone her to death than go to church' Who are you?

How sad is that? Why can't Priest and, Nuns have sex? When God gave them the same body parts, we all have the same feeling we do. You know what I mean. Were the ones responsible for believing that priests and nuns shouldn't get married or have sex?

We have a priest in prison for having sex with young boys and girls. Some older women go after priests even if they shouldn't.

Who are you to judge? You're not God? But he sees all trust and belief. Now that I am older, I hear many people go to church because they need forgiveness mostly before we die and give tidings hoping God will forgive them; they think God will forgive them for their wrongdoing. God doesn't ask for your money for forgiveness. It's in the Bible that God will not accept gifts of any kind to get you forgiven or go to heaven. Don't get me wrong, we all need to go to church and give tidings to help others here in their own home as we give to the church. You never know when you may need their help.

I believe God is everywhere, so he helps those all over the world. I know of a man and his wife who go to Vietnam to help the people because they hope it will get them to heaven. As you know, many of our soldiers had sex with the women while fighting the war, so we got many women pregnant. He was one of them and may need forgiveness. The truth is they're going about it the wrong way. All you need for forgiveness is remembering Godson died on the cross for us and forgiving God. You can talk to God anywhere; just believe. I love hearing the service at Legacy but, in the Summer and, on a nice day, sometimes like to go to the mountain to pray; I feel at peace and not around many strangers. If a church can help others with your money, you can give it to someone in need? Most people need help as their paycheck isn't enough to make ends meet? And it was hard to care for your children. It's worse when teenagers need a cell phone, tablet, which are expensive.

So we can communicate with our friends and family. When I was raising my children, I never let my children know we were hurting for money. It was my problem to solve and, I kept it in my heart. I had to figure out what was needed in their life. My kids didn't ask for much but, I knew they wanted more, we managed. We have to show a happy face but, deep inside were hurting.

Look around and see what you have, not what you don't have. Some churches will drill you before they lift a finger to you before giving a helping hand. It's embarrassing enough having to ask for help. All we need is the shut-off notice of your utilities or an eviction notice. But we want to know why you got behind on your bill and, how will you make your next month's bill. Show proof of income. Then after they help, they say we can only help once a year. I know I have been there. It's not like I hadn't worked most of my life.?

My friend knew I had nothing to eat or pay my bills. And I didn't say a word and put on my happy face as if nothing was wrong. he knew I needed help when no one else would; I felt as if I was using him. I cried and felt terrible, but I knew he could afford to help me get on my feet. If it wasn't one thing, it was another. He could afford to help me, but I still felt like I was taking advantage of him. I will never forget that he was there for me when I needed him, and I will always be grateful. When he gave me money to survive, I had to pay my bills and eat and buy things I needed. Every time I had to ask him for money, it was hard for me. I couldn't sleep at night, wondering how I could ask him to help me. By then, I had a shut-off notice I was desperate. The fear and the thought of him saying I can't help you even if he could. If only he knew how I was feeling and, hurting the thought of him saying I can't help you would have hurt, I had to swallow my pride. I never had money to do anything for myself. I will always be grateful to my friend; he saved my life. I will always keep him close to me. As I say to everyone, he will always come first. I am so thankful for what you did for me and thank you for thinking of me. We are soulmates forever.

When you needed help, how can you explain to the church or other originations that you needed money because you got divorced or your family wouldn't help you? They will ask, who did you ask for help before you came here? Can't a family member help you or a neighbor? I thought to myself, why do you think they're asking? They had no one? People need money sometimes and, I don't mean those who make it a living asking for money on the street corners, with a kart full of stuff they don't need. There shameful what or why do they need a cart full of junk. If they can stand on the street corner early in the morning till late at night, including holidays, damn it, they can hold a job. We're the ones who inspire them to stand on the street corner.

My car got stolen by two white males, homeless men. When three unmarked police officers found my car, I was so happy till I saw my vehicle cherry-picked by the unmarked police. I didn't know what cherry-picking meant. It means the police can take whatever is of value to them and take it for themselves. The female officer refused to cherry-pick my car. The homeless had jewelry, rolls of money it looked like over a thousand dollars, expensive cell phones, college books, jewelry. My back seat was full of stuff. As I watched, I felt sad. The police are supposed to Service and Protect. Not cherry-pick your car.

Most homeless get disability checks and food stamps. They make your city and the neighborhood look dirty. You make them what they are because you give them money to continue living the way they do. After writing, my story on homeless my son got News that his best friend, whom he thought of as his brother, had died. He had a hard childhood life. His parents died when he was young and, his grandmother raised all of her grandchildren. It was hard for her too. She died after her grandkids graduated.

It was the Christmas of 1999. When my son best friend died. His friend was married and had a daughter. Who sent a Christmas card to her father saying, why are you even alive. That may have triggered his death of committing suicide. It would be best if you thought before you said angry words. When you don't know what that person is going through or suffering. Sometimes we're hurting and say things we don't mean, but we do it. Think before you say anything.

When you go to a funeral, the whole family and old friend come out of the woodwork; you wonder where they were when you were alive? Another one of my son's friends died before then and, his sister walked up to my son at the funeral and said that after his brother's death, his father was murdered, and his mother became homeless. A homeless woman gets beaten up and raped. They would have to stay up at night to keep my guard. The only way to survive is through drugs to keep warm and help with the pain. Her family tried to help her but, she didn't want to live with her daughter. It's been over three years since she has been on the streets. My heart ached. I wanted to find her to help, but I couldn't even help myself. I prayed God would help me even if it's been three long years. Shelters aren't what it seems. My god sister lived in one and, it was sad to hear my stories.

You have to stay to know if it's a Shelter you would rather be out in the street. Why do we treat the homeless like dirt? The people who need your help aren't on the street corner. Most of them end up at the ER in the hospital with stress, wanting to commit suicide after getting laid off from work. They can't get a loan to help them till they get back on their feet. You weren't expecting a disaster; that has put them in a bad situation. I knew what it was. I cried and would instead go without food. The food bank's food is mainly expired food and stuff most can't eat. Like a lot of bread, meat that must be cooked right away. Why can't we give them a food card to buy what they need instead? I watch people buying junk, extra toilet paper and, cleaning supplies. When others need to survive, help your neighbor as those who are materialistic.

When you die, you won't take it with you. Trust in God go to church. Get off your ass and stop feeling sorry for yourself; you never know what you may see. When you go out there, people who are worse than you are. You're the only one who can make a difference. You came to this world dealing with our problems.

Have you read what happens to me. Now I see the world differently. Who the hell do you think you are when we're all having to deal with our dilemmas. Stand up for yourself. Life is short and, we only have one life. Try everything that once especially what you wish; try everything. Do it right. I had nothing but the one pair of jogging pants my neighbor gave me, a man whom I didn't even know, just a neighbor.

After being released, Jake and Annie became millionaires by crucifying me and putting me in prison for forty-one years without feeling how I would suffer. I lost everything my home, car, everything I owned, including all my clothes. At the same time, Jake lived like a king with the millions received. God is real and, so is karma. I thanked my counselors and everyone who helped me. While in Camp, my friend and some of the inmates would go to the chapel and gather every Tuesday and Thursday on a prayer circle and pray for early release for non-violent crimes but, it never happened. After my release from the Camp for filing Improper filing of Income Tax.

I was at the bottom of the barrel and ruined my life. I had nothing to live for. Not just did I lose everything owned but, I lost my best friend, my daughter, whom I have not spoken to since this day and, my family, who would rather hear the gossip of others than figure out the truth. I thank God for my son. I got down on my knees and prayed to God and thanked him for everything I didn't have and what I had. I know what it's like not to have food or a place called home. If there was ever a Miracle, I was living proof. I wanted to punish all those who beleaguered me and make them pay. I had a lot of anger and hate. How could God make them millionaires knowing they got the money dishonest and made others pay and suffer? I wasn't the only one who suffered while their lawyer made it possible to win a case that would cost the blood service and, me, it's worse than blood money but, after I got out, I felt different I had to leave it in God's hands and, move on.

You won't believe what happened to me today. I went to the grocery store to get three items on my list because I only had a five-dollar worth of quarters, and, out of nowhere, I found a twenty-dollar bill right in front of me as if it called me. I looked around there was no one. I knew God put it right in front of me to see because I needed it. I said, Thank you, God, then I went home, lit a candle, and, said God, if the person who lost the twenty dollars needed it, please help them as I did not know whom it belonged to, but I needed it too. I could never tell my friends and family that the only one who knew how poor was my neighbor was because it only became gossip. The person who could have helped me had to find ways to help me. You can't imagine how hard it was to ask him for money even if he had money. It was hurting more to help me, greed. I'm sure friends thought the same thing but, there were times he wanted to help me. I went home and cried because they were so good to me and I had very little to give back. he was the best person in my life. I will never forget him. If I wasn't so sick, I could have gotten a job. But I had good days and bad days. I miss my friend. I know he can't help me anymore, but I think of him all the time, giving than receiving, even when I need help. Who would hire a person who is over the age of 57 years old? Since I worked hard most of my life, I would get a big retirement check to live a better life, but it wasn't enough to pay the rent, then your health goes down south, and so does everything else. All you can do is hope that the younger generation will be Social Security and a better retirement plan.

Most of us worked hard. Most Senior citizens have to continue to work and apply for welfare to make ends meet, and some, like my Aunt, are still working at the age of ninety because she said she have bills to pay. Thank God for my health and, high spirits, and wonderful boss. I have to pay rent, gas, electricity, food and, the list goes on. For those of you who pay a little more on your electric and gas bill to help others who need assistance, that will help LIHEAP won't shut off their utilities.

Thank you. Talk about another government assistance. Where does Section 8 housing get its funding? This woman had overheard one of the section 8 housing supervisors say to one of the section 8 families they were getting evicted from their homes. Then the other housing employee found it to be like a power trip to put someone out in the street, but what we should be doing is helping those in need.

The government is throwing away the money in housing, with section 8 apartments are being built, and landlords are buying more properties. Why can't section 8 occupants own their own homes? Section 8 homeowners would only have to call the section 8 office if they had a change in income which is very seldom or not paying the mortgage. Being a homeowner, your would save money by not having all those employees sitting around doing nothing except forcing an elderly to pay more than 30% of her income after recertified housing when I lived at my home for over three years. I was paying 98% of my check went to section 8 housing.

There was a woman who was told she might no longer get help with housing.

You stuck it cost you move to another place, you'll need a deposit, moving cost not just the moving but the time it takes to move and if your old it's hard to pack to get the moving truck loaded. You're living on a steady income; why do you even need to be recertified every year? Your income won't change. You are basically at risk.

If you rent a two-bedroom or a three-bedroom, the rent may be the same in cost. Why is one person qualified for the amount of a two-bedroom worth more than a three-bedroom? It doesn't make sense section 8 housing authority is supposed to help you with rent & subsidy in a living home. However, today, the section 8 housing specialist said re-certification increased her payments on the re-certification appointment. Now your payment will be increased. You have ten calendar days from the date of this appointment to start paying the amount requested. Section 8 housing knew the only income her neighbor received was her social security check. The section 8 housing authority would be taking and leaving her with forty dollars to live off for the rest of the month to pay for gas, electricity, and groceries.

The list goes on; you can't just get up and move because you need at least one thousand dollars deposit for another place. The last apartment took the deposit because housing didn't pay the final payment for the rent. The next best thing to do is set an appointment with the supervisor in the housing authority office, but the supervisor never returned the call? After a week went by, you called and left messages. But, still no return call. Then we go to the office to do a walk-in visit and were advised to see the caseworker, who had just raised the rent. And, if your doctor wouldn't sign the section 8 housing information questionnaire, basically, you are out of luck dealing with section 8 housing? Why are we even renting a home? Why can't the money go towards buying a home?

The landlords are getting their homes paid off by section 8 housing, and buying more homes to rent out on section 8. More apartments are being built, are being rented from the government and profiting for their own? The system should use the money to give those qualified a place called home, not the landlords, to have more properties to rent out for their profit. If these people owned their own home, they would care for it and respect it as an investment home for their Legacy.

Some people are waiting and need a home.

Young people who can work shouldn't be qualified for housing. My god sister, who lost everything and, living in a shelter with two kids, needed a place to go. She was in her late forties and disabled. She wants a home garden and a yard for her kids to play out in the yard not stuck in an apartment the only place to play was in the street or school.

The elderlies want a place called home to have their families come to visit. Section 8 has rules as do the owner do also. Why can't they have a place called home instead of giving the money to landlords, and apartment owners. There not, a reason they should die in a nursing home.

My god sister ends up committing suicide.

I never imagined she would take her life. She was homeless on the street, and only a stranger could help her. Most families don't understand or have the time to help someone like this woman. She needs rehabilitation and counseling to help her with difficulties she had to deal with alone. It's not easy to get food stamps or housing. Section 8 was on her about having to get her doctor to sign a seven-page questionnaire to get qualified to get a room for therapy she was hit by a hit and run driver she was raped in her own home and left to die, she was also a diabetic, and was on pain killers. Then she had a doctor who refused to sign the paper work from section 8. The hell you go through. Sometimes you think being homeless on the street would be a better place to recover and not to continue living an everyday life dealing with people who don't give a damn. Seeing their loved ones suffer from pain and torture. Trust me; It Could Happen to You.

Then we have the attorney called Ambulance Chasers call the 1-800 number you can call if a priest has sexually abused you. We guarantee you money. You won't believe how many people have called. If we reach this number, and we can get you free counseling, who would call? Not a one. But God sees everything trust and believes karma is real.

I had a friend ask me if I could give her a ride home from work as a barmaid.

Then all of sudden she saw her boyfriend with another woman. She yelled, stop the car and, started rolling on the ground, then tore her clothes. She then proceeded to call 911. That she was raped The story worsened and worsened the attention she received and the power she felt. The alligator tears, the poor man was arrested.

The police refused to hear my side of the story.

Then I heard a story from a friend of her brother-in-law. He had sex with her sister-in-law, and she later felt dissatisfied. She feared her sister would find out, so she said her brother-in-law raped her and received ten years in prison. Her sister put her brother-in-law in jail for rape. So she wouldn't blame her for having sex with her husband. Remember, God sees everything karma will follow.

The Bill Clinton sex setup by Monica Lewinsky, the people were too quick to judge. Monica looked for power even if they did not have sex but gave a blow job to a powerful man. Monica was in Clinton's office, so how was it rape or otherwise? Who the heck saves clothing after giving a blow job? She could have called the rape crisis to take a report but, a blow job that's gone wrong is not rape. Could that have happened to a man who wasn't as rich and powerful as Bill Clinton? Monica knew how to play the part with the help of others. This woman should understand. First, she should have advised a counselor of her feelings. The talk shows talk about the humiliation, disgrace, and mortification; Monica didn't have shame or remorse for President Clinton and his family. It had to be a setup. What woman would save her dirty, smelly clothes after a blow job? Monica carried it around like a prize. President Clinton and others have more important things to worry about.

Stop wanting to get a chance in the spotlight. It may backfire. Annie wanted the spotlight, and people were helping her without getting the absolute truth.

The problem with the system is there too quick to judge. Some will put the man who made them famous or supports them are facing prison, while she writes books and goes on the Talk show, television is full of promises. For example, they said poor Monica while she was getting ready for the kill. She got in and out like a snake. If any ordinary woman had sex with another man, the Courts would have tossed the book at them and put them in jail for prostitution. This woman who writes books starts having sex at a young age for money and fame: years have gone by, and they are no longer the young girl. New girls are going to take their place. They will become rich and have fame, as they were given, but she will become jealous the new young girls will get the money and fame and ruin the man who gave her the food on the table. It's the devil's way of controlling evil. Why Now?

Women allow men to have sex with them; then if the sex goes wrong, women have a way of hating a man who just wanted to have sex or didn't love her anymore for their use; women show off their boobs, legs and, whatever else to get a man attention. They look for opportunities. The court system should not mark a man as a sex offender on a one-time sex mishap.

Women will make a one-night stand or mistake look and sound like rape; the Attorneys trained to make it look worse than it was. Have you ever had sex, and it just didn't feel right, or you just wanted to have sex? It's called being horny. Young girls change from little girls to women and have no idea what happened. They get Horney, at the age of thirteen-year-old girl have become a mother. Their life has changed. It's not a joke; becoming a woman is not just growing up but facing life. No more dating going out with your friends,

Protesters who talk about being abused and want to band the outrage child sex dolls. Are they disturbing? Would you rather have a sex therapist have to touch your child after what they have gone through? We need to understand or find out if a child says they handled them for attention from their parents. I worked in a Mental Institute. With children and adults as the office manager, some patients would ask me for advice while waiting for their therapist, to which I could only listen. You need to spend time with your child—not seeing if a doll didn't look pretty enough for you. I think art and sex dolls can help. Again it takes one person to go after their theory of a sex doll or whatever we may or may not like. Get a life. Your child needs you.

When Jake hurt my daughter, I talked with his parents and, of course, they said, oh no, not my baby. I looked at them as if they did not understand their son needed counseling, and he had to stay away from my children. I said, your son is a sick bastard. We were never close after that visit. My daughter went to see a counselor a child sex therapist who should have been the outside person looking inside?

That didn't work out for us.

They say money is the devil's way of controlling the evil ways of people. We now have to face people who want to sue the Catholic Churches, not the only church being sued. Attorneys believe the church can afford to pay cash and glory from those who call themselves victims. Karma is real.

Accusing a person of rape should be investigated because before, a person will be marked for life as a sex offender. It could have been a one-night stand or a sex date gone wrong. When I was a teenager, my friend got pregnant to hold on to her boyfriend, forcing him to marry her. Some get pregnant to move out of their parents' house. Trust me, having a baby isn't easy. Your life has just changed.

Then you have the girls who move out of their parent's homes to have sex, but would they ever say they're not pure. If you are having sex with him in your place, you know what you were doing. Don't blame others for your doing it's wrong and, it's not worth hurting yourself and others. Some women don't care about being in love. They are called Gold Diggers. Without feeling which may even have children for security reasons and refuse to take care of the child. Gold diggers aren't and can never be a parent; instead, they go out and get a job and work to get away from raising their child. The father or grandmother will raise them, the mother will not want to have to deal with a child, but if the child has done something great, the mother will want the credit.

Court: Taking someone to court for money is wrong accidents happen. I remember when I was going to visit my parents and, an older man with a ladder on the top of the hood of his car he ran the red light and hit my car. I had insurance but, the little old man did not. I then noticed he had to be somewhere for a job he wasn't drinking; he said it was his fault right away. While talking to the man, I realized he was a patient in the VA hospital with my father at one time. I knew the police would take hours to get to the accident. The store clerk across the street had called the police. I said, don't worry, I have insurance, and my father can fix my car. The insurance would have taken his home and money. The tow truck came and towed my car to my father's house.

While waiting, I noticed the balloon man who sold balloons on Coors road.

My kids walked across the street and said hi! In Spanish, to the balloon man, that's what my kids called him. My kids always looked for him. He had the enormous balloons my kids had ever seen. I then asked him if we could have five balloons and, he said how many I said five if the kids can't find you and bust, there's and we'll have extras. When the kids were a little older, I noticed the balloon man had opened his restaurant, or I should say I ran into the balloon man and, he remembered them he said you're welcome to eat here for free as you were my best customer but, I said we loved those giant balloons. When we went to his restaurant, he was never too busy to say hello to us. We ate there every Sunday after church because he served the best Mexican food; his family worked at his restaurant.

Then we have the Ambulance Chasers Attorneys asking you to call if you used a particular product. Most of the effects of questioning for years. And now they're saying they cause cancer. Did it also cause deformity? There is no way they can sue a company and say it causes cancer when we can't even find a cure for cancer or diabetic most likely diabetic worked as a picker and worked with weed killer or other chemicals. Most men who work in Mining die of cancer people who work on computers can cause back, neck and, shoulder pain, headache, eyestrain and, overall injuries of the arms and hands. Can you sue the computer company for the use of overusing a computer? I don't think so and, if you're a nurse and get sick from getting a virus, can you sue the hospital? It's wrong to sue for money; if an attorney says you got cancer from some product and were dying, the attorney would say he can sue the company for millions of dollars. What the heck do you need the money for? You can't take it with you when you're dead, but you will leave people hurting for their jobs. Do you realize how many people are dying every day with unanswered diseases we have in the world?

Do you realize people who protest are sick and need help it's a power trip. You're the disease of hurting others and yourself. Do we have right or not can we help others or hurt them. If a person is being charged for murder that's why we have attorneys, and the judge; do you have a degree in the law system or is it hate and violence in you system. Protesters talk about being abused and want to band the Outrage Child Sex Dolls. Are they disturbing?

Would you rather have a sex therapist have to touch your child after what they have gone through? Understand or find out if a child is sexually abused? Some kids say they had touched them for attention from their parents. I worked in a Mental Institute. As the office manager, some patients would ask me for advice while waiting for their therapist with children and adults, which I could only do, mostly listening. You need to spend time with your child—not seeing if a doll didn't look pretty enough for you. I think art and sex dolls can help. Again it takes one person to go after their theory of a sex doll or whatever we may or may not like. Get a life. Your child needs you.

When Jake hurt my daughter, I talked with his parents and, of course, we said, Oh no, not my baby. I looked at them as if they did not understand their son needed to get counseling, and he had to stay away from my children. I said, your son is a sick bastard. We were never close after that visit. My daughter went to see Counselor, a child sex therapist who should have been the outside person looking inside? That didn't work out for us.

They say money is the devil's way of controlling the evil ways of people. We now have to face people who want to sue the Catholic Church's is not the only Church but other religions. They believe the Church can afford to pay them and, the Attorneys wish to cash in on the glory from those who call themselves victims. Karma is real.

Accusing a person of rape should be an investigation because that person will be marked for life as a sex offender even if it was a sex date gone wrong. When I was a teenager, my friend would pregnant or say we were pregnant to hold on to my boyfriend and get married. Some do it to move out of my parents' house. Most girls move out of their parent's homes to have sex, but would we ever say there not pure. Really if you had sex with him in your place, you knew what you were doing. Don't blame others for your doing it's wrong and, it's not worth hurting yourself and others.

Some women don't care about being in love their call them Gold Diggers. Without feeling which may even have children for security reasons and refuse to take care of the child. Instead, we get a job and work away from home, not dealing with a child. Gold diggers aren't and can never be a parent, so the husband or grandparents take the mother's place.

Court: Taking someone to court for money is terrible accidents happen. I remember when I was going to visit my parents and, an older man with a ladder on the top of the hood of his car he ran the red light and hit my car. I had insurance but, the diminutive older man did not. I then noticed he had to be somewhere for a job he wasn't drinking and, he said it was his fault. While talking to the man, I realized he was a patient in the VA hospital with my father at one time. I knew the police would take hours to get there. The store clerk called the police. I said to the man, get in your car and go. Don't worry; my father can fix my vehicle. Besides, the insurance would have taken his home and money. The tow truck came and towed my car to my father's house. While waiting, I noticed the balloon man who sold balloons on Coors road.

My kids, I walked across the street and said hi! In Spanish, to the balloon man as my kids called him. He had the enormous balloons you had ever seen. I then asked him if we could get some balloons and, he said how many I said five if in case of the kids bust, there's and we'll have extras. When the kids were a little older, I noticed the balloon man had open his restaurant or I should say I ran into the balloon man and, he remembered us he said you're welcome to eat here for free as you were my best customer but, I said we loved those giant balloons. When we went to his restaurant, he was never too busy to say hello to us. We ate there every Sunday after church because he served the best Mexican food; his family worked at his restaurant. We left a big tip for the waiter. That made us feel worth our trip to his restaurant.

My Father Died

No one knew I was struggling or didn't care to know; I couldn't see my father. My sister filed a restraining order on Felix and me.

I was arrested for a restraining order I never received. I appeared to the restraining order my sister had filed under my father's name. I was not aware; I had been subpoenaed. My sister told the judge, her boyfriend, a friend, had subpoenaed me. I said if this person subpoenaed me, he should identify me because no one had subpoenaed me. My sister's action set me up and, I knew I did not receive the subpoena for the domestic violence charge against me and, not just me but one of my other sisters was subpoenaed several times by her. I found on the court records and made copies if needed. I later figured it out she couldn't order me out of my father's house. My father had put his house in my name, and my sister Felix whom I had added to the deed. I have the original copies of the house my father gave us. We were both not allowed to see our father. When my father appeared in the hearing, I requested a translator for my father to understand. My father told the judge he didn't ask for a restraining order or wanted any of his daughter or his children's not to be allowed to see him. He said he never signed a paper that would stop my daughters from coming to see him at his home. The judge dismissed the restraining order. When we went to court, I had the judge get my father a translator to explain why we were not allowed to see him. my father said all my children were allowed to see him. The judge dismissed the restraining order; my sister later put up a seven-foot fence around my father's property with a padlock. I went with my counselor to ask to see my father. My sister walked to my father's side of the house and yelled out, what do you want? And my counselor asked if it was ok to see my father, and she said, wait, let me ask him. She then came back and said he was not feeling well. Maybe she can see him some other time. My counselor said maybe we could make an appointment to see your father. If you send her a letter, you should send it certified mail, or she will say she never got the letter. We never got an answer. My son received a call that my father was in the hospital. I didn't receive a call from any of my siblings. I could have missed seeing my father for the last time when my father saw me standing by his bedside in the hospital.

He looked at me as if he had seen a ghost. I said Dad; it's me; I said my name to my father in Spanish. Dad, it's me, and I repeated my name. My father's tears ran down his face and, he moved his hand slowly to touch my hand as I held onto the rail of the hospital bed. I couldn't believe my sister had told my father I had died. I said, Dad, she wouldn't let me see you. My father had never hugged me or said he loved me but, I could see it now he was reaching out to me as tears ran down my face. I couldn't believe I had finally seen my father once again. I then said to my father. She won't let me see you need to let go and go with my mother. We had to go my grandson had a flight to catch. On the way to the airport, my son got a call that my father had died.

* * * A story has three sides to tell
about yours, there and the judge * * * **

Truth and, lie and your secret The Third-party tells the story in their way. Worse of all, what you want to make of it, most of them would instead continue wanting to know the ugly part of the story to benefit themselves, but God sees everything payback forward is accurate.

Stories and Lies

My sister talked to all the members of my family and some of my friends. She tried to get them against me, including my children, but, as they say, what goes around comes around. I won't try to explain to my children that my innocents or what she said about me is invalid. I believe God asks me to wait one day; they will figure it out on their own. God sees everything. I'm their mother; I have nothing to lose.

I was at the bottom of the barrel. Who could have believed this could happen to me. Some habitual gossipers who don't know me and would tell a story about me; be careful they're the ones who say their shit doesn't stink; there was someone who went around talking to others to be aware of me. Their grandparents raised her sons in a small town called Torreon. Later they moved to Albuquerque, New Mexico. They owned a bakery and apartments down the street from their house in the South Valley.

When my daughter was pregnant, the father of her son came after work with

dozens of roses of different colors every day. I had never seen so many roses in one room in my life; he filled my daughter's room with roses, till one day, my daughter caught him with another girl at school. She was sitting on his lap. My daughter walked up to the girl and asked if she was seeing her boyfriend. She answered no. Then a week later. My daughter ended her relationship with him;

She was eight and a half months pregnant. The other girl ended up pregnant.

My daughter said to him; you need to find out what you want in life. If you join the Marine Corp, you can travel. Her uncles were all in Marines; who knows, it may help you and, maybe things will change for you. He joined the Marine Corps; he was glad he did.

Except that the other girl was pregnant and her mother forced them to get married, he took her with him to California, where he was stationed. They weren't getting along and decided to get a divorce. One day we went to take my daughter's son to their father's grandmother's house. We saw his old girlfriend dropping off the babies. His ex-wife became jealous, called the police, and reported having drugs and a gun in his car. It all came out on the police report during his sentencing. When he got out of prison, it changed him.

It's the worse experience you could ever have. The prison was brutal; he was scared, life was never the same after that. He wanted to get away and live in Torreon, New Mexico, for a while till he could get his head straight. He said he had an Aunt named Maggie whom he could talk to and, she wouldn't judge him. There were so many things he wanted to say. He remembered his son would visit his great-great-grandfather in Torreon.

He told his Ta-ta he would have wanted him to go. One day I saw my grandson's father. I had his son with me and, he said to me. His brother and his girlfriend told him a story about me; his brother said I wanted to take their daughter to a pageant. But instead, I was going to take her to court. I started to wonder how did Annie know I was on my way to the courthouse. He said all he knew was that my ex-husband's wife called his girlfriend, his younger brother, went to the News to tell their story of their two daughters; they were both strung out on drugs.

Months before, I had gotten off work and went to pick up my grandson from his grandmother's house.

My grandson was sleeping, so I decided to visit for a while. The phone rang it was the mother of her other grandson's girlfriend. She asked if her husband could come and pick her up at the drug store. Where she had been selling flowers and, if he could bring the girls but, her husband wasn't home yet. The grandmother asked? If I could pick her up at the drug store, it was just up the street. The grandmother didn't drive, and her husband wasn't home. His girlfriend asked if I could take them to their apartment; her boyfriend wasn't home. Then the girl's mother asked if I could take the girls back to their great grandmother's home. I said yes, I had to go back and get my grandson.

Then one day, I ran into my grandson's father. He said his brother and girlfriend were in prison for attempted murder. They were both on drugs; they killed her when they fell asleep on top of one of their daughters.

I am sure it was an accident; drugs are an addiction like smoking, drinking, and, overeating but, worse of all, it could happen to you. I know they love their daughters and wouldn't have wanted to hurt them. They were young and just made a mistake that they will regret for the rest of their life.

That person who spoke badly of me had the nerve to say. Do Not trust her. Later her older son was murdered, his home was ransacked and robbed, and he took all his things. It could have been another setup. It's usually someone close to you.

The most horrifying stories come from families who, because of jealousy, or like to gossip. Little lies hurt and, some think by lying, you're protecting yourself and letting it go to their grave.

The real stories of the death of her oldest son? He was living with a girl who was a stripper. They were selling drugs. There was no forced entry, so he knew the person who killed him. After killing him, they ransacked his apartment and took most of his stuff. It could have been a setup as well. Some girls get greedy and get someone to rob their own homes and, in this case, murder.

Karam will come to be for him. The family did not tell anyone he had been murdered. Stories told that they would take to the grave.

My grandson's great-grandson became attached to his first-born son. They hired an Attorney to file grandparents' rights for my grandson. When we received the papers in the mail, I called my grandson's grandfather on my grandson's father's side, called them, and said they better leave the mother of his great-grandson alone.

She's a good mother; we soon dropped the charge of grandparent's rights.

Then my son asked my grandson. What he wanted for his twenty-first birthday He said he wanted to go on a cruise to Mexico. The three days before the cruise, he texted his father that he had lost his passport and driver's license. I said, how is that possible; why would he be carrying his passport with him.

My son couldn't cancel the cruise on short notice and, the next day would be a holiday. His mother said she would try to get his drives license and passport before the cruise. I felt as if he didn't want to go on the cruise at the last minute. Maybe his girlfriend didn't want him to go, who knows. Well, he finally went but, I heard he had gotten a tattoo on his leg. I immediately knew it was a bribe from his mother to get my grandson to go on the cruise he had wanted. When they boarded the ship, his son refused to do anything with his father, misbehaved towards his father, and treated him horribly. I received a text from his mother that my son couldn't get his bank card to work. He needs her to send him some money to pay for the taxi. She called me to send him one hundred dollars till the bank cleared his card. My son was afraid of missing the ship When they returned to the ship. The lady on the ship helped my son get his bank card to work. I called my grandson's mother, had my son send the information of the nearest Western Union. My son was waiting for me to send the money to pay the taxi; his son was sitting outside a food vendor on the table eating.

His father asked him where he got the money. He said he had one hundred cash on him and his bank card. His father needed eighteen dollars to pay for the Cab. Why wouldn't his son loan his father the money? When they got back from the cruise, I texted my grandson how he could treat his father the way you did? He should know better. And why did your mother have me western union your father's money? When I am living on a fixed income, and your mother is supposedly happily married, with a husband who has an excellent job as a detective, she had the nerve to ask me to send my son money. It's not like my son wouldn't have paid her back.

I sent the money right away but, that was not the point I was trying to make. I wanted to know why my grandson asked to go on a cruise. When he refused to do anything on the cruise with or without his father.

My grandson's mother texted me telling me how she knew what I did to my ex-husband. And other things she brought up against me. when she had invited us to my grandson's graduation in California, my son and I ended up paying for most of the graduation party. then my grandson's mother had the nerve to tell my son's not to mingle with the women in the party and her girlfriends. What did she care? She was happily married and, my son was single. My grandson's mother, who was pregnant, had two sons from two different fathers; her first son is of my son and refused to allow his father to contact his son even if he was paying child support and more. He paid a round trip ticket to have his son visit for a week. she would play head games with my son after he bought the airline ticket. She would call the same day that she changed her mind and his son wasn't going. The second father is in prison for domestic violence and child support. I overheard my using my maiden name. I wonder what she was up to. Her friend, Rosemary's husband, lived in California, and, she said, her husband and her had seen two little boys in the car waiting for hours. Her and, her husband decided to dive into the parking lot and asked the boy. Where are your parents? My grandson said they were waiting for their mother, who was in the Casino gambling. There was no way to contact their mother, and Rosemary didn't want to call the police. His father's hands were tied. Her family wouldn't let his son live with his father in New Mexico. It may be because the state was giving her money to keep the kids with her. Rosemary called me, I have a question for you. What is your grandson's name? This little boy said his father lived in Albuquerque, New Mexico and, he didn't know his phone number and was caring for his little brothers. I said to Rosemary can you watch them till I get a hold of my son. She did. I could give her a piece of my mind. How could she say anything about me when she strung out on drugs and was homeless with my two children. But yet, she had money to gamble. Why wouldn't she let the father of her children take care of them? The answer is that she would have lost the money from the state she got for those boys. Then one of her so-called boyfriends broke the arm of my grandson. I'm sure the hospital has that on file. I feel bad for her husband. He stuck with her as she just gave birth to his daughter. That's one way of trapping a man. His family is having issues with her, so they don't visit him. You kept their fathers from their son's life and, so did her parent's. who live in California could have filed for child endangerment against their daughter. We had to know what was going on. The truth is that everyone who reads Facebook websites has their hidden secrets in what we call skeletons in their closet. The only reason they talk is that they have never got caught. Some could even be doing prison time. Karma is a bitch. All that slander will defiantly come back three times worse. All of you who go on Facebook will be trapped and, their information will go against them. Writing things about others on Facebook and their website is called scandalmonger. What is the real story and, the worse part of all, It Could Happen to You? I wish there were a way we could stop people from writing bad stories of others. Don't you wonder what someone could say about you? Most people write about others because of hatred, jealousy, and, worse of all, to destroy you. You might be next. They will soon do it to you. Karma is real. It will catch up to them. There should be a Law for those who write about a person that is fraudulent and hurtful. The jealously, bulling it's hatred toward your survey your life. The federal law that you cannot blackmail someone you can do prison time in most states. Isn't Facebook and websites the same, even a talk show that spreads lies about a person be considered worse than blackmail? Trust and, Believe Hate crime is equivalent to the website Annie created and should have been charged for writing stories to destroy the Justice System and others as Annie has done. If you have read Annie's website, wouldn't you have wanted to investigate why there were multiple DNA testing? The Judges and a Jury would reconsider the shreds of evidence against me and question the Attorneys' involvement? Facts don't make up stories as Annie has done. Hate Crime is the feeling of the extreme form of anger. That may cause hurt to others but, deep inside; you know why and how to tell a lie that only makes you angry when you get on Facebook or the website to get people to feel sorry for you or to make friends and, cheer you on the power it gives you to destroy the people you don't know. Those people should be arrested, for aphorism, phony stories written or said by a psychotic person against them. Harassment is her pleasure. When you're desperate to write a story from your hurt towards a hated person, you don't know you can only hurt others and, you can't take it back.

My Nephew Died

Felix, only son George, passed on and is in heaven with his loved ones. I never had the chance to say goodbye to my nephew. No, I can't say that I did say goodbye to my nephew. You may not believe it but, when my nephew died. I felt my nephew's presents. I said; I will never forget your smile. It was so beautiful he had these cute dimples when he smiled. I could see him clear as day, standing right in front of me. The radio in the kitchen started to play out of the blue to the oldies station. I said to George, have you ever danced in your room or anywhere? We started to dance.

We danced to the oldies till we were worn out. Just as I was ready to sit down, a slow song played. I held on to my nephew, and we danced. I could feel him as I held him. He was wearing a dark suit, and we laughed, and I cried. It's my miracle to keep. He and I had the last dance and laughed as if it would last forever.

> **Lord, give me your eyes today, let me see the "heart,**
> **in the people I meet, and things I will do.**

They all knew that my nephew was suffering from depression. My parents called it male de Ojo, but you can't help those who won't seek help for my nephew's reasons. It was something he didn't know how to explain without getting hurt again. That would have broken the family, but my nephew should have come first before judging him with gossip and standing up for her son. My nephew lived with my parents in their house till he died. My younger sister rented my nephew the house my father left for me. My father gave it to me when my mother died.

My sister lived next to my parents rent-free. My nephew remained at my parent's place with my sister till he died. We all fear the thought of dying but, life may be more than we expect. My nephew is happier; I feel it in my heart. My nephew's father, James, was called by my sister, who gave my sister money for the memorial service of his son and, she would let him know when they would have his funeral, but, as of this day, we haven't heard of any service made for my nephew or where his ashes are. My sister asked my nephew's father, James, to sign all Georges belonging to her. I took care of my nephew when he was a baby. My sister joined the Army when he was three-month-old. My father got sick. My mother was taking care of my father, then he was admitted to the Veterans Hospital. I also helped take care of both of my sister's daughters. I thanked my sister Eva for coming for my nephew and reuniting him with his mother and grandparents.

Where have all the Roses Gone

Salomon and I met when I was working in a flooring company and, Sal worked in a company that was doing construction work for the company I was working for.

Sal came to the office to bring in some paperwork for his boss. I looked up and, said can I help you and he said, yes, I'm here to see your Mr. Roberts. My boss Mr. Martinez has the agreement that needed his signature. He then asked me if I wanted to go out on a date. I remember telling him I was not interested in a commitment. I was having difficulties with my ex-husband and Annie Sal and, we decided to be friends. Sal called me from work. He said he was feeling sick; I went to his workplace and took Sal some cough medicine. The next day Sal asked if he could take me out to dinner for taking him some medication. Sal called it a date. I guess you can say we dated for two weeks. Sal called and said he needed to talk to me and, I said Ok. We met after work across the street from his place of employment at the church parking lot across the road from where we both attended church; I worked downtown, which was about a fifteen-minute drive away.

When he walked toward me, he got on one knee and took out a ring from his pocket then he said will you marry me?

I looked down at Sal and, said No, you can't ask me to marry you. It's complicated. Sal looked up as he was on one knee and said why.

Then a few days later, we had taken my father to Furr's Cafeteria to eat. That's was my father's favorite place to go. When I went to get my father a plate, Sal took the opportunity to ask my father for my hand in marriage and, my father said, why do you want to marry my daughter? Salomon said because I love her. My Dad just laughed with joy.

Later I heard that Sal had invited my best friend, my soulmate, out to lunch and wanted to ask him what kind of girl I was. Sal used to call me his baby girl.

I later heard Sal ask my soulmate to lunch to ask him what kind of a girl I was; we had been dating for seven months. I couldn't believe it. What could my friend have said to Sal about me when he was in love with me too. When I was asked if I was single, my answer was always the same.

I would say Yes, I'm single but not available. I had too much going on in my life; I couldn't allow myself to have a relationship—the fear of hurting him.

Jake and Annie haunt me.

When I had gone to lunch, the IRS Agent went to my employer and reported that I was under investigation. My supervisor felt terrible having to let me go, but they didn't want to keep an eye on a person whom the IRS had reported as a problem.

You know, even a person on probation is most likely a better employee. Most criminals will have a transparent background check. The difference is they haven't gotten caught. A person with a clear (background check) knows how to be dishonest., it's true.

The federal agent made it hard for me to get hired for a job. I was facing charges for Improper filing of Income Tax, not murder.

Sal loved fishing, camping. My son liked Sal. He would have been a great person to take camping and hiking. That's one of my son's favorite things to do.

Sal worked in construction, driving heavy machinery. He had a drinking problem: I couldn't detect being I had never been around anyone who had a drinking problem; he seemed normal to me.

Sal had a hard pass he suffered with anxiety; apprehension drinking was his place of peace. There was nothing in the world Sal wanted more than to please his father. Sal went to Rehab Center. He had a drinking problem. He stayed at rehab for several months till Sal's situation was under control. I maxed out my credit card but, it was worth it.

Sal was finally able to get a job in construction. Sal loved to cook his mother's stew. He called it Caldeo. Sal would cut up the meat and add all kinds of ingredients in a big pot, and some call it Sopa. He made enough for lunch and put the rest in the freezer in a small container. When I cooked for Sal, he said, you did a great job in Spanish every time we ate.

It was a Friday, and Sal had gotten paid. He wanted to make me a special dinner on his way to the store. He met a friend who gave him a ride to the grocery store.

Sal put all his groceries in his car. When he went put the cart away, his friend drove away with all the groceries.

I couldn't believe it. We just laughed, and Sal said I better not ever see that so-called friend of mine again.

The week before Sal died, the strangest things happened. It was as if he knew he was going to die.

My friend, daughter, and grandson came to visit me from Carlsbad, New Mexico. I invited them to go with us to Legacy Church, where we attended service every Sunday. My son had introduced me to Legacy. He knew the Pastor. That Sunday, the five of; participated in the service; We drove to the Central location. It was a twenty-minute drive to Legacy.

The strangest thing happened during the service. Everyone was singing then Pastor Steve Smothermon started to preach. During the middle of the service, Sal got up and yelled out I feel it; I feel the Holy Spirit.

That wasn't like Sal. At first, I was embarrassed and said to Sal, what's wrong? Are you ok and, he said it again I feel it, I feel the Holy Spirit? We had attended Legacy several times before and, Sal never acted the way he did. The next day early morning, Sal got up and kissed me before he left to work, but that morning Sal said, Viola, Thank You for everything you did for me. You're the best thing that ever happens to me. I felt something was wrong. After he left to work, it started to rain hard that morning. An hour later, Sal came home and said they couldn't move any of the equipment in the rain; his boss said to take the day off.

I said, do you want me to make you breakfast and he said yes; I went to the kitchen to make breakfast, and Sal left to the bathroom to shower. Suddenly I heard a big bang and ran to see if Sal was ok when I checked on him; Sal had locked the bathroom door. I yelled, Sal, are you ok open the door. I started to worry and asked Sal, are you all right again? He had never locked the bathroom door before. I couldn't get Sal to answer. I then ran to get a screwdriver to open the bathroom door and found Sal bent over on the bathtub passed out. I couldn't pull him out. He was too heavy for me. I called my son to help me; my son tried to give Sal CPR; Sal wouldn't respond. I called 911. My son said Mom is dead. I got on my knees and held Sal on the floor where he lay dead. They came to take Sal's body, I stood outside the house, and I cried.

I couldn't believe Sal was dead. I looked up in the sky and, seen a double rainbow as I stood crying; I swore I had seen Salomon up in the clouds. Salomon said I'm here. Look, that's my Mom and my dog. I think he called his dog Zeus who stood next to Salomon. He looked happy.

The Coroner came to retrieve Sal's body said his death was caused by drowning. I said that not possible he was a good swimmer, and there was only a couple of inches of water in the bathtub. The shower had been running. He said it only takes a small amount of water for someone to drown. My friend heard that Sal had died and she came back to my apartment to stay with me.

I called Salomon's father; his sisters came to my house. His sister asked if I needed anything. I said yes, I want Salomon ashes. Sal wanted his ashes taken to a particular area but, his older sister said the Catholic Church doesn't allow cremation. Sal's ashes were buried. The service was in Las Cruces, New Mexico, where Sal grew up. My son and my friend, her daughter, and grandson, and my soulmate all went together.

My friend was mad at the Salomon family and scolded them about how they treated Sal. We stayed behind and didn't go to the cemetery. I never knew where they took Sal's ashes were taken to the cemetery. Sal lived a hard life.

Sal's family didn't understand him; however, one of his brothers cared for Sal and was sorry for his loss.

I stood outside of the church when everyone had left to the cemetery. When this old lady who wasn't part of the family said, it would be ok. And put her two fingers pointing between each eye, meaning God sees all. She made me feel at peace for some reason.

Sal's kept his boat and water jet skis in storage at Elephant Butte. His sister, and her family had been using them. I remembered Sal asking them to sell them and send the money for his boat and the jet ski they were still using; they wouldn't send him money.

After Sal died, there was a big flood. At Elephant Butte, Salomon's boat and the water jet ski's his family had taken from Salomon were destroyed in flood.

I thought to myself, Oh God, that was Sal claiming his boat. I felt his presence that day. Sal could have been a good person if his father hadn't made him an alcoholic at seven or eight years old. I guessed his mother feared his father and didn't do anything to help Sal.

The Strangest Thing that Happened

I had seen the love of my life. We had history. I started to walk towards him at a gathering in Torreon, New Mexico, from a distance, My best friend from my past. It had been years since I had seen him. I started to approach the man who loved me and, I loved him. I started strolling towards him. When I overheard a woman announce he was getting married. I walked away, never to see him again.

I was a teenager when we met. I then moved away and, he went on with his life.

I had started to play in an all-girl band called Leather N Lace, where all my old friends lived in Santa Fe, New Mexico. My best friends and I had the best time of our life; we were also on a magazine. That changed our lives forever.

I played in a band and watched others dancing with the person they were dating or those who wanted to have fun after a long week of working. I always wondered what my soulmate was doing? He knew the songs as he read them to me when a song was playing that reminded him of me. I listen quietly with a smile on my face.

My soulmate and I met once a week or more. I helped work on my son's car and, mine then we would go for a ride on his son's car. Sometimes we got in his car and parked and lesson to music together.

We went to fix his son's car and stayed at his son's apartment in Arizona. He took me to his son's college and around town. He went to California to get his father and mother. They left for his son's graduation. He texted me a pic of his son's girlfriends and of the ribbons his son received at his graduation. He's so proud of all his sons; you know he is responsible for their accomplishments. While his wife left to work, he raised his sons and continues to support them every day. She argued after his son's graduation on the way and back —she Nagged about whether his parents had given him money and what he did with it.

My next prediction will hurt him so much that he'll end up hating what his wife has done, being she will be responsible for, as her sister and mother have already ratified their waits to pay the villain. I hope it won't come to pass. To me, one of his texts reads, you can't imagine what it's like to live with a spy. She asked her son to help her use the camera on her cell phone to spy on him and have pictures to show the judge for the divorce hearing and, She would have thought I had a nasty divorce hearing. I said your too old to live life like that; I hope one day he'll be free. I hope your sons will love you and see why their father lives the life he does his looking for happiness and, I hope he finds it. The scares she drove into his life will never heal the horror will always haunt him for the rest of his and his son's lives. The controlling hand over them was worse than a ball and chain he carried for many years. I asked my soulmate to write a couple of things he disliked about his relationship with his wife. I couldn't believe he wrote over nineteen things. Wow, that's sad; I couldn't believe it; I still have the list. And most of his text.

My soulmate texted me that when he was eating dinner, his wife said to him. What's Yours is Mine and, what's Mine is Mine.

Now that I've written the story of my soulmate and our dilemmas, it would make our life more manageable to live in peace. When he read it, I could feel the hurt in his eyes.

The truth of being afraid to speak up for himself and make his own choices I know his sons knew how his wife treats him. I hope he will get the courage to speak up for himself and stop her from mistreating him. My soulmate said his wife gave him an ultimatum to marry her, or she would end the relationship at the time; he felt he was getting old and knowing. He hadn't heard from me; he still loved me and, it wasn't going to be easy to keep me out of his life; believe me, I tried too but, his love for me was more substantial than before. It had been over twenty-eight years later when we did finally meet again. He then said we were soulmates forever. When he texts me, he calls me goddess. I saved all his texts he would text me, and the letters I still have the stuffed lion with blue eyes he gave for Valentine's Day. when Forever Young played on the radio; he texts me forever young.

I know everything about him as he knows about me; we're soulmates forever, as our story goes. I know him more than his children, wife, parents, and sister, who has passed on.

We've even talked about how we want to be buried and come back in our reincarnation form. I know about the other persons in his life and, the lady who asked him for a kiss, I asked why you kissed her? The answer he wanted was to stop her from yelling, kiss me, kiss me. I may never be the woman in his life but, I will be his soulmate forever because we embrace a secret that no one can take away from us, not even his so-called wife. I know his life history that only he and I know about and will take to the grave. My soulmate and I will never be together as his interest are not the same as mine. I have stepped out of his life; I asked him several times to work on his marriage. He said to me, she a greedy woman as her family is, it's not about her loving him but about the MONEY. His wife was mainly worried he would have to pay child support, not who he was—the fear of greed. I'm not the jealous type jealousy is evil; it causes terrible vibes. Even if his wife yelled at him every time his phone rang, who's that? Is that your girlfriend? she yelled at him like a madwoman, not like a jealous woman would but of greed? The way she treated him in the past and the future has left a scar.

He wanted out of the marriage, but his wife continued to hang by his side and make his life a living hell. The memory of his wife literally making that noise like a kiss sound. The minute he got home from work, if he didn't go straight to her and kiss her when he walked into the house. She became angry; he said to her he believed a kiss should come from the heart. If not, let it go. My soulmate kissed me when he had the feeling too. I never kissed him because he was married; he loved holding me every time we were together as if he needed a hug.

She acted as if the marriage was satisfactory in her mind.

His wife had her sons spy on their father at his shop. She then drilled them. Did he get any calls from a woman? Did he leave the shop?

His wife worked for the probation office. She sat in front of the entrance door, handled the offenders sign in, and issued them a cup to collect their urine for drug testing; now, she works at a drug store. She transferred to the drug store closer to home to keep an eye on her husband, lucky for her after being fired at the drug store for disobeying her bosses. She was able to transfer herself back to the store she was last employed. His wife had a problem with the last boss. She was caught having an affair after that; his wife asked him to transfer out. Then there was the letter her son received at school. She read it then announced to her son that some woman wrote to her to stay away from her husband at work. She was having an affair with the manager at the drug store. I would have never shared that information with the school employee; you know, the whole school heard the crazy woman confessing she did not have an affair with her boss who worked at the drug store with her. Because of her actions, she would punish her son as he had to deal with the school, knowing his mother's reaction when his wife worked. I wonder how she had paid vacations for months and weeks to visit his parents as she wouldn't allow him to see his parents without her tagging along. The manager with whom she was having an affair ended, but she could accrue paid time off to go on all her trips and visit his parents. I worked one year to get a two-week vacation.

When his mother asked my soulmate to take her to see her daughter in home. New York she couldn't fly alone from California, so he got on a flight to California to take his mother to see his sister dying of cancer. His wife surprised him at his sister's home in New York. He had gone alone to take his mother to see his sister when she suddenly appeared with my sons to check-up on him. I won't allow him to visit his parents in California without her or visit his sons. He can't talk to his son alone. Then he had a business trip he had to attend for a week for training and, she tagged along, acting as if her marriage was great. He said to his soulmate. He was just glad to see his sons. During the training, his wife starts her sad story about why she didn't attend college. She made up stories. She blamed her father for telling her she wasn't college material. She called herself a Dumb baba meaning stupid; It wasn't her father's wish that she moved out on her own to be with her boyfriend's, so how was it her father's fault she didn't go to college? She went all over the United States with her boyfriend/husband. Now, why couldn't she have gone to college? She should have proven to her father and gone to college, yet she gave her boyfriend an ultimatum to marry her. A relative of hers asked my soulmate for a favor to go on a blind date with her. You know she had sex before him as she had her apartment. She was looking for the right man to entrap. Her other male companions saw right through her as a gold digger.

My soulmate was now trapped but thought of me as his soulmate, yes, he did not once but several times ask me to marry him with his ring. My soulmate wanted out of his marriage. Do you know what's keeping them together? It's not their children or their love for each other. It's called greediness.

It's the Entrapment of Mat-er-i-a-list-tic life. What's you have here on earth you can't take with you when you die.

His wife and her sister and brother-in-law heard about my ex- and Annie's story. She decided to make me look as if I was using him. Annie and Jake on my back, wanting to destroy my life? That I had taken my ex for child support, Annie wanted to become the headlight of attention. Why doesn't his wife talk about what her mother and the two daughters hold a big secret of power and now will reuse it to keep me from ever speaking to my soulmate? Karma is closer than you think.

Even if he wants the divorce, she remains with him as each one passes by their side with bitterness. He hopes one day he will be free of her. Not to be with another woman but to be free to do as he wishes and not have her yapping at him. I tell him all the time you're not a child for her to treat you like that. It's unfortunate because you can't force a man to love you if the feeling isn't equally shared. She is the last person she should worry about me. There was someone who cared for him even though we had a history together; I couldn't compare with that person; it didn't matter because life had passed us by. My soulmate wondered if his sons would be happy for him if he told them of his dilemma. The secret his wife held back, not including how he felt about the woman in his past life and present. It's too bad her life was a mess, and she wasn't ready to go on with a new life.

I was at the store when I ran into an old friend. Who used to go to school with one of my friend's older sisters. I had loaned him some money when we were teenagers he was so happy to see me we started to see each other's he wanted me to move in with him and maybe get married, but I wasn't ready to continue to live life as it is. I never asked him for the money I had loaned him. It didn't matter anymore. All that mattered was that I had my old friend back again in my life.

It wasn't enough of her nagging at my soulmate. I couldn't believe it when my soulmate called me.

I got a text from my soulmate telling me he feared for his life and couldn't explain over a text. We met at a restaurant. Oh my God, he said his life was over his wife; threatened to put him in jail. I asked why he said she accused him of stealing her money from her safe and gave me the money. I said, what? He said I took her two-dollar bills, dollar pieces, bonds, and two guns his father had given him. He said she was going to call the police and have him arrested. I told him you needed to file a police report but, he was afraid to do it because the only person in the house was him. If someone gets a hold of those guns and uses them to kill someone, the police will go after your father.

He then said that might work. I can say I filed a police report if in case someone may use the guns. I couldn't believe he was afraid of his wife and didn't want to make a police report, yet she was going to put him in jail for stealing her bonds?

I said you should tell her she needs to report the saving bonds stolen at the bank and, you should tell her you to have to go with her to the bank to report the stolen bonds. After all, she is accusing you of taking them.

She had been buying The saving bonds every pay period for over twenty-five years or longer. There had to be over ten thousand dollars' worth of bonds or more. She bought them in her name and her sons. She didn't include her husband when she bought the savings bonds; she should have had his name on them as well. Isn't that community property? She said his name was not on the bonds because he would spend it with another woman if she died. The safe only had her stuff in it.

She bought the safe from the drug store where she worked and kept her bonds, cash. She had her nest and, you have nothing. Can't you see what kind of a person she is? Her father told you to watch out for her. She was a Gold Digger.

She's a woman who engages in a type of transactional relationship for money rather than love. When it turns into a marriage for her, she doesn't love you. It's sad when you married, and you give her everything, and she is never satisfied.

She nags at you because the thought of her being stuck in marriage till to Death do us part. The thought of being with a man who she doesn't love when a woman loves a man, she treats him good. You make her sick she wishes you were dead, and you will die from being stressed. I know because you tried to commit suicide.

That entrapment will drive you crazy Now that your son is grown up and moved on with their life. She won't cook for you or do your laundry and, she won't let you do anything on your own. she can't control you and, you don't know what she'll do next. How can you trust her? How could she accuse you like that? I was glad I made a copy of his text so he would remember what had happened. He said she agreed to go to the bank with him. He said the key she gave him would go in but wouldn't turn. He decided to call a Lock Smith but, he would not be available for three days.

How was it that he never had a problem opening the safe before? The locksmith finally came to open the safe. I figured that Would give her enough time to put everything back in the safe. My soulmate texted that She had given him a key but, it didn't work. It wouldn't open. I said if the safe didn't open, how did she open it to see you had taken her bonds and money. When the locksmith came to open the safe, they had to wait for over half-hour. Then suddenly, his wife ran into the house with the keys to the safe in her hands. She gave the locksmith the key; he got the key from his wife, put it on the safe, and turned; it opened the right way. She must have given the locksmith the original keys. I said to my soulmate. I knew it just like I said after you asked her to report the bonds stolen at the bank; she didn't want to report the stolen Bonds. She had the keys all along. You need to talk to your sons about what's just happened; she wanted to put you in jail and, if you don't report those guns. I don't want to hear your dilemmas with your wife.

How could you trust her after accusing you of stealing her bonds and money?

My God, She wanted to put you in jail. How could he trust her after that?

She had the nerve to say she planned a trip to California to celebrate his father's 94th birthday. He drove to California with his parents, Casita. Without saying a word all the way. When they got to the Casita, they met his sons and had his father's birthday party at the hotel.

She acted as if nothing had happened two days before. They didn't say a word to each other on the way to California. She stood close to him to make sure he didn't mention a word. His sons were there with their girlfriends. After they got home, she asked him didn't your parents give you any money for the hotel yet—what a Gold Digger. She a piece of work; the truth is, what is in life trust your heart. What good is money if you're never satisfied? I have always believed in trust in God as he will provide we are here on this earth for a purpose make the best of it. Only you can make life what you want to be, what's more important than being happy. When you earn your money, it's magical and, you're careful about how you spend it. Trust me; it's better to give than to receive. Why do you think that is? I always articulate to my soulmate.

Have you ever heard of the saying. Did you ever see a Hearse pulling a U-hall? Trust me; you came to this world with nothing and, you're leaving with nothing. Share your treasures with your loved ones now so you can see them enjoy them as you can't take them with you. Greediness is the devil's way. Giving is a gift from God; to give is better than to receive. You'll feel it in your heart.

To my soulmate, may your broken heart heal, and know life is what it is. I hope you will live life as you once wished one day as we are not getting any younger and life is passing us by.

* * * Words once spoken can never be recalled * * *

* * * Life is like a ladder;
every step we take is either up or down * * *

I agreed to send his story to his family as my soulmate thought it to be fit. His wife had made my soulmate believe I had sent the envelope to his parents.

Yes, I knew of it, but I did not send it. By someone else to help my soulmate's family regarding his wife's affair, someone else took the liberty to send it for the reason would have helped him when he went to visit his parents, and they would understand, and understand what he was dealing with. His sons should know too.

He sent it to the company address to the employee who stayed on.

Enclosed was a note then the second envelope was written across the envelope confidential, delivered by hand to Mr. & Mrs. This trusted co-worker took the liberty to read the article instead. Subsequently, he decided not to deliver as he found the article was inappropriate and would keep it from the family.

The person who sent the envelope said it's against the law to open the mail as stated on the package. He made a few calls and chose not to file charges at this time as his parents are too old to deal with that kind of dilemma with the federal law for tampering with other people's mail charges would be pending.

Then he started to wonder what else has this trusted employee was capable of doing. He may be sabotaging his family business.

This person who took the letter had a high position in the company. He did a little investigating and found out the trusted employee's wife was working in the company, where she later managed to marry this man. Instead, he discovered a secret: his wife had a lover who played volleyball with a man she yearned over after the game. There were pictures of the two but, had witnesses who spoke of the two being lovers. His wife had mentioned to her friends her husband was not a handsome man but had money. Is that another Gold Digger? How sad is that? She didn't marry for love, so as they say, karma is a bitch. The story goes that no woman would have him, and if her husband were to die, she would be rich. He had a daughter but, she died, so there was no one else to leave his money. It's never enough; you want more and more never satisfied there call gold digger or heartless. These stories have been taken to the grave by many businessmen who have endured, over other people's business, primarily attorneys.

For example, there was this old woman who loved dolls. Her father bought her a doll every birthday, Christmas. And when he went on business trips. She had them at a well-known corner house where children would go to her exhibition. She had hundreds and hundreds of dolls from one room to another from all over the world. The dolls were of all sizes colors shapes.

She then hired an attorney; as she had no living relatives, she was getting too old; her last wish was for her exhibition to continue to have the children enjoy her dolls as she died. The attorney closed the display and converted it into a law firm where he opened his law practice. The poor woman must be rolling in her grave.

When we move on, we hope someone would care their pets taken care of or children given a better life, but, as most of us believe, an attorney or a Living Will would grant your wishes. That is why it's essential to have a second plan talk with a friend, someone whom you can trust. That's why it's necessary to communicate with others about what goes on in your life. We all wish for the best of what you have left behind. A second wish list is mandatory for all who have a dream as we can't take it with us but hope someone can continue fulfilling our dreams. Make out a will you never know when life ends.

My soulmate talked about coming back in a reincarnation form. Time after time, even if I was there for you as well, I Thank my soulmate for being there for me when I needed him and for all the good times. Thank you is not satisfactorily of a word, and know that life has changed us. I have decided to move on and leave him with his dilemmas as I will with mine. Just don't promise me anything you can't deliver. So long, my friend, till we meet again.

CORONAVIRUS: What the heck happened? All of a sudden, the world fell to its knees. Everything was closed and, the News aired the death, and people in the hospital, what do you mean the hospital the minute they hear your positive with the Coronavirus. Their advice is to stay home. Do not come to the hospital. Really go home, and die. My God that sounds horrible. The News is fake since they had president Trump by the tail. Someone will someday leak the truth. There will be a Whistle-Blower on the actual facts and reason of the Coronavirus. Those who hurt the business and the ones who lost their jobs. Our city looked like a ghost town, and we were kept in our own homes as prisoners. In the dark, they say one thing, then they change it how many times have. They played head games with us fist no plastic bags; then they started charging ten cents for plastic bags. Then, they told us to take off the masks in less than a month; we had to wear our masks again. The Casino was allowed to open, but we couldn't go out to eat unless you like fast food. What's the difference? I said I refused to hear the News talk shows whoever was hungry for publicity. Look at the facts were not idiots.

The lie of the Coronavirus will get their karma. All it takes is one person to control our lives as Hitler did to his people; protesters become one of the leaders. There should be a law for no protesting; they cause riots, damage homes, cars, and most of all, they should be there for their families. No one else should matter.

We need to work things out with our government, who should listen to the people. The News should announce what our needs are, not fake News.

It took one person to destroy my life Trust and, Believe. I'm living proof.

I wanted to die because I had no voice, and no one could see me. The pain and suffering, and most of all the shame Annie and Jake brought to me and my family, they didn't care what I was going through.

Shame on the sick persons who started this bogus Coronavirus. We're not idiots. We're human beings. The Coronavirus can be seen as a good thing; because before the Coronavirus, most of you worked, worked, and worked. They didn't have time for the most critical thing in their life, God comes first, then your family and friends? Now with the Coronavirus were spending time with our loved ones and missing their family and friends. We're dealing with the Coronavirus that is not real but an eye-opener.

We don't need to wear a mask to hide from the truth. How is wearing a mask helping when we stand six feet apart and stand where the person in front of us stood. Then we walk into the store after waiting for hours on the cold, windy day to get into the grocery store. When we shop, the stocker touches the items, as does the person before them, then comes you with your mask. How did the mask help?

A friend said to me this man had his house built and, no one has ever farted in it, meaning they were moving to a house no one had lived in, it was as clean as a whistle and, then I said to my friend that's not true the carpenters had farted in the home before.

We're fakes too, believing what you hear, not what you see, no one will stand up and say what they feel the News should air the names of the people dying of the Coronavirus? That does not exist. Why is this happing? Why is it when you were waiting in the long line for hours to get in the grocery to get water and toilet paper that was all gone? I didn't see one person drop dead or catch the Coronavirus. I caught a cold but, I do every year. Some people say yes, it is true my wife died of the Coronavirus. Who are they to say we're not medical examiners? If I died today of diabetes, they would announce my death of the Coronavirus.

I had been paying my life insurance for years. Then I received a letter from my life insurance stating that they would not honor my insurance to your family if I died of natural death during the Coronavirus.

The Real Story

For those of you who worry about wearing a mask? It would help if you worried about our men and women at war, right—those who have a reason to fear for their lives. Every minute of their life wonders if they will see tomorrow. They stay up 24-7, hoping there won't be a bomb fall from the sky or a trap take their life of losing a leg or any body part? They will have to live with the injury but, worse of all, see your best friend, who is now like family to you, killed, and you can't do anything except hope you won't get killed or, worse, captured as a prisoner at war. When you come home to your family, they can't understand the fear of what life was like in the war. The memories will never leave the minds of our brave soldiers who are suffering in fighting in a war so that you can wear your mask. What are the numbers of or brave men and women? You think you have stress in 2020, try spending one night in combat. They face watching their best friend, their family, blown to pieces or left behind dead; then we have the injured soldiers. Who will care for them?

The rich will keep their son in college to live as a coward and become some bigwig while a real man or woman is out there defending your life.

Most of you don't care as all you face is street violence, but when it's someone you have gone to war for, you genuinely love someone close to you after what they've seen. No one will ever honestly know depression as it is in mind the rich the poor live life. When a little simple thing goes wrong, you panic about what this world would be like without having a bump in your life. Deal with it only you can reach inside of your self-bull-shit if someone can face a tragedy like our young men and, women do they should be your president that private is a general in my eyes. Why do we elect a president who is on their death bed? The men and women who are at war are the suitable candidates for us. We need to face the music. Deal with it yourself. No one can see what's inside of you. I know from my own knowledge watching and hearing psychiatrists laugh at how pathetic you are.

There is no mask for the war we're fighting now. We don't need a degree to figure it out. Wake up, America. What happens to our country.

You are more worried about dying of the coronavirus but, you don't worry about those who have cancer, or diabetes and, heart disease, or even being born with a deformity. We have coronavirus experts, physicians, researchers, epidemiologists, analysts, educators, and healthcare providers. It is not yet known how long COVID-19 vaccine protection lasts. What happens over six months?

How is it that we have a vaccine for the coronavirus?

There are now booster recommendations. For all three COVID-19 Vaccines is recommended that certain people are eligible to receive Moderna and Johnson & Johnson/Janssen. is it safe to say the vaccines will help even if they were developed rapidly? Oh, and don't let me forget about the vaccination card your tracking device. We wear a mask for what? As we touch everything and bring it home, there is nothing in this world that someone else hasn't touched before you. No matter what, life is what it is. Nothing can stop you from becoming sick or dying and, you won't take your hoarding with you when you depart. Dead is dead. You won't see a U-Haul pulling your toilet paper and water behind your hearse when you die. Karma is real.

Do you take the flu vaccine every year? Has it made a change in your life? I've taken it for a while and, I almost died a year ago. I took the flu shot and, I got sick with a cold. I ended up in a coma, then being in the hospital was a disaster.

I checked myself out.

How can you find a vaccination for coronavirus but? There is no cure for cancer, people with diabetes, the illness the people face worldwide, including the United States.

The Scientist who developed the Covid-19, a husband, and wife behind the vaccine from Turkish-German, has heart problems who are more than 90 percent more likely to die. What is coronavirus? Is it a cold, flu? Why is it mandatory to wear a mask? Why haven't they mentioned any side effects, but you're running to get vaccinated; you don't know anything about whether you are taking it because the governor said it would keep you from getting the coronavirus. Why take a vaccine when you're Not Sick or see others sick. It's a mental trip. Before you know it, you will believe you have the coronavirus.

We have men and women who are scientists here in the United States but, we trust other countries to protect and serve our own. Have you noticed that your over-the-counter medication, like Bayer Products, is now run by Japan? Read the labels. We are trusting Germany to find a cure for our families. Who are they? We need to stand up for our own. We are taking a vaccine of what? that been tested. How do you test the coronavirus when we don't know what's causing it. I choose not to trust as I would be a follower. I want facts. If your positive. is specifically created to neutralize the virus and its ability to infect. That is Fake. The government is the devil that we have made.

They run the News to the world that we believe. When our people wanted to tell us about the UFOs, the government stopped them until most died. The ones left behind with most of their families are dead as most of the people who threaten them with the secrecy of the UFO but, how late is it? And why did they hold back what we could have learned or helped in our future? Why does our president travel to other countries when the United States is falling apart? Why were our best presidents, including president Kennedy eliminated and, why are we prosecuting Donald Trump to keep us against him so he can't speak? We need to know all the facts. Stand-up America, we need to help our own. I hope my grandchildren will have a better life. Don't fail them.

The coronavirus is facing whether you live or die. It's God's will and, no one can change that. If you get sick right now, the doctors won't help you; instead, your death is a coronavirus. We should pray to God that He will heal our minds to think clearly. If there is a virus? God should come first. How is it you believe the News before God? What a hypocrite you are? The demon who reported the churches for not wearing masks will have to answer to God, who reported those who won't allow you to attend church unless you wear a mask in God's house. Wow, how pathetic is that. To the News, the Numbers are fake; people were in the hospital when they asked you if you have the coronavirus stay home. People have died, and how will wearing a mask help figure it out on your own were not idiots.

Do the math. For years the most Brilliant people have tried to find heaven or figure out where God is and if miracles are real. The coronavirus's truth is that we're alive even if so many of us are without work and can't pay the rent. Don't get stressed out. It won't help; instead Stand-up and do something for someone else. Just talking can help but be optimistic. We need good News in these times of hardship. I have very little money but, I called and helped a mother who needs pampers for her child with my last few dollars.

During the coronavirus, the government gave the Natives money. Why aren't the casinos helping their people? They make over millions of dollars a day instead of building their casino bigger. Help your people and others in need who supported their casinos. Do the Natives get new Trucks? How could they afford it now? When most of us have eviction notices in our homes and, businesses. Navajo Nation News was fake as the people who watched the News has mentioned most natives are living in the city. Since the coronavirus commercials, most of us are talking about whether you saw the nice white truck and where the garden came from was fake. Did you see the commercials he brought the grandmother boxes of brand food not like the one the food bank gave out?

The Natives have been seen driving a new truck and are buying freezers to store food.

The first lady visits the Navajos in New Mexico in April 2021. They dressed in ceremony clothing.

The First Lady should help the Mexicans who had their children taken away from them. Can you imagine your child being taken away? The first lady, it's not about entertaining—it's about life. The Mexican has missing children, hear their cry, and help reunite them with their families. That's not fake News God keep our children safe. I don't listen to the News. All my information comes from the people I talk with.

Who is benefiting from the coronavirus? The minimum wage went up, but then the store's prices went up so did the rent. What good is getting a raise if you are still where you started? The stimulant check won't get you back on your feet. Most of us have to pay the credit card, and if you try to get back on your feet and get your children back in a home. Now you've gotten two stimulant checks, and you can move your family out of the car; you had to sell everything to eat and live till the coronavirus is over to do that, you're going to need back rent, a deposit and, first-month rent.

Your house is now empty. You need to start over. Don't try to get it at Goodwill, as everything costs more than going to Wal-Mart or a yard sale.

Poverty: You can never help the homeless. It's wrong to keep them in the gutter by providing them with money to stay on the streets. Help them stand up for themselves. Most of them have mental problems. We need a rehab facility to help those who can be helped and let them smell the coffee. We can make it most of the homeless stand on the street in bad weather, holiday if we can do that, why can't they keep a job. America has miles and miles of land that homeless people can live and grow vegetables to survive and sell to make a life. It would be a safer way to live. The Natives did it when they traveled from place to place. We can make housing miles away from the city and be brought to town once a month to get supplies or get what they need and visit families. Counseling should be mandatory. Most homeless people are brilliant and just lost their way, losing family members, or as an example, some just lost their job and, hopefully, after counseling, they can get a job. Homeless people aren't under the age of seventeen years old that the age most parents tell their children you're on your own.

At twelve, the kids who call being homeless are spoiled brats who want their parents to suffer, as my daughter did at sixteen. She went to stay at a friend's home. I was lucky one of the parents called me that she was ok.

The News and, Talk Shows need to STOP airing out bad News about the coronavirus Miss-Information and try to cheer us up with good News. I sure could use a joke now and then. We need a talk show that doesn't talk about killing like the News or the coronavirus. I could hear the fear my friends had and wonder what was going on. We want me to tell them the Good News, but you can't say anything; bad News is more vital than good News, just like we remember all the bad things in life instead of the good thing. Look around for what you have, not what you don't have. I had a rough life and loved my family. Think of all the good even if we don't care. I talked with my soulmate and, he said, you know if you need more toilet paper, I'll get it for you. I said I had plenty. I didn't ask him for any but, it was nice of him to offer.

When I was younger, we were outside most of the time. Now you don't see any kids playing outside or the adults sitting on their porch waving at their neighbors passing by or sitting down with friends having coffee. They have in prisoned us in our own homes.

We now stand six feet apart. I like about the six feet apart; people aren't pushing their baskets, bumping their baskets up my butt. During the coronavirus, we ended up cleaning and getting rid of stuff to make space in their garage. I had this dollhouse I had started to build. My brother started it for me but made it worse, so I had to finish it. Since I didn't have the time and, with my son telling me it was a piece of crap, like a wood carving of a saint, I finished painting. Then I lost interest; first, I enjoyed my hobbies. My son can't stand dolls. They make him feel creepy, so I can't have a doll around him either. I decided to put my dollhouse outside in the front yard with a sign saying free. Hoping someone would take it, and maybe it would benefit some little girl and their families. Now that we're on lockdown and, it could become a family project. I hope it brought joy to someone special.

In December, my prediction will be we will have a new vaccine number four for the coronavirus. It's like giving them an insulant with sugar water and, we believe it has healed us. It's called mind over body. If you think you're sick, then you will get sick. If you think you're ugly, you make yourself unattractive. I asked my son how they made a vaccine to cure the coronavirus in less than three months? What is Hydrochlorborite? Why haven't they found a cure for people with diabetes and cancer patients? My brother's youngest daughter was 28 years old when she died of cancer a year ago; my other niece just had surgery for breast cancer a week ago.

Where is the CURE for them? Do you realize how many people are dying of cancer and diabetes each hour?

Would we rather die than live in pain? The only reason they're still alive is that they're hoping for a cure to heal them. You can't imagine what diabetic nerve pain is like, or having Gout is the worse pain ever and, there is nothing you can take or do but sit back and take it. Our elderly worked hard most of their life and, now they're struggling to make ends meet.

When I first heard of the coronavirus, I was so sad that I had to use a mask and be incarcerated in my own home and away from my family and friends. I kept telling my son, who started this rumor, that the coronavirus is a bitch.

I received a letter from my insurance company it said we would not pay your family if I died during the coronavirus or natural death.

Thanks to my cell phone and the computer or it would have been hard for me.

I prayed for those who were suffering from stress and those who were work alcoholics. They devote their lives to work and live alone. I thank God I have my son and two small dogs to keep me company and get my exercise by taking them for a walk. We need to get out. We have been incarnated in our own homes. I sat at home looking out the window; I noticed my neighbors out riding their bikes with their kids and jogging and, some are walking their dogs. I went out around the block with my two small dogs. And, would you believe it, people who were driving by actually took the time to wave hello their usually in a hurry to get somewhere. I was standing by the door watching the neighbor tree. When a white car came by my house and dumped the mother cat and five kittens, I saw a dog out on the street because people thought their pets would give them the coronavirus. Karma, Will get them back as these animals need tender loving care. I couldn't run fast enough to catch any of them. I put out milk and bought cat food. I was so happy to see the cat food and milk gone. Till the next day, I noticed it was a squirrel eating my cat food. I never found out what had happened to the kittens.

There are diseases of all kinds; suffocations are the most dangerous in the body; it is in mind for the brain, an actual person to whom you may impart griefs, joys, fears, hopes. Suspicions counsels, and whatsoever lieth upon the heart to oppress it in a kind of civil or confession.

The nursing homes kicked out the patients, not for the coronavirus. The elderlies were told they were at risk and kicked out of the nursing home without notice. The orders came from the governor.

The News aired a nine-year-old boy. He died of the coronavirus. In a small town outside the city limits, his brothers and sister and his parents not infected by the coronavirus? What does that tell you? Is it not contagious? How is it that staying six feet apart, helping, or distancing's from others wearing a mask isn't safe? It's terrible for you. Someone could die from it, especially if it's hot outside. The coronavirus isn't real who is playing the part of Hitler. One man; destroyed so many lives. It took only one person to assassinate the big and the mighty. There will always be history, and when their history their death—unwanted death when we could have prevented it by believing in each other. Don't keep your distance from your family and friends. If my family was dying, I'd want to be there for them; if they're sick or dying, I could never forgive myself if I wasn't there.

And, if my loved ones were dying, I would want to live off of a vaccine I would like to give my life to God. Besides, do you have control of keeping yourself from not dying? Will wearing a mask give your life? What Would God Do? Will a mask allow you to live life to the fullest? Do the math. It doesn't take a genius to figure it out. The numbers there give us on the News are all considered the coronavirus.

Fake News Even if you died of old age or a car accident. The number for the coronavirus deaths list. Mis-Information. People walked around as if though everyone had Leprosy.

The News announced the coronavirus was hospitalized 127; no one is hospitalized. They sent you home to dye, recovered 8,343 and 3 deaths in the state. Get real. A 12-year-old boy died of coronavirus. His brother, sister and, parents are doing well. Then there was an 11-year-old boy who committed suicide. The parents said social isolation was a factor. The total number of deaths sounds like nature, car, suicide, accidents, some elderly, illness, and killing. Then the Great News will be a cure for coronavirus by the end of the election or late December Bull-shit what treatment. I was at home for six days. I was out of everything. My son made me wear a mask when it was 93 degrees outside. It was hotter than hell. By the time I got to the line at the supermarket, I had almost passed out. You won't believe the new rule at the supermarket is. First of all, wearing a mask and shopping isn't fun when you finally get to the cash register and bag your stuff to get out. Then all of a sudden, you have another line to show your receipt that you just paid for your property. I saw women pass them as she had to get home after standing in line for an hour. She had to get home to my children. The employees at the supermarket ran after her and got her license plate number of the car. She later got a warrant for her arrest. First of all, there is no sign stating Caution must check out with clerk and show receipt. What you just paid a few seconds before walking out. I wondered what the outcome would be with the judge's ruling.

Then we have security driving around the parking lot. You would think there making sure no one breaks into your car during your shopping. No, that wasn't the case for me and, my friend when I took mine to the store, she had put the handicap sticker on my view mirror. It expired, but after making an appointment at MVD to renew my sticker, they told her it would come in the mail. So she used the old sticker. We got a citation the day before the security guard gave me on my vehicle for $300.00 and, since my friend lived almost an hour away, the ticket had doubled. So we decided to take it to court. Thank God they dismissed it.

Then there is a woman driving around, The apartment complex checking the license plate for expired stickers, and will put a boot on your tire and, the sign says to get the boot off, you need to pay $78.00 cash.

Fake News I just heard about a man and his wife were on the News standing at the nursing home window trying to communicate with their parents by standing outside the nursing home window. The News said both parents had the coronavirus.

When he heard the News after it aired that his parents had corona, the truth was they didn't speak English and, the News reporter made it seem as if they were sad that his parents had the coronavirus. The truth was they couldn't understand. Why their son couldn't visit, had to wear a mask? They had to explain what was going on and why they were in lock and, the nurse made them wear a mask and gloves. I'm sure they were scared.

I said to my son. You better hope I don't die on you now because I just got a letter from my Life Insurance Company; if I die now, they won't honor my life insurance during the coronavirus. It stated, we are living in unprecedented times and must inform you that your insurance does not include coverage for COVID-19 related claims. Please see the enclosed state notice for details on the limited nature of coverage for COVID-19 CONDITIONS. They did not sign the letter on the bottom that said Customer Care- Insurance. There was no signature or name. I was so angry with the governor I said there going to start charging a fine or jail time if you didn't use a mask.

Power trip It's for your good. If it was for their good and the governor cared so much about us, why didn't she have my staff issuing masks for those who could not get one? Then people started making masks and sanitizers, selling them for profit shame on you. It's not like you can take the money with you. It's so wrong when your brothers and sisters are in need in a time of crisis. We should work together to stay alive. It's the right thing to do. The hoarders took a lot of the stuff we needed to feed their children for those who bought all the food and cleaning supplies. Shame on you, do you now see it was a Test; What do you plan on doing with all the stuff you hoarded when you were left alone in the world. If we don't care for others, what good is it to living?

Now you can sit locked up in your home and enjoy all the food like a pig. While most families didn't get much food as they had to wait till Friday, they lived paycheck to paycheck, no savings for a rainy day. It's not because they're out spending their money, but because they're on the lowest-paid scale. Even with all my education and on-the-job training, I wasn't a high-paid employee. I was paid minimum wage even with a college education and on-hand experience. I know the feeling I've lived it. My kids never knew how hard life was for me. It's was my responsibility to care for them. World; it isn't easy. Now we're facing another problem called coronavirus.

Food Drive: I heard that a friend got the extra snap and more food from the food drives. The food drive should be for working and receiving minimum wage while the coronavirus is on lockdown. Not for those who already get assistance or like the ones saying I'm getting more on unemployment than working. Kids don't eat that much. My kids ate and snacked all day but, it's not like they're starving. The ones who need the help are those who are on minimum wage. I know because that was me. No help from family, friends, or don't qualify for assistance. It would have been nice if, on one paycheck, we didn't have to worry about paying my bills; kids nowadays don't realize how life works because their parents wanted them to have what they didn't or couldn't afford to have. We're not helping them. I went to work sick and never missed a day no matter what; I had to work to make ends meet, then go home, cook, and clean the kids ready for the next day.

I used my vacation to attend parent-teacher conferences or if my kids were ill.

I got off work to care for my children when they were sick.

I had a three-day weekend off. We went on road trips to Carlsbad Cavern, Las Vegas, Nevada, to visit my uncle and grandmother, and, to Texas, whatever would work for us but, what I loved the most was on the weekends when we went to the mountains for the day hiking and, having a cookout. It was mostly the three of us.

The food drives during the virus, people who needed help with food couldn't go because they had to work and earn their minimum wage to pay the rent, utilities, and food.

You may want to consider giving out a gift card for the local grocery stores, and you can keep track of everyone who needs it. Those who drive and get food from all the food banks stay home and get government assistance. Most food banks give out bread, junk food cake, and expired food; you have to eat it before it goes bad and tastes terrible. Most of the food you don't eat red beans or lots of canned fruit. When you open it, it has a horrible taste. One food bank gave out five jars of peanut butter. Those of you who give to the charity as seen on TV are not Real? You may think that you're helping someone, but someone is going on vacations or buying nice things for themselves and, going to other countries with your money, you can make a difference. Give to food banks, utilities, or any other cause you don't know if you're helping. Why can't you do it yourself and enjoy being a part of helping that person? When I heard that my neighbors didn't have toilet paper, I walked to her house and took toilet paper even if I only had a twelve pack.

I saw on the News; food bank was an hour wait for food you weren't sure you were going to get and, worse of all, gave it to most immigrants who receive government assistance most get double as they have a spouse who works you see them at the store.

I walked to the store, and three Mexican boys almost ran me down, riding their electric skateboard worth two hundred dollars each. The mother didn't ask her sons to say excuses me. They made me feel as if they were better than me. As an American, I couldn't afford what this kid had. The Natives were buying bicycles for their kids and grandkids with the stimulant check the president granted, but worse of all, I saw a woman at the casino with one thousand dollars on the machine. She was playing five dollars a hit. I pay fifty cents a hit and go once every other month with twenty dollars; if I win, I get to go to the casino restaurant to get something to eat. She must have got the money from the government assistance for her kid's school. If you ever go to a casino, you'll see immigrants gambling as the government supports them. Their kids live like kings and queens. They have the best cell phones, kids' tables worth a hundred dollars on the market, best brand on their computers when most of us have to go to the library to use their computers. The stimulant check should be for the hard-working immigrant, Americans, and most of all, the elderly who work hard and I was paid. It's not the people who plan to get government assistance and will never work or pay taxes. The immigrants know the system better than we as Americans do. It's not fair to us who can scarcely pay their bills. We shouldn't be worried about immigrants who come and get government assistance. Some immigrants truly work and pay taxes.

The Navajos in the reservation received extra food stamps and, then they had food boxes delivered to their home, plus the Federal Government gave them money. They don't even pay federal taxes. About 90% of the natives live in the city. During the coronavirus, I ran into three different natives at the gas station who had just bought a new truck, and here we are hurting our Mamas, and Papas businesses are closing. We need to start bringing businesses back home; it sounded like a political thing. We, the Americans and the immigrants who pay taxes and don't get government assistance, are hurting.

I don't care much for voting after what they did to President Trump, and now we have a great grandfather Biden with one foot in the grave running our country. After talking to many people who believed in a particular person, we voted for lost.

Is the voting machine safe? Why do we need to hide behind a small booth with curtains to vote? When I voted for the first time in my life for Trump, it was my freedom to vote for whoever you want; it's your freedom of choice.

Do your family and friends question you if you're a democrat or republican? Or who are you voting for? What is it to them they don't pay your bills or live your life where are they when you need them? How many of your friends will stand up by your side in court and say he is my friend, and I believe in him. Instead, they would turn your back on them. Trust me; it's easier to walk away or gossip about them. Will they ever remember the good things their friend did for you in life?

If you give to your favorite charity, do the leg work and see where your money goes towards the cause you're supporting. Since I was a little girl, I have seen the same commercials about babies who are malnutrition. I asked myself, how could a mother see their child suffer and will die yet continue to bring another child into this world. I couldn't bear to have a child knowing my child would suffer. There is no cure as the commercials are still airing. The person that needs your help is right in front of you. It could be your employee, an old friend, someone you may never believe needs help. I watch the game shows on TV. Steve Harvey shows you have to think fast and have a good memory for the answers but, it's fun to watch and, Jeopardy is educational. Then there Goes Whammy; that's an old show it looks like fun. But most players have a great job and can afford to fly their whole family to the studio. These game shows are for people who have money and want to go on TV, like Let's Make a Deal. I wonder if there are actors? When do you ever see someone who needs to pay the rent or can't afford a new car? Now that the person who should be on a game show to win. It should be for someone struggling to work hard and use the money to pay their bills or win a vacation they could never afford. Hey, if you love the game show, Go Whammy is a fun show, not like the rest, but it looks fun. I remember my Aunt Nana, who my Dad called Trinidad, wanted to go to the game show Let's make a deal but, she died and never had her wish.

Loss of Hope

There was nothing left for me to do; I lost so much of my life. My children were all grown up and, times had changed. I tried to forgive those who hurt me and made my life a living hell. I hope writing my manuscript will help me make it through life. It is almost like going to counseling; my true feeling comes out and, most of all, the truth of what I live for and what we lose in this life and can gain. When you get to my age, you don't give a damn. You tell the truth. Whether you want to believe it or not, you learn to say what is real and not live for others. We have a voice. You can now say the word F--- you, and if I want to vote for Trump, what the F--- is it to you. Now that I'm retired, people will ask what did you do all day and, my answer is what the F--- is it to you. What do you care what I did all day? It's my choice and my right to do or not do anything. I'm not your puppet. No matter what I do, they will never be satisfied. We work hard to please our boss, who doesn't give a damn and gives you more work than credit. The number one rule I learned is don't overdo yourself at work.

You'll just end up wearing yourself out. Do your job and get the hell out of there. It's not your company. If they choose to fire your ass, you're out in the door for being such a brown noser. Now you're a red noser from crying. Will the people at work come to your aid hell no, they have a job and your history? I was only fired once in my whole life. Wow, did it hurt? I felt like a loser and as if I had been blackballed. That federal agent had no right to get me fired but, what the heck?

I couldn't fight it. I had no voice and those who could didn't lift a finger. People who have power don't work; most bring their problems to work and take them out on their employees. If it weren't for your employees, you wouldn't have a job or a company. They kick back and smell the roses. Life is like running in a circle, same old shit. In the end, it won't matter but, it matters now live life.

Remember M and, **remember** E put them
together and, **remember Me**.

On February 11, 2022, I got a call at 8:07 am that my youngest brother who lives in Arizona had died. His organs had shut down. I said to my brother why would you leave me so soon. I had decided to give the News of my brother's death to a loved one but waited till the traffic was slow. I was heading to the other side of town when all of a sudden my car was heading towards the wall. I looked upon the freeway and, I saw the exit wall, I blacked out. The next thing I remember was the doctor at the emergency room. He said lady you must have angels around you I couldn't understand what he meant. Till my son came to see me in the hospital, he said how did you get ejected out of the passenger side window, you laid on the side of the road. The first person who stopped at my accident was a doctor and behind him was the EMT. I thought to myself who called them to my aide. I believe it was my brother Robert who helped me. No one better than the two persons I would have needed, My dog Ziva was with me I asked the girl in the hospital to call my son Ziva is in the car he went to get my chihuahua her leg was hurt so he took her to the veterinarian to have her checked she said her leg was broken and, my son asked how much will it cost she said about $6,000.00 he took Ziva home hoping he could do something for her after I got home Ziva was walking with her little leg dangling when she saw me trying to walkshe started to walk but when she saw my son she would start limping. I think she remembers my son going to get her at the accident she and I are getting better every day. I have a perfect driving record and I'm a professional driver of 23 years. The X-ray showed I had fractured L1 to L4 vertebrae and my lower ribs were broken on my left side I did not need surgery; I didn't have any movement on my legs. I left the hospital with no pain. I was traumatized and feared getting up to walk on my own. I was sent to a rehab center the night after my accident. The first night I asked if I could get help to the bathroom, no answer so I sat on the side of my bed and said God please don't leave me now. I need to walk help me. I got up without fearing I could fall and then I took my first steps toward the bathroom. I was at the rehab center for seven days. The rehab center refused to release me. The night shift didn't help they had my call button shut off. When my physical therapist came in on Monday morning I asked if he could check my call button and he said it was unplugged and he plugged it up for me I told the girl that brought my medication that my call button was off she said no the front desk will be alerted. I said no I have my visitor and the therapist who noticed it was unplugged, and he pugged it up. When I was at the rehab I asked the lady what medication are you giving me she said I don't know I just follow the list given to me. I asked if she was a nurse she said no.

This had to be a miracle.

As seen when the tow truck is taking my car there are Spirit Orbs there were three small ones that didn't come out on the picture.

VIROLOGY

	Collected Date	2/16/2022 12:55 MST	2/14/2022 17:25 MST	2/10/2022 18:57 MST	Units	Reference Ran
Procedure	Collected Time			Not detected		[NDE-NDE]
Influenza A PCR		Not detected	Not detected	Not detected		[NDE-NDE] [NDE-NDE]
POC Flu A PCR		Not detected	Not detected	Not detected		[NDE-NDE] [NDE-NDE]
Influenza B PCR			See Below			
POC Flu B PCR		Not detected	Nasopharyngeal swab			[NDE-NDE]
RSV PCR		Nasopharyngeal swab	Not detected	Not detected		
COVID-19 Source		Not detected	See Below			
COVID-19 PCR		See Below	NO	Unknown		
FLU+RSV+Covid-19 Comment		NO	NO	Unknown		
Patients first test		NO	NO	Unknown		
Healthcare worker		NO	Not Applicable	Not applicable		
Patient symptomatic		Not Applicable	YES	Unknown		
Date symptom onset		YES	NO	Unknown		
Patient hospitalized		NO	NO	Unknown		
ICU patient		Unknown	NO	Unknown		
Congregate resident		NO				
Patient pregnant						

Textual Results

RSV: 2/14/2022 17:25 MST (RSV PCR)
      Test not performed per current protocol.
CV: 2/16/2022 12:55 MST (Flu+RSV+Covid-19 Comment)
      Testing performed by Real-Time PCR.
CV: 2/14/2022 17:25 MST (Flu+RSV+Covid-19 Comment)
      Testing performed by Real-Time PCR. (The COVID-19 PCR test is for in vitro diagnostic use
      Emergency Use Authorization (EUA). This test has not been FDA cleared or approved.)

Order Comments

CV: Flu+COVID-19 PCR (FAMC)
      Swab in Universal Viral Transport Media.
CV: Flu+COVID-19 PCR (FAMC)
      Swab in Universal Viral Transport Media.

BLOOD BANK

Type and Screen

	Collected Date	2/11/2022	2/10/2022			
	Collected Time	02:12 MST	18:51 MST	Units	Reference Range	
Procedure						
ABO Rh Type		O POSITIVE	O POSITIVE			
Antibody Screen			NEGATIVE			

Patient:	Trevino, Viola
DOB:	12/23/1952
MRN:	398537

Report ID: 130062617
Print Dt/Tm: 4/7/2022 15:57 MDT

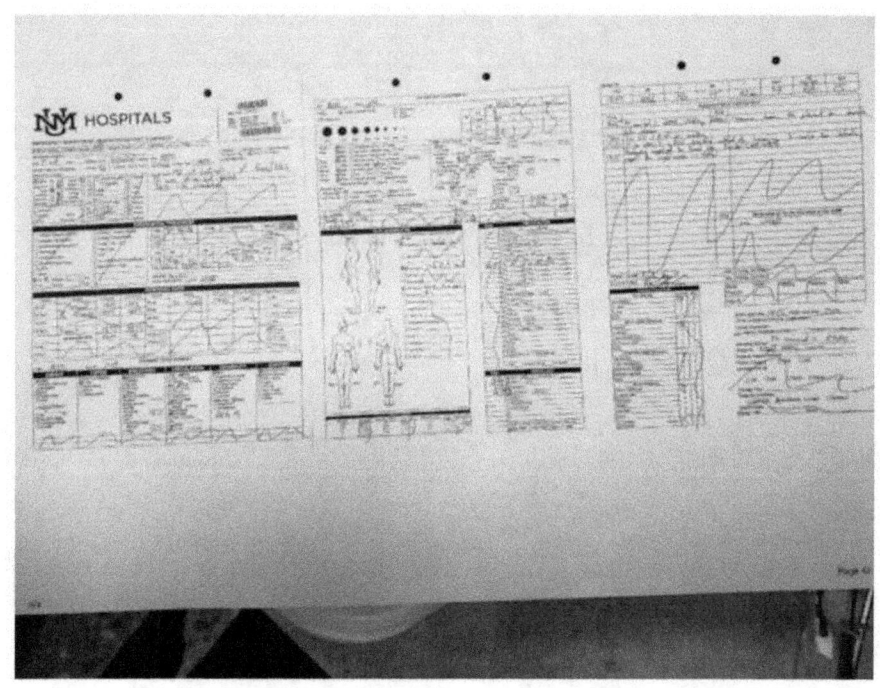

The Heart

A strong person knows how to keep their life in order. Even with tears in their eyes. They'll say it with there heart as it is bleeding with sadness they will manage to say **I'm Ok**. As they say hard times are over we thank, God, for never leaving us, and help those who are in need. We can make a difference it won't cost you a penny to give a helping hand to your bother, and sister as we are God children. Most of us just need a friend, happiness, joy, peace and, love. It all comes from the heart.

May the road rise up to greet you
May the wind be at your back
May the sun shine warm upon your face. May
the rain fall soft upon your field and, until we
meet again.
May God hold you in the palm of his hands till we
meet **again** good-bye, my brothers and sisters.

The End

www.ingramcontent.com/pod-product-compliance
Lightning Source LLC
Chambersburg PA
CBHW070905120626
46546CB00001B/138